YOU'VE *GOT* TO READ THIS BOOK!

55 People

Tell the Story

of the Book

That Changed

Their Life

YOU'VE *GOT* TO READ THIS BOOK!

Jack Canfield

Gay

Hendricks

with

Carol Kline

HARPER

An Imprint of HarperCollins*Publishers*

See Permissions (page 284) for credits and individual stories.

YOU'VE GOT TO READ THIS BOOK! Copyright © 2007 by Jack Canfield and Gay Hendricks.
All rights reserved. Printed in the United States of America. No part of this book may
be used or reproduced in any manner whatsoever without written permission except
in the case of brief quotations embodied in critical articles and review. For information,
address HarperCollins Publishers, 10 East 53rd Street, New York, NY 10022.

HarperCollins books may be purchased for educational, business, or sales promotional use.
For information please write: Special Markets Department, HarperCollins Publishers, 10
East 53rd Street, New York, NY 10022.

First Collins paperback edition published 2007.

Designed by Ellen Cipriano

Library of Congress Cataloging-in-Publication Data

You've got to read this book : inspiring stories about the life-changing power of books /
[compiled by] Jack Canfield, Gay Hendricks with Carol Kline.
    p. cm.
ISBN: 978-0-06-089169-5
    1. Books and reading.   2. Life change events.   I. Canfield, Jack, 1944–
II. Hendricks, Gay.   III. Kline, Carol, 1957–

Z1003.Y68 2006
028.8—dc22   2006040287

ISBN 978-0-06-089175-6 (pbk.)

13 14 ❖/RRD 10 9 8

This book is dedicated
with gratitude to all the authors,
past, present and future,
whose books make a positive difference in people's lives.

Contents

Acknowledgments

CREATING A BOOK such as this is always the result of many people's efforts. First, we would like to extend our most heartfelt gratitude to our spouses and families:

Jack Canfield: I'd like to thank my wife, Inga, first for always being there to support me on my search for more knowledge and wisdom; second, for always being there with love and support for this project, including reading stories and always offering her honest feedback; and third, reminding me through her playful nature that there is more to life than books. I also appreciate all of my children—Oran, Kyle, and Christopher—for sharing the same love of books and reading that I do.

Gay Hendricks: I'd like to thank my wife and creative partner for the past quarter-century, Kathlyn Hendricks, for providing a loving space in which I can think out loud about anything under the sun and moon.

Carol Kline: Unending thanks to my husband, Larry Kline, who creates beautiful spaces for us to live, entices me away from the computer to "smell the roses," and makes all of it worthwhile. And to my stepchildren Lorin and McKenna, for their love of beauty, words, and books. Thanks also to my sisters Barbara Pearson and Holly Zurer, for their enthusiasm about this project and for suggesting people to interview whose stories have added so much to the book!

We'd also like to thank the following people for their invaluable input:

Lisa Hotchkiss, whose top-notch organizational skills, good humor, and energy made this book possible.

Jai Collins for his quick work turning disjointed transcripts into brilliant first drafts.

Cindy Jevne Buck, a wise and gifted editor and dear friend, for her many hours wading through stories in all stages of completion and masterfully structuring and polishing them so that they sparkle. You are a gem beyond value.

Our friend, Marci Shimoff, whose insightful comments always improved the stories and whose presence in our lives we consider a great blessing.

Bonnie Solow, our literary agent extraordinaire, for her assistance in crafting the original vision of this book, and for conveying that vision to our publisher. Bonnie also helped in so many other ways as we created and perfected the manuscript, from helping us locate and enroll many of the contributors to giving us valuable feedback on the title and the manuscript. Bonnie is also a splendid exemplar of how to bring heart and soul to work.

D'ette Corona, for her capable, efficient, and loving assistance with getting all of the permissions that were needed—a huge job for which we are eternally grateful!

The following people at Jack Canfield's office for their help in creating this book and preparing the manuscript: Patty Aubery, for being there on every step of the journey, with her love, laughter, wisdom, and endless creativity; Russ Kamalski, for his sage advice on several points; Veronica Romero, for assisting the coauthors in keeping everything on track in the midst of their busy lives; Jesse Ianiello, for her insights and logistical support; and Kacie Mutscheller, for her assistance in typing.

Gay Hendricks's magnificent support team of Monika Binkley, Marija Crabtree, Otelia Rodriguez, and Chris Foley.

Computer genius David Christian Wolfbrandt, Carol Kline's indispensable "tech support," as well as Jeanette, Tara, and the rest of the transcribing team at Oldfashionedoffice.com.

Our publishers, Jane Friedman, President and CEO of HarperCollins, Worldwide; Joe Tessitore, Group President, Collins; Libby Jordan, Senior Vice President and Associate Publisher, Collins; and Mary Ellen O'Neill, Vice President and Publisher, Collins, for valuing books and reading as much as we do and for sharing our commitment to bring this book to the world.

Toni Sciarra, our wonderful Executive Editor at Collins, for her diligent work in helping us enroll several of the contributors and for editing this manuscript quickly and efficiently under huge time constraints. And her assistant, Anne Cole, who was always there to help if we needed her.

The following people in the marketing and sales departments at HarperCollins for their magnificent efforts to make sure this book gets into as many hands as possible: George Bick, Senior Vice President, Sales; Tony Valado, Online Marketing Manager; Tara Cibelli, Marketing Coordinator; Diane Burrowes, Director, Academic and Library Marketing; and Virginia Stanley, Associate Director, Academic and Library Marketing.

Paul Olsewski, Vice President, Senior Director, Publicity, and Larry Hughes, Publicity Director, HarperCollins, for their efforts in getting us radio, television, and print coverage to promote this book.

Colleen Houghton, Information Center Manager at HarperCollins, who helped in the research for this book, and who helped us contact some of the more difficult-to-reach celebrities whose stories appear in the book.

The following people in the HarperCollins Production Department— Donna Ruvituso, Executive Managing Editor; Diane Aronson, Copy Chief; Amy Vreeland, Senior Production Editor; Leah Carlson-Stanisic, Design Manager; Karen Lumley, Associate Director, Production—for their talent in creating a book that looks, reads, and feels as good as the content it contains.

The following people in the Art Department—Georgia Morrissey, Art Director; Victor Mingovits; and Erica Heitman-Ford—for their talent, creativity, and unrelenting patience in producing a captivating book cover.

Dahlynn McKowen, for going above and beyond the call of duty to help us in the acquisition of several stories.

Shannon Tullius for her help in contacting several authors whose stories we have included.

Matt Adams, Paul Gilbert, and Pat Williams, for their efforts in helping us contact people in the field of professional sports.

Marty Becker, Tom Lagana, Kate Ludeman, John St. Augustine, Ken Browning, Bob Bender, Marci Shimoff, and Elizabeth Cogswell Baskin for their help in securing stories.

Tony Esparza, for helping us track down some of the harder-to-find people.

Lastly we'd like to acknowledge the following people who worked with us to share their stories, which for reasons at the end we simply didn't have the space to include: Carol E. Ayer, Elizabeth Cogswell Baskin, Meg Charendoff, Susannah Crowder, Hale Dwoskin, Jo Gibson, Lori Johnston, Dr. Dennis Kimbro, Vice-Admiral Keith Lippert, Joanne Morrison, Laura Murphy, Judy Prang, Hilda Robbins, Bob Scheinfeld, Marci Shimoff, Robin Shope, and Shirley Oscarson Wood.

Because of the size and duration of this project, we may have left out the names of some people who contributed along the way. If so, we are sorry, but please know that we really do appreciate you very much.

We are truly grateful and love you all!

Introduction

Man's mind, once stretched by a new idea,
never regains its original dimensions.

—OLIVER WENDELL HOLMES

W E LOVE BOOKS, and we bet you do, too. We especially love books that inspire, heal, and transform lives. It has been our long-held dream to put into your hands a work that carries the essence of what we believe to be most valuable about a book: its potential to change your life. This collection of stories is the fulfillment of that dream.

We've all found that life becomes richer when we're reading a great book. You go to sleep at night feeling that your time on Earth is more valuable, your experience here more worthwhile. You wake up seeing yourself, other people, and the world differently. This is real magic—and in this book you will read story after story about the effect of this magic on people's dreams, goals, careers, and relationships.

Working on this book has been magical as well; it has changed our lives profoundly. In the course of bringing it together, we were exposed to powerful new insights and discovered new worlds to explore. It is our great hope and highest intention that this book will do the same for you.

HOW IT BEGAN

It all started with a fascinating conversation. Twenty-five transformational leaders, business consultants, and authors had gathered at Jack's house to discuss ways we could work together to make the world a better place. During a lunch break, a number of us were sitting in the living room when the subject of books came up. Several people mentioned how difficult it was, with the thousands of books being published every year, to know which ones were really worth reading. Others mentioned how much they loved to read and how reading had transformed their lives, but unless a book was recommended or referred by someone they respected, they often didn't make the time in their busy schedules to read.

Gay picks up the story: "As I listened to our friends talk about their love of books, a question suddenly flashed through my mind: What were the books that had transformed the lives of these remarkable people sitting around me? Everyone in the room had written books (and some, such as John Gray and Jack, had written best sellers that had sold in the tens of millions), but what were the books that had changed *their* lives? My wife, Kathlyn, was sitting beside me, and I leaned over to whisper to her, 'Wouldn't it be great if we could read all the books that the people in this room considered most valuable?' Her eyes widened in agreement, and in the next moment I asked the intriguing question out loud: 'What was the book that transformed your life?'

"What happened next was wonderful to behold. We all listened in fascination as one person after another told of a book that had changed his or her life. One striking thing was the look on everyone's faces. They absolutely glowed as they talked about their special books and told stories of the profound changes these books had inspired in their lives. What was truly remarkable, though, was that we found we hadn't read many of each other's favorite, life-changing books! In fact, we hadn't even *heard* of some of them. This discovery had an electrifying effect on the group; it was as if we had opened a door to a roomful of new treasures."

That conversation led to a yearlong journey in which we conducted in-depth conversations with dozens of inspiring people—some famous, others less well known, but all doing valuable work in the world. You can see from the names listed in the Contents that they come from many walks of life: politics, medicine, healing, psychology, business, entertainment, the arts, sports, and more. What they have in common is a passion for reading and a personal experience of the life-changing power of books.

THE POWER OF TRANSFORMATIONAL READING

What is it that gives certain books the awesome power to change lives? Noted author Deepak Chopra once said that reading has a special transformational power because "it gives you the opportunity to pause and reflect." Opportunity for reflection is a rarity in today's world, dominated as it is by visual media such as television, which fires a constant stream of images at you point-blank. And even if you are nimble with the mute button, the silenced visual stream still requires continuous mental processing. This is not the case with books: When you hold a book in your hands, you're in charge of the pace at which you read and the images you choose to form. You can stop and digest concepts and try on different perceptions and feelings.

But even that doesn't guarantee transformation. As our friend Bernie Siegel writes in his story in this book, "To be honest, I really don't believe any book can change your life—only *you* can. Look, two people read the same book: One is inspired while the other is bored. It's the person—not the book—that creates the transformation." When time for reflection is combined with the willingness to be transformed by what you read, the possibility for real growth is created.

This is why a book can have different effects if read at different points in one person's life—and why two people can learn different things from reading the same book. In the following pages you will find stories that illustrate situations like these, as well as many other examples of that most powerful of combinations: books plus people open and willing to receive the ideas contained in them.

Motivational speaker and author Charles "Tremendous" Jones once said, "You will be the same person in five years that you are today except for two things: the people you meet and the books you read." With that in mind, we are excited to help you meet 55 people who have had an influence on today's world—each in their own unique way—and to introduce you to the books that have profoundly shaped their lives. We know that you will be inspired by their stories and moved to read many of the books they write about. And whether you're exploring books new to you or finding hidden treasures in old favorites, we are confident that you will also find your life transformed for the better.

May this book bring you all the delight reading provides—from the joys of entertainment to profound insights and inspiration. Happy reading!

—Jack Canfield, Gay Hendricks, and Carol Kline

THE STORIES

Jacquelyn Mitchard

Jacquelyn Mitchard is a critically acclaimed *New York Times* best-selling author. Her first novel, *The Deep End of the Ocean*, was the first book selected for Oprah's Book Club and was made into a film starring Michelle Pfeiffer. She has written five other novels and three children's books. A newspaper reporter since 1976, she now writes a nationally syndicated column for Tribune Media Services and travels to promote awareness of colorectal cancer, which took the life of her first husband, award-winning reporter Dan Allegretti. Jacquelyn lives on an old farm south of Madison, Wisconsin, with her husband Chris Brent and their seven children, who range in age from 4 months to 22 years. ▪

A few years ago, on my birthday, a simple box arrived in the mail from my dear friend and agent, Jane Gelfman. When I opened it and saw what it contained, tears welled up in my eyes. It was a first edition of the book that I loved more than any other: *A Tree Grows in Brooklyn*. The copy was inscribed lovingly by the author, Betty Smith, to her own agent, and tucked inside were letters she had written, preserved just as they were 60 years ago. At this point, even my children, gathered around the dinner table, grew misty eyed. They knew how I felt about this book, its author, and its heroine.

Some months before, I had herded my three teenaged sons into a budget screening of the newest movie production of *Little Women*. They entered that theater as willingly as accused felons being led to jail while TV cameras rolled—their coats hunched over their faces, lest they encounter anyone they knew.

Afterward, however, they realized why *Little Women* was required reading in our house full of little men, along with a couple of other "girl" books, including *National Velvet* and, of course, *A Tree Grows in Brooklyn*. My son Dan, who, before puberty and Limp Bizkit hit simultaneously, was known to us as "the sensitive one," said as we got into the car, "I get it. When you were a kid, you wanted to be Jo March, didn't you, Mom?"

I had to admit it—I did want to be Jo, the brilliant young heroine of *Little Women*, growing up with a gentle, endlessly patient mother and a brave, wise, and superbly educated father; surrounded by books, piano music, genteel poverty, and noble breeding, in a large house shaded by old trees and with handsome boys next door. But I knew, and my children knew, I was Francie Nolan, the plucky, resourceful star of *A Tree Grows in Brooklyn*.

Like Francie, I'd been an urban child; I recognized the Brooklyn tree that Betty Smith describes in the book's epigraph:

"...Some people call it the Tree of Heaven. No matter where its seed falls, it makes a tree which struggles to reach the sky. It grows in boarded-up lots and out of neglected rubbish heaps. It grows up out of cellar gratings. It is the only tree that...survives without sun, water and seemingly, without earth. It would be considered beautiful, except that there are too many...."

There were trees like that on the West Side of Chicago, too. I'd lived in an apartment there when I was small. My aunt and uncle lived downstairs and my grandparents lived one building over. Everyone was either a plumber or a bricklayer. Our family, though always employed, definitely aspired to the lower-middle class. But I was the daughter of parents who never finished high school: a mother devoted to books and to my only brother and me, and an alcoholic father who worked so long and played so hard, we barely saw him. Our extended family was large, sometimes raucously loving, and sometimes raucously violent. The laughter was often too loud; the songs beautiful, but the words often slurred. Books were a shelter and a friend to me when that shelter wasn't available in real life.

My mother sought that shelter, too. Long before *Oprah*, she read the great books: *Anna Karenina*, *The Brothers Karamazov*, and *Crime and Punishment*. She didn't realize that she was too uneducated—that those books were not meant for her. She always brought home the very best things to read from the library. She gave me the message that nothing was off limits for me, that the circumstances of my birth would not contain me, and that as long as I could learn, I could never be a prisoner of my circumstances.

One day when I was 12 she gave me *A Tree Grows in Brooklyn*. Since that day, I've read it 11 times. I have a tradition of reading it before every book that I write. A work of fiction, it's a beautiful portrayal of urban poverty, and very gritty. We think of it as a book for little seventh-grade girls, but it isn't. It's a book in which there are terrifying things: alcoholism and child abuse and children in terribly dangerous circumstances caused by neglect.

Yet Francie's mother, Katie, makes Francie's life a stable place and points her toward education—in Francie's case, secretarial school, though she wants to be a writer. Katie teaches her that education is the only way to leave behind the kind of life in which she's grown up—the life of a tree forcing its way through the cracks in the cement, surviving on not much more than its own fierce will to live. Her mother was the person who best understood Francie's life ambitions and how difficult they were going to be to achieve. I was struck by how understanding her mother was of Francie as she matured—it reminded me of my own mother, who was the same way with me until she died when I was 19.

Francie Nolan did grow up to be a writer. Reading her story as a child, I felt she was showing me that education was my way to have what I wanted, too, and that I was going to have to fight for it. I always knew I wanted to be a writer. I learned quickly, as Francie did, to embellish the sometimes sad—and, to me, shameful—realities of my own life. I made up some startling expeditions and some glamorous relatives. (We did actually have some glamorous relatives, but they didn't speak to us.) And like Francie, I eventually learned from wise teachers and compassionate peers to "*tell* the truth and *write* the story."

Had it not been for Betty Smith's consummate understanding of mourning and shame, pride and love, and hard work as the only sure passage to dignity, I might not have ended up a writer of fiction; I might have ended up a pathological liar. I might have ended up not a woman who cherishes many friendships and enjoys some respect for the validity of her word, but a person mistrusted and alone.

So many times I've turned to *A Tree Grows in Brooklyn* for its wisdom and simple, clear, pure-water understanding of real life. There is no book that has inspired me more as a writer, as a person, and as a mother. Betty Smith's portrayal of a girl with her hands outstretched toward the key, the word, the message, the love that would make great the grit of her life is for me a mirror within a mirror. Like Francie's mother Katie, I was widowed early and poignantly.

A year after my husband's death, before my own first novel, *The Deep End of the Ocean*, was finished and before anyone knew it would be published to acclaim and then blast off as the inaugural book of Oprah's Book Club, I decided to adopt a baby daughter. The most polite response to my news was: "Have you snapped your cap entirely?"

After 18 months of grim, by-the-fingernails survival, which included the necessity of meeting a magazine deadline on the night of my husband's death, I finally had the hope of some freedom, some hard-earned time for myself. Why would I take on another lifelong burden? And how would my four children, still stricken by grief over the loss of their dad, like having to share the only parent they had with yet another needy soul?

They had no father, I was reminded. What I needed was a social life, a little fun, maybe even a husband; not another child. But I was not deterred. And when I first saw her—dark and big and bold—I knew she must be given a name that would comprise the sum total of what she would certainly face, and what she dared hope: the rumblesome brothers, the unscheduled departures and disappointments of a mother sliced thin as waxed paper, the necessity for allowing trust and love to grow among caring and kindly grown-ups beyond the core of our family.

I knew what to do: I named her Francie Nolan. And so she has grown up, another of those lush trees that seems first destined to be regarded as a weed, lifted from the most ragged streets in El Paso to a great green farm in Wisconsin, where she has learned to tie her shoes, ride a two-wheeler, and tell a dramatic whopper—all well before her time.

Our Francie has heard countless times the story of how she came to have her unusual first and middle names. She knows what book the name comes from, the shape of its cover, the yellow capital letters that make up its words. But she is not yet old enough to read it; not yet old enough to ache as Francie Nolan questions her regret for not having let her soldier lover know her body fully, only to be consoled by her mother's understanding; or to feel the family's fears over the wild brother, Neeley; or to hear the sound of fights and song in the streets.

Some day, in her turn, she'll read the book. For now, she refers, in her child's reckoning of common phrases, to the character Francie Nolan as her name-"saint." As a writer, I call Betty Smith mine.

Kenny Loggins

Musician Kenny Loggins, winner of multiple Grammy Awards, is one of the most successful songwriters and performers in the world. With a career spanning more than 30 years, Kenny is a musical powerhouse, attaining 12 platinum-plus albums and 14 gold albums. He has written and recorded songs for movie scores, including the Academy Award–nominated "For the First Time" from the film *One Fine Day*. His song "Conviction of the Heart" was declared the unofficial theme song for the environmental movement. ■

The silence was driving me crazy. I was vacationing with a girlfriend in the Poconos, but I was having a miserable time. Just days ago, Jim Messina and I had finished recording *Sittin' In*, our first album. For months, I'd been high as a kite, buzzing with the energy and euphoria that comes from the flow of creativity—expressed in my case through music. Now I was coming apart. I had completed a lifelong goal and had nothing to replace it. The nothingness was terrifying.

I cut the trip short, and we headed back to California. At home, things just got worse: I couldn't sleep, and after a while, I couldn't hold any food down, so I stopped eating. That was when I just climbed into bed. I spent weeks there, unable to leave the house, firmly in the grip of an emotional breakdown.

In an effort to distract myself from my pain, I reached for the book on top of the stack by my bed. It was *Siddhartha*, by Hermann Hesse. I opened it and started reading the story of a young Indian man on his path to enlightenment.

I read it twice through. Reading *Siddhartha* was the only time I felt calm—actually, the only time my hands stopped shaking—so I just sat there in bed and read and read. That's mostly what I remember from that period of my life: just devouring that book.

When I finished *Siddhartha* the second time, I reached for another book. Paramahansa Yogananda's *Autobiography of a Yogi* was next on the stack: another story of someone in search of a higher truth. I don't remember if I'd purchased these books or someone had loaned them to me, but there they were by my bed, waiting to ignite my spiritual path.

The combined impact of the two books was compelling. I realized that although I'd had success on a level that I thought would make me happy and complete, when I was left with just myself, I'd come unglued. Reading those books made it clear to me that I needed a stronger spiritual dimension in my life. They described a peace that I was searching for and inspired me to take action to find it. I called a friend who taught meditation, and not long after, I finally got out of bed and learned to meditate.

It immediately affected my writing. The meditation, the books, and the breakdown itself all made me much more empathetic; there was a new level of compassion in my music. I knew what a rough time was and I knew what peace was, and this new awareness imbued many of the songs I wrote after that—from "Celebrate Me Home" all the way through "Conviction of the Heart" from the *Leap of Faith* album. If you look at the songs from that period, you can trace the evolution of someone feeling more and more connected to other people and to life.

Reading *Siddhartha* and *Autobiography of a Yogi* helped me see everything in my life—performing, writing songs, relationships—in a more spiritual light. In the beginning of *Siddhartha*, the main character leaves home, seeking enlightenment. After a long search, trying every conceivable avenue, he becomes disillusioned and bitter and finally gives up. At one point, he actually runs from the traditional sources of enlightenment. He ends up living by a stream, and it's the sound of the stream that triggers a spiritual transformation and opens his heart. Every morning and every night Siddhartha hears the stream, and it speaks to him. The stream becomes both his path and his enlightenment.

Now I see that my stream is my music, which has become my primary spiritual practice. I still meditate today as a way to calm down, to catch my breath. It has helped to keep me grounded through all the ups and downs I've experienced in the last 30-plus years. Yet the main thing I've leaned on in times of trouble has been my music.

My songs have become messages to myself from my Spirit. Every time I perform, I get onstage and sing them not only to the audience but also to myself. I go into my center—and into the moment. Going into each moment, which singing and performing forces me to do, is like a meditation. I have to be clear about the note I'm singing, the word I'm singing, right now. Whenever my mind starts to wander, I have to bring it back to the note, to the feeling within the note, and the word.

Through this practice, the stage has become the place where I best communicate with my higher self and with others. I've become aware of an internal voice that speaks to me when I am out there. It constantly focuses me back on "this moment, this moment, this moment, this note, this note, this note." The pivotal element of performing has become how present I can be, and from that place, how much I can allow my heart and my spirit to be available each night I go on stage.

I remember the night I first realized the power of this experience. I was about two songs into the show, and I couldn't seem to make the connection. The audience response was okay but bland. All of a sudden, to my right, I saw two eyes lit up like lights. I looked over, expecting to see a fan—you know, the male–female thing. Instead, I saw a young girl, about 10 years old, whose face was radiant. She was just pouring love at me. I looked in her eyes, and my heart opened.

As I sang, more eyes lit up, and then more and more. Each time I looked around, I saw another pair of eyes light up—children, women, guys, older people—it was like candles coming on all throughout the audience. All of a sudden, about three quarters of the way through that song—I was singing "It's About Time"—I got a standing ovation. Everybody had caught on fire. I felt totally connected to those people, and my heart was completely open. My inner voice said, *This is where you are headed: to live with an open heart.* There was an "of course" feeling about it. This is where I had been going my whole career, my whole life.

When you get there, when the heart opens, you know: *This* is what life *really* is. All that other stuff is a big overlay of fear. In the end, it comes down to experiencing inner peace; whether gained from the music of a stream or from the music of the heart, it makes no difference.

Catherine Oxenberg

Award-winning actress Catherine Oxenberg is the daughter of HRH Princess Elizabeth of Yugoslavia and the granddaughter of the former Regent King of Yugoslavia. She began her career as a model and has been featured on the covers of *Cosmopolitan*, *Glamour*, and *Interview*. She has appeared in numerous films and television programs and is best known for her role in the popular television series *Dynasty*. In 2005, she and her husband, actor Casper Van Dien, and their family were featured in the reality series *I Married a Princess*. ■

In 1991, I was going through a particularly difficult time. I had already experienced the high of being on the hugely popular television series *Dynasty*, and had then suffered through the crash of leaving the show. I'd also had my first child—a daughter I'd named India—and I was struggling to redefine myself in all areas of my life. My priorities had shifted so much. As a single mom, I needed to maintain my career, but it was no longer what fueled my ambition. The things that had motivated me before seemed less important, and I was trying to figure out where to find the passion to go forward again. What's more, I was still struggling with an eating disorder. I was bulimic—and had been from quite a young age. Although I'd fought against it most of my life, I had never been able to conquer it.

I was clearly in transition. Feeling that I needed to reshape my vision and put the present moment in context, I did what I often do in those situations: I looked back over my life to see what had gotten me from point

A to point B. Understanding that process usually helps me to figure out what to do next, but this time, I wasn't coming up with any answers.

Then, a book came into my life. My daughter's father, who was still my good friend, was an avid reader; he was always recommending books for me to read. One day, he gave me *The Power of One*, by Bryce Courtenay. This book, which is a work of fiction, literally transformed my life. It changed the way I approached my future by giving me a new perspective on my past. It helped me understand the significance of some of the key events in my life—especially the role of a certain person in shaping my path.

The Power of One is the story of a young boy, called Peekay, growing up in South Africa during World War II. At the age of five, while traveling home alone from boarding school, Peekay is befriended by Hoppie, the conductor on the train, who is also a champion boxer. The ebullient young Hoppie has a passionate drive to be a world champion, and during Peekay's two-day journey, Hoppie instills the same commitment to become a boxer in Peekay's heart and mind, along with a powerful set of values. The interaction with Hoppie—though brief—defines who Peekay becomes as a human being, illustrating "the power of one": the power one human being can have in a person's life.

When I read this, I suddenly realized that my life had been touched in the same way—though I had never really understood it till just that moment. When I was 13 years old, my mother was engaged to the famous actor Richard Burton. He was the only male figure in my childhood who talked to me as if I were an adult, and we had many fun times, just the two of us.

Richard and I were always doing creative things together. He taught me Shakespeare, helping me rehearse for my role in the school play as Mustard Seed—one of the naughty fairies in *A Midsummer Night's Dream*—practicing my lines with me and giving me a deeper understanding of iambic pentameter, as well as Shakespeare's genius. I even directed him in a home movie, casting him as the evil king and my mother as the evil queen in a story I'd made up. Richard and I loved to work for hours at a time creating giant, six-foot crossword puzzles. We'd invent the clues and the answers and make them fit together. Everything we did was imaginative, cooperative, and fun—and deeply nourishing to me. I'd never had an interaction like that with an adult. He was probably the only person in my childhood who gave me 100% of his attention for any length of time. The quality of his love, expressed through his attention and interest in me, is what inspired me to follow in his footsteps and become an actress.

I also wanted to be like Richard because I wanted to treat people the way he did—except when he was drunk. Even at that age, I could see what he was going through with his alcoholism and thought, *I wonder if it's possible to be a great artist and not be consumed by your darkness.* Yet in spite of his addiction, his soul called my soul to action, igniting something in me that said, *That's what I want to be in my life.*

I was 16 the next time that I saw Richard. He and my mother had broken off their engagement long before. It was 1977 and I was in New York. Richard was performing in *Equus* on Broadway. To make the play more interactive, they had some of the audience sit on risers right on the stage. Richard had arranged for me to sit up there, and at the end of the performance, after he took his first bow, he came over to where I was sitting. He took my hand and led me out to center stage so I could take a bow with him.

I was so embarrassed! At that point in my life, all I could think about was that I was five pounds overweight. I was also too startled and overwhelmed by the clamor of the applause to understand the significance of what was happening.

That was the last time I saw Richard. Now, as I read *The Power of One*, I suddenly understood my relationship with him in terms of one individual's power to change the course of a person's life—even through a passing encounter. In my case, I was lucky to have more time to spend with Richard than Peekay had with Hoppie. Still, it was only in retrospect that I could appreciate his gift to me: He was interested in me—in what I had to say and in my creative process—and he treated me as if that process matched his. Richard inspired in me a self-respect, a dignity, and a belief in myself as a creative being that I'd never had before. I saw then that his gift had led to the many magical successes I'd enjoyed as a young adult—including my admission to Harvard and my debut as a model via a 10-page spread in *Vogue*—and later, my role in *Dynasty*.

Looking back, I could also see that Richard was my angelic guide—pointing the way to what I could do. When he led me out onto the *Equus* stage, he was handing me the audience; it was a real passing of the torch. *The Power of One* helped me understand that in that moment, Richard had symbolically passed me the baton in what I now considered a kind of spiritual relay race.

I'd come to the end of that leg of the race, and it was time for new inspiration. Whom could I turn to? As soon as I asked that question, I knew the answer: I had to honor myself as my own best guide. I thought again of Peekay, who ultimately learned that "the power of one" is the power to believe in yourself so deeply that you can prevail against any opposition. I saw that I had to access my own wisdom and my own magic, and connect to a higher source within to take my life to the next stage.

The first thing I did involved my battle with bulimia. Since India's birth, I had been trying so hard. Now that I had another life I was responsible for, I knew I had to stop throwing up—but I just couldn't. I had spent time in therapy. I understood the root causes of the disorder, but that had never set me free, and since Richard had never fully conquered his alcoholism, I'd reached the end of his ability to guide me. I was on my own. After reading *The Power of One*, I checked myself into rehab and stayed for six weeks.

Rehab helped dramatically, but didn't completely free me. I saw that I needed to deliberately sculpt what I wanted my future to look like—to become more fully the captain of my own ship. I wrote down a plan and made a commitment: For the next six months, I would read that plan out loud, morning and evening. I would create my own future.

After a few days of reading my plan, my inner voice became very loud, saying that if I didn't stop throwing up, I was going to die. There was a great deal of emphasis on the word *die*. Something inside me just snapped, and I felt *I got it!* That day, I stopped throwing up. That whole compulsion ended, effortlessly and spontaneously, and I started on the next leg of my journey. My new proactive approach to my future has led me to a far more joyful life, one based on creativity, family, love, and service to others.

This entire shift began with Courtenay's book. Reading it, I realized for the first time what an amazing gift Richard had given me with his nourishing and loving attention. He had shown me the power one person has to change another's life, just by believing in that person deeply. Richard was the power of one for me at a young age. Today, I know that I am my own power of one.

Jim MacLaren

Jim MacLaren, a Yale graduate and a former all-American lacrosse and football player, has survived two nearly fatal accidents, losing a leg in the first and becoming an incomplete quadriplegic as a result of the second. After the first accident, he went on to become a top marathoner and Ironman triathlete, racing against and beating able-bodied competition and earning the rank of the fastest amputee athlete in the world. Today, Jim is a motivational speaker, a doctoral candidate, and founder of the Choose Living Foundation. (For more information, visit www.jimmaclaren.com.) Jim has appeared on *Oprah* and in 2005 received the Arthur Ashe Courage Award, which is presented annually to individuals whose contributions transcend sports. ▪

In 1985, I was 22 years old and living in New York City, my future spread out and glittering before me. That spring, I'd graduated from Yale with a degree in theater studies and had moved to New York to pursue an acting career. Physically, I was still at the top of my game. I had been a six-foot-five, 285-pound defensive lineman on the Yale football team, and because I was fast for my size, I'd been an all-American lacrosse player as well. My athletic abilities were a source of great enjoyment and pride for me.

Then, in the space of a minute, my whole life changed. One day as I rode my motorcycle down Fifth Avenue, I was hit by a bus. I was thrown 89 feet, though I don't remember a thing. When I came out of my coma three weeks later, my left leg was gone below the knee.

I dove into physical rehabilitation. Although it was painful, I pushed myself not only to walk but also to run. Within a year, I was running 10-K road races and later ran the New York City and Boston marathons, breaking the records in both for amputee runners. Encouraged by my success, I decided to compete in triathlons. That meant swimming 2.4 miles, biking 112 miles, and running 26.3 miles—a full marathon—all in one day. Again, I trained intensely and soon I was breaking records once more. I loved the feeling of passing two-legged competitors, showing the world what a disabled athlete could achieve.

Fast-forward eight years. I had become the fastest one-legged man in the world. When I wasn't training or competing in marathons and triathlons, I traveled all over the country giving talks to various groups about persistence, determination and overcoming obstacles. Then the unthinkable happened—again.

I was in San Diego, competing in the bicycle portion of a triathlon. The streets were closed to motor traffic, but as I rounded the corner on my bike—racing to break my own record—I was hit by a van that had somehow gotten to the wrong place at the wrong time.

Unlike my first accident, this time I saw the vehicle coming. As the grille of the black van loomed toward me, I heard the sound of the driver hitting the accelerator instead of the brake. Then I blacked out as I was hit and flung across the street, smashing my head into a signpost and breaking my neck. My next memory is of coming to in the ambulance on the way to the hospital and noticing I couldn't feel my arms and legs. When I woke up after surgery in the hospital, I learned the devastating news: I was an incomplete quadriplegic. Although I still had some limited nerve activity that allowed me a small amount of movement, I would never walk again.

That was 12 years ago. As soon as I was able, I once again threw myself into physical rehab. Within 6 months I was living on my own. Since the accident, I've had physical challenges most people can't imagine. I have what I consider a "tragic gift": limited mobility and full sensation. As a result, I deal with constant pain, due to extensive nerve damage. I wake up every morning feeling like wet cement that's plugged into the wall: heavy, electric, and painful. On a good day, with 3 hours of agonizing effort, I am able to get out of bed, bathe, dress, and feed myself. I work out as often as I can, talk on the phone, write and answer e-mail, and drive a van specially outfitted with hand controls. In spite of the pain, I enjoy engaging in this daily ritual and in these activities that stretch my mind and body. But on a bad day . . . well, you don't want to know about a bad day.

Yet even with these limitations, today I am still a motivational speaker, as well as a doctoral candidate in mythology and depth psychology at Pacifica Graduate Institute. I was recently presented the 2005 Arthur Ashe Courage Award and appeared on Oprah Winfrey's show. Obviously, these aren't automatic outcomes for someone who becomes a quadriplegic; I could easily have become bitter and sorry for myself. I owe the initial redirection of my energies—the rechanneling of my fierce need to do and accomplish—to a book I read shortly after my second accident as I struggled to build my life yet again.

I found the book in December of 1993. I had just been released from rehabilitation at Craig Spinal Cord Institute in Englewood, Colorado, and had returned to Boulder, where I was living at the time. It was a snowy afternoon and I was at a beautiful, brick walking-mall. It was the first time I remember being by myself since the accident, and I was using a manual, or nonpowered, wheelchair. (Even though I don't have the use of my triceps, I can move my arms a little.) As I pushed myself slowly through the mall, I saw a bookstore and decided to go in. This proved to be difficult, as there was a little incline leading to the store's entrance. I started to roll backward but managed to stop myself. It was a huge physical and emotional victory when eventually I was able to push myself up into the store. My hands were cut from the ice on the rims of my wheels, but I hardly noticed.

Inside, I looked around. It was one those wonderful bookstores with brick walls, comfortable sofas, a fireplace, and wood floors. I wheeled myself over to the bookshelves. Being in a wheelchair was still new for me; I was adjusting to the fact that my eye level was now at four foot five instead of at almost six foot five like before. I came upon a display of new releases. Next to each book was a tag that explained briefly what the book was about.

I was instantly drawn to one book, *The Passion of the Western Mind: Understanding the Ideas That Have Shaped Our World View*, by Richard Tarnas. Described as an explanation and discussion of Western thought from the Greeks to the present, the book had a number of glowing reviews on its cover. I saw that Joseph Campbell—one of my favorite authors—was one of the scholars who had written an endorsement: "The most lucid and concise presentation I have read . . . of what every student should know about the history of Western thought." I managed to pull Tarnas's book off the shelf on my own—another victory—and began reading.

Before the second accident, I'd read philosophy and books on self-knowledge—including works by Campbell, Krishnamurti, Socrates, and Plato—and the concepts had started to make a lot of sense to me. I had even incorporated them into my speeches, but I was really speaking from my head, not my heart. I was a 27-year-old guy with one leg, trying to be superhuman. As I spoke about Krishnamurti and self-knowledge, I was picking out the woman in the audience whom I was going to ask out to dinner that night. My speeches definitely affected people, but in those days it was probably more important to my psyche that they come up to me and tell me how amazing I was. I wasn't as deep as I could have been.

Now, as I read the first pages of *The Passion of the Western Mind*, I felt the stirring of a new level of interest and curiosity about these concepts. The book triggered a desire to understand my own belief system and how it connected to the universal issues of being human. I took the book home and began to study it.

Since becoming a quadriplegic, I have sometimes been asked, "Why do you think you had two accidents?" When I answer, "Maybe I finally needed to sit down," I'm only partly joking. Over the next few weeks, as I read Tarnas's engaging and thought-provoking book, the ideas in it—which before had engaged me only on an intellectual level—began to settle into the depths of my psyche and my spirit. Socrates says, "The unexamined life is not worth living." From the moment I was put into this chair, its gift has been to make me go inside myself. *The Passion of the Western Mind* shaped that process and was the catalyst for me to really begin examining my life. The book lit me up and made me eager to learn more about the history of religion, philosophy, and psychology. I saw that all these disciplines centered on humankind's search for meaning, which suddenly seemed relevant to my own situation. My life had changed so abruptly and completely and I was still scrambling to make sense of it all. What was the meaning of my life *now*?

Reading the book, I discovered that I wasn't as alone and different from everyone else as I had thought. Although my situation was certainly more extreme, I saw that human beings have been searching for life's meaning for a very long time: It's been humankind's central quest. I even had the thought that many of my earlier achievements might actually have been distractions. Now—because of my physical limitations—I had an opportunity to focus deeply on the one thing in life that was most worth doing.

I credit *The Passion of the Western Mind* for inspiring me to begin my graduate studies. My first step, after finishing Tarnas's book, was to enroll in a writing workshop at Naropa University. During the workshop, I was amazed at what came out of me. I discovered a whole new side of myself—one that was sensitive, introspective, and expressive. My body had been effectively taken away from me—in two installments—but my mind and heart were more than intact, and I used them to explore the depths of my own personality and being.

After that, I began attending Pacifica Graduate Institute, studying world religions, mythology, and depth psychology, which is the study of the deep, archetypal elements of our psychology. Over the years, as I've taken more classes on mythological archetypes, I've seen that my struggles to live with my constant pain and my frustrations with my limitations are *my* journeys to the underworld—where I battle inner demons and fight for my life. I return from these journeys with more wisdom about the human condition and more compassion for others' wounds.

When people hear my story, they sometimes comment that I am a modern-day Job: How much can one man take and still love God and the life he is dealt? But I don't look at it that way anymore. After a lot of study and soul-searching, I have come to the conclusion that Job's troubles were not God's way of testing Job's love for Him, but a way to bring Job closer to God—and to force Job to come to a deeper understanding of himself. In this same way, my accidents have brought me closer to God and to a place inside myself where I am finding peace and a fulfillment that go beyond outer achievements.

So many things in my life have changed in the last 12 years—and remarkably, some for the better. In the old days, when I was only an amputee, if I didn't get in the 20-mile run or that 100-mile bike ride, I felt guilty. Today it's enough to engage with another person, to meditate or write or speak or learn something, for me to feel good about the day. If I simply reflect on my life, the day, this moment, or the beauty of the sun that I'm sitting in right now, I am satisfied. I have become a more loving human being since that snowy afternoon in Boulder when I first found *The Passion of the Western Mind*.

I can only speak from my own experience, but there are two things I do know: One, we can never know what our lives are going to look like, and two, as long as we accept what happens to us and move forward, we will always be okay—maybe not in the way *Merriam-Webster* defines okay—but in the larger sense. For I have no doubt that unless we fight it, we are always moving toward a better, more whole state of being.

Wyland

Wyland, the world's foremost ocean artist, has been a pioneer in the marine art movement since 1981. This painter, sculptor, and muralist is one of the most prolific artists of our time. To date, in addition to his spectacular paintings of a wide variety of marine life, Wyland has completed more than 93 of his landmark murals, the renowned Whaling Walls, throughout the United States as well as Canada, Japan, Australia, Mexico, France, and New Zealand. It is estimated that more than one billion people are exposed to Wyland's art each year. There are approximately 500,000 collectors of his work in more than 30 countries, and perhaps more than any other artist, he has raised the planet's environmental consciousness with regard to the oceans and their inhabitants. ◼

I was born and raised just outside Motor City—Detroit, Michigan. Considering that my life is dedicated to making the art of the ocean visible for the whole planet, my birthplace seems a mistake. I've always felt I should have been born on the West Coast, closer to the whales and other marine life I've come to love so well. But in truth, it hardly matters where I was born, since my love affair with the ocean actually started with a book— *The Silent World*, by Jacques Cousteau.

I was around 13 years old when I read it. Even then, I knew that I wanted to be an artist. At the age of 3, I had painted my first murals— on the back of the headboard on my parents' bed. I would slide underneath the bed with the paint and brushes and paint these detailed landscapes of the world of dinosaurs. Later, my mom let me set up a studio in our basement, and I spent hours there painting. It was a way for me to relax after sports and schoolwork.

I didn't go out looking for *The Silent World*; a friend of mine just handed it to me. I had no idea that I would find it so compelling. The book was first published in 1953 and has sold more than five million copies in 22 languages. Cousteau is mainly known for his films, but his writing is tremendous. Using words, he paints an incredibly vivid picture of the undersea world. I believe Cousteau was able to do this because he knew that world so well. He had an emotional bond with the sea; people often say it was like his mistress. His descriptions of his encounters with marine animals are powerful, too. He writes about swimming with sharks and manta rays. At the time his book was published, most people feared the undersea world, but he made it very clear that the most dangerous animals in the sea were not the sharks or whales, but us.

Cousteau transported people into the marine world in a way that nobody else had. I immediately fell under the book's spell and couldn't put it down—I was up until two, three o'clock in the morning reading it. When I finished, I knew I wanted to be just like Jacques Cousteau. *Someday*, I vowed to myself, *I too will be an ocean explorer and diver*.

After I read *The Silent World*, I began to lobby my mother to take our family on a vacation to California to visit her sister, my Aunt Linda. It took a year of pushing, but when I was 14, we finally went. When I saw the ocean for the first time at Laguna Beach, my budding interest in it, inspired by Cousteau's book, blossomed into a full-fledged passion. As we stood on the beach, the waves crashing onto the rocks and the sand, I looked out to the horizon. A few hundred yards out from shore, I saw two black backs covered with clusters of yellow barnacles, accompanied by magnificent sprays of water blowing up into the air. I was looking at living whales for the first time. I couldn't see the entire body of each whale—only their backs as they surfaced to blow. But that was enough for me. I was ecstatic. I had never seen an animal that large in the wild. I felt as if I were seeing something very rare and beautiful—as if it were a miracle to be there when they swam by. Words alone can't describe how this first sighting affected me; I can only say I'll never forget what I saw that day. I was changed by each and every detail of it. I told myself that one day I'd live here. Sure enough, 10 years later, I moved to Laguna

Beach and painted my first Whaling Wall mural not more than a hundred yards from the very place I'd seen those gray whales.

When I returned to Detroit, I began painting ocean scenes. Over time, I found that when I painted the marine creatures, I grew closer to them and understood not only their anatomy but also their spirit. I remember thinking about dinosaurs becoming extinct, and being afraid the same thing was going to happen to the whales. Soon, I became passionate about wanting to play a role in preserving the oceans and the marine environment.

I came up with my own way to accomplish this. At the time, members of Greenpeace were going out in small Zodiacs and putting themselves between the harpoons and the whales. My method was different. I wanted to draw attention to the delicate beauty of these creatures by painting them and then sharing my art with others. I believe that if people see the splendor in nature—in this case the undersea world—they'll work to preserve it.

Reading *The Silent World* had other life-changing effects, including introducing me to diving. Cousteau, along with a French engineer named Gagnan, invented the aqualung, or scuba (self-contained underwater breathing apparatus), and he was one of the first people to swim unrestricted: without an air tube connected to a remote oxygen source. In the book, he shares his experience of that remarkable underwater freedom in this beautiful description of his first scuba dive, taken in the Mediterranean Sea in June of 1943: "At night I had often had visions of flying by extending my arms as wings. Now I flew without wings. . . . From this day forward we would swim across miles of country no man had known, free and level, with our flesh feeling what the fish scales know."

Although *The Silent World* is mostly text, it has one great photo of Jacques Cousteau diving. That photo, combined with Cousteau's description, intensified my desire to learn to dive. When I started a few years later, it was everything Cousteau said it was—and more. Diving has become a spiritual experience for me. Like Cousteau, I feel that I am actually flying underwater. Each dive has its own magical moments.

I think diving has an even greater power for me because of the physical limitations I had as a small boy. Born with a severe clubfoot, I underwent

11 major surgeries before the age of five and was continuously hobbled by a corrective cast that prevented my swimming. I wasn't able to go into the water like everybody else; I could only dream about and imagine it. When all the casts were finally off and we took our first vacation to Cass Lake, I couldn't wait to get in the water. The very first time I jumped in, I was swimming well; it felt so natural. In fact, I'm more comfortable in the water than out. I'm more of a sea mammal, I guess.

It's amazing how important a book can be. Before I read Cousteau, I mostly read books about all kinds of art; I was inspired by artists such as Salvador Dali and Robert Bateman. And although I loved the water, I hadn't made a connection to the ocean. Reading *The Silent World*, art and nature came together for me. It was "the barnacle that broke the whale's back" and changed the course of my life. Cousteau inspired people to respect, love, and protect the ocean and its inhabitants with his artful use of words. Today, I do the same thing with a paintbrush.

Lisa Nichols

Lisa Nichols is a motivational speaker, personal coach and the founder and CEO of Motivating the Teen Spirit, which conducts breakthrough trainings for school systems, leadership programs, the juvenile justice system, and youth agencies. Lisa's work has affected the lives of more than 55,000 teens, prevented more than 1,100 suicides, reunited thousands of teens with their parents, and influenced hundreds of teen dropouts to return to school. She has been recognized with several awards for her dedication to bettering the lives of teens—and adults—all across America. Lisa is also the coauthor of *Chicken Soup for the African-American Soul*. ▪

It has been 16 years since I first read Stephen Covey's *The 7 Habits of Highly Effective People*. If you asked me today how I came upon it, I would probably say that it floated down to me from the sky with lights glowing all around it and landed in my hands after much prayer. Perhaps that will give you an idea of the enormous effect this book had on me and how it has shaped my life since then.

What actually happened was that a colleague from work recommended I read it. At the time, I was in my early twenties and worked for a software company. It was a decent job and I was good at it, but it didn't really express who I was. I was searching for my purpose, my passion—for who I wanted to be in the world. I still felt defined by who I had been in school and who I thought other people wanted me to be.

The woman who recommended Covey's book was a senior person at my office. She was 15 years older than I was and I had a great deal of respect for her: Not only had she been in corporate America much longer than I had, but also there was a groundedness and peacefulness about her that I wanted in my own life. Everyone at work, including this woman, saw me as a professional, a mover and a shaker. She wanted to add value to my life and felt that this book would do that.

When I heard the title, I became very excited. "Highly effective" was what I wanted to be. At the time, I felt I was only "partly effective." All the self-help books I'd read before were affirmation books, spiritual books, or daily meditation books. I had never read an intellectual, cognitive-learning-type book. It was my first "big girl" book!

To be honest, I was slightly intimidated by the idea of reading Covey's book; just contemplating it was a big step for me. In school, I hadn't been a huge academic success, and at that point, I hadn't yet recognized my true gift of speaking and communication. All I knew about myself were my academic challenges and limitations. I had heard opinion after opinion and label after label, none of them inspiring. Inside, I believed myself to be someone bigger than who I'd been told I was, but at age 23, I didn't yet have any tangible evidence of that.

I bought *The 7 Habits of Highly Effective People* on the day I left for a business trip to Spokane, Washington. I remember sitting in bed in my hotel room early the next morning, reading the part of the book in which Covey asks you to go through a meditation with him. He asks you to imagine yourself walking into a parlor. You smell the flowers and hear the organ music. You walk down the aisle of this parlor. (He kept using the word *parlor*, which I found strange.) You see the faces of people sitting in the chairs, and they're all people that you know, including the ones you love the most. Everyone has a look of reverence on his or her face, a look of appreciation, and a look of sadness as well. You're not quite sure why they're there. You walk up to the front of the room and see a casket. Looking into the casket, you come face-to-face . . . with yourself! You are at your own funeral!

At this, I felt a shock ripple through my body, but kept reading. Covey goes on to explain that there are four people who will speak: a family member, a friend, a work colleague, and someone from your civic circle. What will they say about you at your funeral? What kind of friend were you? What kind of sister were you? What kind of coworker were you? What kind of neighbor were you? He finishes the section by saying "begin with the end in mind."

The whole thing was so incredibly startling to me. I had never once thought about my life in that way. I wasn't bad or mean, but I knew that I was essentially selfish and self-absorbed; my agenda was Lisa-driven. I'd always been a giving person, so I could mask it very well, but underneath it all, I was into living my life right now. I wasn't into leaving a legacy.

A couple of hours later, as I was driving to a meeting with my clients outside of Spokane, I suddenly became consumed with emotion about that part of Covey's book. I began to cry and couldn't stop. I realized *in my heart* that I wasn't living the way I wanted to be remembered. If I died that day, on that road—which because I was crying so hard was very possible—I wasn't sure what they would say about me at my funeral. Although I wasn't leaving any blatantly horrible impressions, I wasn't leaving my best impressions, either. I was deeply upset at the unconscious way I was living my life.

The other thing that struck me was that there were so many things I still wanted to do. Not physical things like start a business or travel to Africa or Jamaica, but things I wanted to do and be *with people*—like sit with my mom and paint her toenails or laugh hysterically with my dad until both our stomachs hurt. I wanted them to have those memories, but I was too busy for those kinds of things at the time.

I cried for the entire two-and-a-half-hour drive. When I got to the client's office, I immediately went into the bathroom and put on a fresh coat of makeup. My shirt was stained with brown spots from my foundation, which had dripped off my face with my tears. I couldn't hide those spots or the puffiness of my eyes—and I couldn't hide my excitement, either. I needed to share what I had discovered in reading Covey with someone else because it was so big; it couldn't stay inside of me. So I told my clients about the funeral exercise in Covey's book and what it had meant to me. It sparked a great conversation about how we were living our lives. For the last 16 years, I've been sharing that same lesson in one form or another with everyone I meet.

I flew back to California and started trying to live the way I wanted to be remembered. It was a two-step process. Before I could do my mom's nails or laugh with my dad, I felt I had to stop doing things that I wasn't proud of. They weren't terrible things, but they weren't what I wanted to leave as my legacy. I had been throwing lingerie parties on the weekends to earn extra money. While it was a great venture and people had a lot of fun, when I really went to my core, I didn't want to be remembered as the person who sold a lot of lingerie to young women. So I dissolved that business. I also had a talent for writing steamy romance novels, but I put aside any idea of pursuing that occupation. It was simply another thing I didn't want to be remembered for.

Some things were easier to let go of than others. It took me a long time to give up my unhealthy relationships with men. I started by looking inside myself for the reasons behind these behaviors. What was it that made me feel I needed to have three guys all chasing me at the same time? Eventually I got to the place where I could say no to a gorgeous guy if I knew he wasn't right for me. I was more and more aware of the long-range effects of my behavior on all levels.

I think the most important thing *The 7 Habits of Highly Effective People* gave me was the permission to write my own life. Before I read the book, I hadn't let myself "stand inside" the gift of speaking that God had given me. But I could tell that I had something special to give by the way people reacted to me when I spoke. As part of my job, I trained the staff members of alcohol and drug recovery agencies to use the company's software. Everyone was so afraid of computers at that time—this was 16 years ago—that I always gave them a little inspirational session before I started the software training. No one ever wanted the motivational part of the training to end—including me.

Giving inspiration made me feel more alive than anything else. Every time I did a motivational session, I felt this little person inside me just screaming, "Yes, *yes*, *YES!*" When I sat down at the computer to start the software training, I felt that little person die. My clients began to ask me, "Can you give us a second motivational session at the end of the day?" I realized that they didn't want training for the computers—they wanted inspiration to deal with what was waiting for them at home. Afterward they would tell me with tears in their eyes how much I had helped them.

I thought of that when I read the passage in *The 7 Habits of Highly Effective People* that says "Begin with the end in mind." I knew that when

I went to my grave, I wanted people to say, "She was a great speaker." So I quit my job and began my speaking career. The first thing I did was to sit down and start writing. For 15 days, all I did was write. When I was done, I had written five speeches. Then I went back to those same clients, the alcohol and drug recovery agencies, and said, "Can I come speak to your clients and your staff?" They all agreed and allowed me to do staff motivational sessions as well as client sessions. From the start, my speeches were always well received, and my confidence in myself grew. It was the beginning of the successful speaking/consulting/coaching business I have today.

I still feel the effects, both professionally and personally, of "attending my own funeral" so many years ago. In fact, every important decision I've made since reading Covey's book has been based on that one question: How do I want to be remembered? Today, I am literally writing my eulogy with the way I live my life. Of course, I'm not perfect. I've fallen short on many things, but I can honestly say I have no regrets. If God took me home tonight, I would leave here dancing.

Rafe Esquith

Rafe Esquith has been teaching fifth grade for the last 25 years, the last 22 in Central Los Angeles. In addition to teaching his students Shakespeare—Rafe's students have opened for the Royal Shakespeare Company, have appeared at the Globe Theatre in London, and recently performed in front of Congress—he also helps them achieve academic success: Many have gone on to attend outstanding universities all over the world. Rafe's teaching awards include the Walt Disney American Teacher Award for *National Teacher of the Year* and Oprah Winfrey's *Use Your Life Award*. Queen Elizabeth invested him as a Member of the British Empire, and President George W. Bush presented him with the National Medal of Arts in the Oval Office—the first teacher in history so honored. Rafe is the author of *There Are No Shortcuts* and *Teach Like Your Hair's on Fire: The Methods and Madness Inside Room 56*. ∎

I should have been walking on air. In 1992, the Walt Disney Company had made me their National Teacher of the Year. The attention was overwhelming: phone calls, letters, media requests—wave after wave of accolades and praise. I smiled for the cameras, but inside I was absolutely miserable. I felt like a sham and a failure.

At that time, I was 38 years old. I had been teaching for nine years, the last six of them at Hobart Boulevard Elementary School, which is in a very rough neighborhood in Central Los Angeles. Over 90% of the kids in my fifth-grade classes were (and still are) from families living below the poverty level. Nobody speaks English as a first language, and everybody is on free breakfast and lunch programs. At Hobart, I had been trying new things with my students and had been successful at getting them to come to the classroom at 6:00 AM for a before-school math clinic. Not only did their math scores shoot up, but also many of them discovered that they loved math. They also showed up in large numbers for my lunch-period lessons in playing various musical instruments, and they were wild about our after-school theater program.

I knew that the kids grew a lot during their time in my classroom, and that their experiences gave them a chance to see much more of what was possible for them. But I also knew that when they went off to middle school, many of them went right back into gangs and drugs. This knowledge ate me up inside. In addition, there were plenty of other kids whom I felt I should be reaching but wasn't. I felt I wasn't successful at all.

I also discovered the dark side of acclaim. The Disney award brought me new fame and exposure. I was horrified by the many people—some of whom had never even met me—who sent me hate mail, who left notes on my windshield, and sometimes even smashed and dented my car. Many didn't like that I upset the status quo, while others felt it was unfair that I should be singled out for recognition. Between my own internal sense of failure and these hurtful incidents, I was a wreck.

In those days, my favorite book was *The Adventures of Huckleberry Finn*, and it's still one of my favorite books. I love how Huck and Jim make a trip down the river, running away from the racism, violence, and hypocrisy of society. At the end of that book, Huck has a chance to go back and be civilized, but he refuses, saying, "I been there before." Instead, he decides to "light out for the Territory." In my youth, I used to think, *Yeah, you tell 'em, Huck. Screw the world, because people aren't worth it. Walk your own path.* But now as a teacher, Huck wasn't giving me the answers I needed. I understood why Huck would run, but his solution didn't fit my situation. I was in my classroom; I wasn't supposed to be running away. I was left with the bleak option of continuing to give it my all—though my all was clearly not enough—while battling the angry and venomous tide that swirled around me. I soon felt that I couldn't do it anymore.

One night, I was sitting in bed, bemoaning my fate, when my beautiful, brilliant wife, Barbara, said, "Maybe it's time for you to read this book again." And she handed me *To Kill a Mockingbird*.

I knew I wouldn't be able to sleep, so I took the book and went into my study to read. There, in my gym shorts and T-shirt, I sat up all night, reading.

I had read *To Kill a Mockingbird* several times before and loved it. When I was a teenager, I'd always thought that book was about a trial and the search for justice for Tom Robinson, the innocent black man accused of raping a white woman. Of course, the book is about that, but that night I realized it's about much, much more. And it was in the character of Atticus Finch that I found the answers I was looking for.

Early in the book—something I'd never noticed in my previous readings—when Atticus is handed the case, his children ask him, "Are we going to win the case?" Atticus says no, very quietly. Yet Atticus doesn't run; he doesn't light out for the Territory. He goes into the courtroom and fights anyway, knowing that he is going to lose, knowing that the town despises him—they spit at him, they terrorize his children, and so on. But Atticus has a personal code of behavior. He doesn't do things for anybody else. In his code, you stand up and defend innocent people, even if everybody disagrees with you. You fight the good fight. The parallels to my own situation hit me like a thunderbolt—the classroom was my courtroom!

Excited, I kept reading. Soon I found another passage that went off like a small bomb inside of me and forever changed the way I taught my classes. In this passage, Atticus comes home from work one day, and Scout, his young daughter, asks him, "Do you defend niggers, Atticus?"

He responds, "Don't say nigger, Scout."

She says that everybody in school uses that word and is criticizing Atticus. Atticus explains that he is defending a Negro, much to the town's displeasure. "Then why are you doin' it?" she asks him.

Atticus answers, "For a number of reasons. The main one is, if I didn't I couldn't hold my head up in town . . . [and] I could never ask you [or Jem] to mind me again."

Reading that passage, I understood suddenly that this book wasn't only about a trial but was also about the raising of children—and that the number-one rule in raising children is to be a role model. I saw that if I wanted to be a truly great teacher, I had to be the person I wanted my students to be. If I wanted them to work hard, rather than lecture them, I had to be the hardest worker they had ever seen. If I wanted them to be kind, I had to be the kindest person—*even and especially when times were bad and others were unkind.* If other teachers were mean to me, it didn't matter. That wasn't what I did. It sounded so simple, but I knew it wouldn't be easy. Still, it was what I had to do to become the teacher I wanted to be, and I resolved to do it.

In the final section of *To Kill a Mockingbird*, Atticus and the sheriff wrestle with the dilemma of Boo Radley's fate in the presence of Jem and Scout. Boo, a mentally challenged man, has saved Atticus's children from a physical attack by a loathsome man who lives in the area. The sheriff wants to hush the facts of the situation up, because he knows that the attention—even though it is positive—would be terribly damaging to the extremely shy Boo. But Atticus insists that the truth be told no matter what the consequences. He has worked to instill in his children a deep respect for the truth and is afraid his children won't understand the subtleties of the situation. Then Scout pipes up, saying that they have to hush it up, otherwise it would be like "killing a mockingbird"—a bird that never harms anyone—which they have talked about earlier as an example of a true sin. Scout's comment signals to Atticus that his small children have learned a more important and more complex lesson: that doing the right thing in the larger context trumps all other considerations. They have an even deeper understanding of right action than he'd realized. This passage had a profound effect on me, teaching me to have faith in my students' ability to understand and achieve even beyond my hopes for them.

I finished the book as the sun was coming up. With tears streaming down my face, I closed the book and stared out the window, my mind whirling with insights but my heart calm and peaceful at last. The book was the same book I had read so many times before, but I was not the same person reading it. All the life experiences I'd been through had made me see the world differently. Reading *To Kill a Mockingbird* that night affected everything in my life, but most especially it affected my teaching. Although the change didn't happen in one day, it started that day.

I decided to begin teaching ethics and moral development in my class. In those days, I, like so many young teachers, made the understandable mistake of focusing mainly on academic excellence: If you can improve a child's math test scores from 60% to 90%, then you feel you are a good teacher. That's a wonderful thing, but does it help to create good people? This is the bigger issue, and it's one that is not often discussed because it's far more difficult to achieve. It's not hard to raise students' math scores. What's hard in this time, in my students' neighborhoods where there is gunfire every night, is to teach kids to be good citizens.

I started reading everything I could on Atticus, which led me to the work of social scientist Lawrence Kohlberg. Kohlberg delineates six levels of moral development that explain why people do what they do. Today, I use this simplified version of Kohlberg's model in my classes:

1. Level one: We do things because we want to avoid trouble
2. Level two: We do things for a reward
3. Level three: We do things to please other people (i.e., to stroke our own egos)
4. Level four: We do things to obey external rules
5. Level five: We do things to be considerate of others (because we care about others' feelings)
6. Level six: We do things to live by our own sense of what is right

When I present this information to my kids, they get it! They walk around identifying the different levels: *There's level-three behavior! There's level-five!* Everyone in my class understands that becoming a level-six thinker takes a lifetime, but it is something we aim for. Atticus is the model of morality and of living a level-six life. I use other examples of "acting from level-six" from a wide variety of sources—including *The Shawshank Redemption* and *Death of a Salesman*—to inspire my students to act not for recognition but for the fulfillment to be found in doing what is right.

A number of years ago, I had a clear demonstration that my students were absorbing this lesson. I was in class one morning, teaching math, when the mother of a first grader in the school—not a woman I knew—came to the classroom searching for somebody. The day before, the woman's child had been beaten up on the way home from school. The child had been kicked and terrorized. While a group of kids stood around laughing, an older girl had come by and, seeing the situation, had picked up the little girl, brushed her off, and walked her home, leaving her at her door. The mother was going from class to class trying to find the student who had helped her child, so she could thank her. As they listened to the mother's story, my class of 32 kids was looking around to see if anyone would come forward, asking each other, "Did you do it? Do you know who did it?" Nobody knew. I looked around, too. I noticed that one of my students, a girl sitting in the back of the room, had been working intently on her math homework the whole time and had not lifted her head once. That struck me as odd, since this girl hated math! When the mother left, she looked up and our eyes met. She gave me a look that said, *Don't say anything*. She was clearly displaying level-six behavior. That student, who went on to attend an Ivy League college, is still in touch with me today, but we've never discussed that incident.

The final aspect of the personal transformation I experienced after reading *Mockingbird* was the knowledge that no matter how many times I failed—and I fail all the time—I wouldn't quit. Today, I don't even think about it—ever. This is where I make my stand. Atticus would never leave the town, never leave the courtroom. For the same reasons, although I've been given incredible offers to leave my school for enormous sums of money, I refuse. If I take them, I'm lost. I tell the children that Room 56 is an important place, a place where we can create opportunities for them and change their lives. If I leave, what does that say to them? What does that say to the hundreds of former students who continue to give me unbelievable support?

Still, there are times I ask myself, *Is it worth it?* The answer? *Not always*. There are days when it is definitely *not* worth it, and days when I really question whether it's worth it, but in the end, this is what I do. It's what all teachers do. The difference between the good teachers and the others is that the good teachers don't give up. Just one more lesson I learned from Atticus.

Chellie Campbell

Chellie Campbell is a former bookkeeper and musical comedy actress who combined her acting and financial skills to create the popular Financial Stress Reduction® Workshop. A full-time speaker and seminar leader, Chellie is the author of *The Wealthy Spirit* (Sourcebooks, 2002) and *Zero to Zillionaire* (Sourcebooks, 2006). ▪

"You're so stupid!" my boss screamed at me. "If you can't do any better than that, don't come back here tomorrow!"

His face was bright red, the veins in his neck as thick as ropes. Like many powerful motion picture producers, my boss—let's call him Oscar—had a reputation for screaming. As his executive assistant, I was a handy target. Terrified, I fled to the bathroom, closed the door of the stall, sat on the toilet, and broke down crying. I was so unhappy. What was wrong with me? And I was so angry! What was wrong with *him*?

But mostly, I was so scared. How was I going to stand up to him?

In 1981, I hadn't had much practice at standing up to people—especially if they were angry. My marriage had recently disintegrated because every time my husband got angry, I got quiet. But my retreat into silence only made him yell louder. Finally, I could cope with his rages no longer and I left.

Now, here I was with a rageaholic boss, having jumped out of the proverbial frying pan only to find myself plunged right into the fire. As I realized that, I started to giggle, my sobs punctuated with hiccups of laughter. Isn't that always how growth happens? We recreate the circumstances

CHELLIE CAMPBELL / 39

we can't handle over and over until—finally—we choose a different way to behave that solves the problem. I recognized my situation and knew it was time to change. I knew it because of a book I was reading.

When I Say No, I Feel Guilty, by Manuel Smith, was one of a number of books I picked up after my divorce, looking for guidance and help. There were a number of questions on the book's cover—including ones asking if people walked all over you or whether your requests for raises were unsuccessful. My answer to each of these was yes. I knew these weren't good answers. *Is there help for me?* I thought.

I bought the book and soaked up its "Bill of Assertive Rights," 10 statements that set out healthy personal boundaries—such as having the right to stop justifying your behavior with reasons and excuses, the right to change your mind, the right to say "I don't know," and even the right to make mistakes—and take responsibility for them. The author concludes this list of rights by reiterating the title of the book: You have the right to say no, without feeling guilty.

I couldn't believe what I was reading. Page after page gave me explicit instructions on how to please myself before pleasing others. It said that I had the right to choose my own happiness first. That I could say no. And more importantly, that I had the right not to *explain why* I was saying no.

All my life I had been a people-pleaser. I thought everyone had to like me and approve of me, or I was doing something wrong. But this book suggested that my first responsibility was to myself. And that trying to please everyone else was an impossible task doomed to failure anyway.

I eagerly absorbed these lessons. But you can't train yourself to do something new without attracting to yourself the circumstances in which to actually do it. So here I was, sobbing in the bathroom, an angry boss waiting by my desk like a disturbed wasp ready to sting me into submission.

I knew I had to fight. I armed myself with my "Bill of Assertive Rights" like a housewife with a spray can of Raid. What was the worst that could happen? I could get fired. So what? I had survived getting divorced from my husband, so I guessed I could survive getting divorced from my boss. I knew for sure I would not survive being yelled at every day.

I washed my face with cold water. I took several deep breaths. Then I headed for my Big Confrontation.

He was sitting at his desk as though nothing had happened. Didn't he know this was a life-changing event for me?! No. He didn't know.

I walked into his office and said, "Oscar, could I talk to you for a minute?"

He nodded and I shut the door.

"Oscar," I said, "I respectfully request that you please not yell at me again. I just had to go cry in the bathroom for half an hour, and this isn't effective time management for you or for me."

Poor dear, he looked completely taken aback. I don't think anyone had ever asked him not to yell at them.

"Oh, you shouldn't mind that, Chellie," he said. "I like you. I think you do a good job. The yelling doesn't mean anything."

"It means something to me," I said. "It's very upsetting and makes me cry. So I'd appreciate it very much if you didn't do it again."

"All right, all right," he muttered, shuffling some papers on his desk.

I went back to my desk in shock. I had asked him not to yell at me, and he had said, "All right." He hadn't fired me. I was dazed and amazed. I couldn't believe it was that easy.

Three weeks later, he yelled at me again. I cried in the bathroom again. Same routine: sob, laugh, wash face, deep breath. I remembered a quotation from Shakespeare: "Once more unto the breach, dear friends."

I walked back into his office and said, "Oscar, could I talk to you for a minute?"

He nodded, and I started to close the door. The door hadn't shut before he started apologizing.

About four months later, he yelled at me one more time. I yelled back at him. He never yelled at me again.

But not getting yelled at is not the same as getting ahead in your career. I had more work to do with the principles outlined in *When I Say No, I Feel Guilty*.

One day, in a cost-cutting measure, they fired the office gofer (the person at the bottom of the company roster who would "go fer" this and "go fer" that). They weren't going to hire a new one, and the rest of us were anxious about who was going to get the gofer assignments from then on.

I decided that it wasn't going to be me. I knew that if I started doing any of the gofer's tasks, I would get all of those jobs. Respect for me would disappear, along with any dreams of advancement. I realized that if I was asked to do this work and refused, I might get fired. But if the price of working there was that I had to be in the lowest dead-end job, then getting fired would be a blessing. Every night I read from Smith's book and practiced how I would say no.

Several days later, Oscar and an up-and-coming young producer (who later produced many fine motion pictures) had a meeting scheduled at MGM. The young producer always drove the two of them to these meetings, and the gofer would pick up Oscar after the meeting and take him to his next appointment. Oscar knew someone had to be given this assignment, but he didn't want to make the choice. He just walked out of the office saying, "Somebody's going to have to pick me up at MGM at five o'clock."

The entire staff froze.

The young producer knew then that he had to pick the new gofer. He turned around, saw me, and said, "Chellie, pick Oscar up at five o'clock."

My heart pounding, my throat dry, I looked him straight in the eye and said, "No."

Nothing else, just no. Smith's book said not to give your reasons for saying no, or the conversation would degenerate into an argument over the validity of your reasons. I knew better than to think I would win an argument with this producer. So I didn't give him anything to work with. I just said no.

He was totally taken aback by this, and he laughed. "You have to!" he said. "Pick Oscar up at five o'clock!"

I said no again. Smith calls this technique "broken record"—just repeat your position.

He stared at me for a long moment. I could see the wheels turning in his mind: Should he fire me? I held my breath.

Then the producer turned to a young man seated near him and said, "Fine. Then you do it."

That young man said, "Okay." And he became the office gofer from then on, until he was fired six months later in another cost-cutting effort.

You know what happened to me?

The next morning, Oscar walked directly to my desk.

"Good morning, Chellie," he said with a smirk.

"Good morning, Oscar," I replied, straight-faced.

"Will you do me a favor, please?"

"Sure." I nodded.

"Will you call Jerry for me?" he asked. Jerry was a bigwig at MGM.

"Yes," I said, and reached for the phone.

"Whew!" he exclaimed, and mimed wiping his brow. "Thanks!"

Laughing, I said, "You're welcome," and we had a great day, working as a team with spirit and energy. From that moment on, I got better assignments and more respect from everyone in the company.

My career path shifted not long after that, and I left Oscar's office to take a position managing a bookkeeping service. With my new ability to stand up for myself and what I believed in, I grew the business from 2 employees to 13. Then I bought the company. I designed a workshop to help others have wealth in their work and serenity in their spirit. In order to help others as I had been helped, I wrote a book, and then a second book. From very humble beginnings, my life has exploded with passion, purpose, and prosperity. I say yes when I want to and no when I must, without feeling guilty.

It all began on that long-ago day when, sobbing in the bathroom, I remembered the lessons I had learned from a book. Some people sneer at self-help books, saying that they don't really help anyone make lasting change. I smile to myself whenever I hear that—because I know better. I was drifting on a gloomy highway to nowhere, and a book showed me how to shift gears, turn left, and speed up the freeway to success. Now every day is a glorious ride in the sun.

Malachy McCourt

Though Malachy McCourt—brother of Frank McCourt—first became a published author at age 66 with his best-selling memoir, *A Monk Swimming*, he has long been admired as a teller of tall tales and personal anecdotes of growing up poor in Limerick, Ireland. Among other things, he has been a longshoreman, an actor, and a radio talk show host. He also owned New York City's first singles' bar, Malachy's, a hangout frequented by such Broadway stars as Grace Kelly, Richard Harris, Peter O'Toole, and Richard Burton. As an actor, Malachy has appeared in a number of films, including *Gods and Generals*, *The Guru*, and *Ash Wednesday*, and on the HBO television series *Oz*. ◾

In 1950, when I was 18, I lived in Limerick, Ireland, and worked as a houseboy in a Jesuit residence. There I was, mopping floors, washing out bathrooms, and shining shoes, while the priests were drinking fine wines out of crystal glasses and tucking into prime rib with their silver knives and forks. I used to watch them and wonder, *How is it that they can live this way and I can't?*

I had just returned from England, where I'd had a similar position in a monastery, as well as a few stints as a manual laborer. I hadn't been much of a student and felt there was little hope for me ever amounting to very much in my life. *What misfortune of birth put me into the poverty class?* I would say to myself. *I'm intelligent and I appreciate some of the finer things in life, so why am I at the bottom of the human heap?* It all seemed so hopeless.

To top it off, like most young men my age, I was terribly interested in the girls. Ninety-nine percent of teenage boys admit they think of nothing but sex—and the other 1% are liars. It's a universal phenomenon, and yet this natural human urge was made out by the Church to be sinful. Though the clergy blabbed on about the love of God and what have you, it was really all about shame and punishment. Catholicism—at least in Ireland—seemed to me obsessed with the sins of the flesh.

You had to swear you would never masturbate, touch yourself, or even have an impure thought. Otherwise you would end up burning in hell for eternity. You went to confession and did your penances, but you knew you were only postponing the inevitable: With that storm of impure thoughts raging continually in your head, what were the chances that you'd die in a state of grace? Suffused with remorse and weary of feeling ashamed and of considering myself doomed in this world and the next, I began to question what I now saw as the Church's dogma.

My saving grace in life was that I'd always been a reader. As a young child, I learned to read all on my own, before I even started school. When I was about seven, I got my hands on a copy of *A History of India*. It took me a whole year to read it, and it just fascinated me—all the practices, the colors, the different religions, the variety of gods, the festive marriages, the ceremonies, and the strange foods. Then at 18, while I was working for the Jesuits, I came across a tattered volume about the life of Mahatma Gandhi. Because of my fascination with all things Indian, I gobbled up the book.

What a man! Of course I loved how Gandhi pissed off the entire British Empire. We Irish have to admire the man for that because we've also suffered at the hands of the British. I read how Gandhi organized nonviolent marches and protests—risking his life to help the Indian people overthrow British rule. The Brits had an empire stretching all the way from Ireland to India, and the Irish and the Indians were united in their resistance to it. That struck me as being so beautiful and awful, all at the same time.

But the main thing about Gandhi's life that absolutely stunned me was his spirituality. Here was a man who was a vegetarian, who dressed in simple clothing and talked in simple terms, and who was not afraid of death. He went to jail many times, sacrificed everything, and yet condemned no one. He never talked about hell or eternal damnation but loved all people equally and believed in their fundamental goodness. I could not imagine a greater contrast with Catholic doctrine. For the first time, I glimpsed a difference between religion and true spirituality.

But I wasn't ready to make a big shift in my life. I would say that the book planted a seed in me, which came to fruition in its own good time. At that point in my life—age 21—I still lumped spirituality in with religion, so I left Ireland exclaiming, "A plague on all your houses," and set sail for America, the land where I was born. On the ship, before even setting foot in New York, I went on a binge that lasted 30 years. I drank, womanized, and spent money like water. I lived just a crazy, wild life.

In my late twenties, on one of my more outrageous adventures, I became a gold smuggler and got to see India, the country that so fascinated me. I'd always wanted to visit, and I knew this was the only opportunity I'd ever get, so I took it. The country was everything I had imagined as a little boy. I went to funerals and watched the singing processions and the corpses being burned on the sandalwood, but I kept my distance because I was still wary of religion and ritual. The food and clothes and colors were all infinitely more intense than anywhere else I'd been. And the smell! There was a smell in the air like none other on Earth: a sweet aroma with elements of decomposition in it.

While in Delhi, I visited Gandhi's memorial. He doesn't have a tomb because he was cremated and his ashes were spread all over India. It was a quiet, somber moment for me. Here I was, up to my eyeballs in hedonism and profligacy, standing in front of a memorial to a man who was austerity personified. *In honor of this man,* I told myself, *I'd better mend my ways.*

But I didn't. I went back to my dissolute life until I was in my early fifties. Along the way, I destroyed a marriage with a wife and two children. Then I remarried but still didn't get on the straight and narrow for another 15 years.

By then, I was in a horrendously bleak place in my life. Everything had gone wrong—my marriage and my career were on the rocks—and the drinking and the hedonism weren't fun anymore. I took a trip to Ireland and stormed around the place in a vile mood, angry at the country and at the crazy-making religion it had been hosting for centuries. I was determined that everyone should get down on their knees and beg my forgiveness, but nobody seemed inclined to say they were sorry. I nearly drank myself into an Irish grave.

When I returned to the States, I made an appointment to see my doctor because I was feeling so bad. I thought he'd diagnose some disease, but he just said, "You know, you're drinking too much, smoking too much, and eating too much." I said, "What'll I do about that? Will you give me something for it?" He said, "Yes. I'll give you a bill if you don't get out of here and clean up your life."

That was the turning point. The seed that had been planted in me when I read Gandhi's biography finally germinated. I made up my mind to be a better man and got sober. That was over 20 years ago. Today, I'm not exactly thin—I'm about twice the size of Gandhi because I still eat too much—but I don't drink, don't smoke, and don't eat red meat. I'm quite a loving husband and father, still married to the woman I wed 40 years ago. Life is good.

What's more, all my distrust of ritual and religion and fear of death are gone. I realize now that rituals are fine. People need a place and a time to get together, so we can celebrate and mourn. Both are important in community. And without all that fear about hell and sin and sinners, I'm curious about death. I've come to view it not as an ending but merely a transition.

I have always aspired to Gandhi's frame of mind, particularly his ability to forgive his enemies. I've come a long way toward that goal, though my brand of forgiveness is more in the vein of my fellow Irishman Oscar Wilde, who once said, "Always forgive your enemies; nothing annoys them so much." Who knew that being sober could be so much fun?

John St. Augustine

John St. Augustine is the creator and host of a daily nationally syndicated radio talk show and has been called "the voice of America" by veteran broadcaster Bill Kurtis and "the most influential voice on radio" by best-selling author Cheryl Richardson. A motivational speaker as well, John addresses a variety of audiences on the subject of human potential and is the author of *Living an Uncommon Life: Essential Lessons From 21 Extraordinary People*. ▪

The Victorian-style home I grew up in on the northwest side of Chicago boasted a massive floor-to-ceiling bookcase in the main hallway. Every day on his way to work, my father would stop for a moment, select a book, and be out the door. Back in the 1960s—before the advent of video games, cable television, and computers—the stories and ideas that fed our imaginations came from the many books in our home.

Today, as I look at my own extensive home library, I see a collection that ranges from a rare and deeply prized first edition of the spiritual classic *The Life and Teachings of the Masters of the Far East* to personally autographed copies from some of the numerous guests I have hosted on my radio show over the years. And though there are well over 500 books lining the shelves, there is only one that I have read for the last 36 autumns without fail: *Instant Replay: The Green Bay Diary of Jerry Kramer*.

The little paperback is barely recognizable as a book. It's been taped and retaped countless times, in an effort to keep the cover in place. The pages are severely dog-eared from dozens of late-night thumb-throughs, and there are two "autographs" inside—Jerry Kramer's in the front and Vince Lombardi's in the back—scribbled by me when I was 10 years old.

To a kid growing up in Chicago, the Green Bay Packers were the evil men to the north. I lived and breathed the Bears and was at home with names such as Sayers, Butkus, and O'Bradovich. To even speak the names of the Packers was considered a sacrilege on the playground. All through the years that the Packers regularly pounded the Bears, I managed to hold my ground—until the summer day in 1968 when my dad needed a shave during our vacation.

Every summer we went to Wisconsin and stayed just outside of Appleton in a little place called the Dreamland Motel. The name said it all. For those 10 days every year, life was a dream. Appleton seemed very far away from Chicago, and for a kid who spent most of his life in the city, it was life with no boundaries. We stayed up late, went fishing, shot a .22-caliber rifle on my aunt and uncle's nearby farm, and ran in the cornfield until we were exhausted. My dad and Uncle Ron had an ongoing bet every year about the upcoming football season—the Bear–Packer thing again—and it usually had something to do with a case of beer.

The day before we drove back to Chicago, my dad went to the store for some supplies and returned with a book in his hand. "I didn't buy this. It came with the razor," he explained as he set it down. "I would never buy a book about the Packers." There on the table sat the paperback edition of *Instant Replay*, attached to a Personna "Electro-Coated Blade" razor as a promotion.

When we left the next day, my dad placed the book among some bags on the floor in the back of our 1959 Chevy Impala. While my sister and I fought for seat space in the back, I uncovered it. Without thinking, I opened the book to the black-and-white photo pages in the middle. There were Jerry Kramer and Fuzzy Thurston leading Jimmy Taylor on a classic Packer sweep. There was Kramer in the pit battling Merlin Olsen and Alex Karras. I gave in and began to read.

On that warm summer day in 1968, as my dad headed the family car south for Chicago, I devoured *Instant Replay*. My life would never be the same. As I read, the lessons began to sink into my young subconscious mind. Although it was a book about football, it was also a book about life: about the will to win and do your best—and then find another level to perform on. It was about going within yourself and digging deeper than you ever thought possible. And it was about teamwork and struggle and discipline and effort.

Reading *Instant Replay* allowed me to relive the 1967 championship season from beginning to end with the most successful team (on and off the field) in the history of sports. I quickly learned the names that were verboten in our neighborhood: Forrest Gregg, Bart Starr, and Max McGee, not to mention the feared but respected name of a short Italian named Vince Lombardi. I observed these men in action, through the eyes of right guard Jerry Kramer. I felt like one of them, which is a tribute to the skill and candor of Kramer and his coauthor Dick Schaap. I began to think that becoming the best I could be should be the number-one priority in my life—no matter what I decided to do. It was pretty powerful stuff for a 10-year-old.

As the years passed, *Instant Replay* became a must-read every fall. I applied the lessons of the book to my high school football career and was named cocaptain in my senior year. Leadership, commitment to a goal, and playing until the final tick of the clock gave me a pattern of discipline that moved me through college football, semi-pro and coaching careers, and a four-year tour of duty in the United States Coast Guard. Every fall, like clockwork, *Instant Replay* took me back to the Lombardi years and the oft-repeated themes of winning and losing and how important it is to challenge myself every day. These lessons became a part of me.

In the late 1980s I connected with a former Chicago Bears player and cocreated a magazine called *Pro Athlete Insider*. As we were putting together an advisory board, one name immediately popped into my head. If there was an athlete who understood the importance of this project and what it would take to make it work, it was Jerry Kramer.

After a lot of digging, I found Jerry Kramer's phone number. He was living in Idaho. I steadied myself as I prepared to make the call. *What will I say to him? How can I possibly thank him for being such an important part of my life?*

I dialed and held my breath. Then a husky voice barked, "This is Jerry."

"Mr. Kramer? I—my name is John and I . . . uh, just wanted to thank you for writing *Instant Replay*. Because of that book—and the way you blocked Merlin Olsen—I learned that I have talents and abilities that I might never have found. I was wondering if you would consider being part of a new magazine that makes sure ten-year-old boys know how important it is to dream big—even if they hate the Packers."

Jerry laughed. As I remember, that call lasted about half an hour. He invited me to a roast of Packer defensive end Willie Davis in Appleton the following weekend. As I drove north from Chicago, the memories came flooding back. Many of the old landmarks were gone: The Big Boy Restaurant on College Avenue had a new name, condos had replaced the Dreamland Motel, and a massive mall now stood where corn once grew. But none of that mattered because I was going to spend the evening with Jerry Kramer and the Packers. That trip was a turning point in my life.

The roast was a glorious evening—listening to the tales of days gone by from a group of men I had only read about. Their humility and camaraderie were infectious. We stayed up late listening to war stories: how Max McGee and Paul Hornung sent Lombardi into fits of anger over their late-night forays into every town's watering hole. Or the time that Jerry Kramer tried to tell Frank Sinatra how to sing. We relived the Ice Bowl victory over the Dallas Cowboys into the wee hours of the morning.

The next day I drove farther north to Green Bay to attend an event at the Packer Hall of Fame as Jerry's guest. It was Bear–Packer week, and as we all sat down at the long lunch table and introduced ourselves, it quickly became clear that I was the only Chicagoan in the room. The man next to me, sitting in a wheelchair and hooked to an oxygen tank, became animated and energetic as he described a lifelong dedication to the Packers. He vented his hatred of the Bears and Coach Mike Ditka, saying that if he could get out of his wheelchair, he would do unspeakable things to the Bears coach. Then he turned to me and said, "Where are you from, son?"

To save my backside in hostile territory, I replied the only way I could: "Denver!"

Since that day in Green Bay, Jerry Kramer became a real presence in my life. He has advised me on numerous projects, and we have collaborated on a few. He visited me at my home in Upper Michigan, and one of my fondest memories of Jerry is the warm summer evening when, after a day of golf and a great dinner, we drove lakeside singing John Denver's "Some Days Are Diamonds" at the top of our lungs with the windows down. I'm sure the wildlife appreciated our harmony.

As Jerry's stay ended and he headed home, I realized that the dreams I held as a 10-year-old boy had indeed come true. Since 1997 I have hosted a talk radio show I created to remind listeners that life is just like a football game: If you are lucky, you get four quarters to play; you will be challenged on a daily basis to adapt to and overcome the obstacles life puts in our path; you need to create a good team to win; and having a great coach is all-important.

Thousands of guests have brought their unique talents and perspectives to my show, and we estimate that since the show began, we have given away over 5,000 books, ranging from *New York Times* best sellers to self-published works. There is something sacred that touches the human spirit between the covers of a good book—a place that only words on paper can find. When we read a book, our most essential trait—imagination—is given the opportunity to soar. And although the words in a book remain the same, their meaning changes as we grow from reading them over and over again.

There have been more than a few challenges in my life: a severe electrical shock at 19; a near-fatal auto crash at 27; the loss of everything in a bad business deal at the age of 36, which forced my family to live in a motel for a year; an 800-mile walk from Upper Michigan to Chicago and back that started out as fund-raising venture and turned into a life-changing adventure; and the life-giving donation of a kidney to my daughter when I was 43. Through all that—and more—*Instant Replay* and the lessons it contains has gotten me through. If Jerry Kramer could endure all his operations and still play, I'd also heal from my injury. If Vince Lombardi could persist until he attained his goal of coaching a world championship team, I, too, could begin again no matter what.

One could say that I am in the early third quarter of my life now—more than a few autumns have come and gone. I live 300 miles north of Chicago; my parents have both passed on. Jerry Kramer is in his early seventies, and some of the men whose names appear in *Instant Replay* have, like my folks, gone to their next adventure. The game clock keeps ticking.

Yet every fall, when the leaves begin to turn and the wind has a bit more snap to it, I pull out my tattered copy of *Instant Replay*. The moment my fingers touch those familiar pages, I am 10 years old in the back of my dad's 1959 Impala and my whole life is ahead of me.

Sheryl Leach

Sheryl Leach is a producer, entrepreneur, and the creator of Barney, one of the most successful children's characters of all time. Sheryl was named Entrepreneur of the Year by the CNBC cable network and has received a National Freedoms Foundation Award and a national humanitarian award from B'nai B'rith International—the first woman to receive this prestigious award since Eleanor Roosevelt. She has been a featured guest on many talk shows, including the *Today Show*, *Good Morning America*, *CBS This Morning*, and *Donahue*. Today, as cofounder of the Shei'rah Foundation, Sheryl supports visionaries, media projects, and entertainment channels producing programming that inspires, uplifts, and challenges the human spirit. ■

When my son Patrick was a toddler, I was always looking for ways to entertain him and keep him busy. Sometimes videos would do the trick, but at that time there were few on the market for the very young child. The old adage "Necessity is the mother of invention" proved true: I was able to create a children's entertainment property, and a new business, as the result of my early motherhood experiences. I felt that if the storylines worked with my son, they would work with all children—Patrick was an excellent focus group of one! And that is how Barney, the six-foot purple dinosaur, was born.

Putting a team together and building the *Barney* series was the start of a wonderfully creative and exciting period in my life. Today, almost 19 years later, Patrick has grown up—*Barney* has grown up—and we've all moved on to other exciting projects and endeavors.

Three years ago, our family took a trip to the Turks and Caicos Islands. Just before we left, a girlfriend told me about a book that she just couldn't put down: *The Power of Now*, by Eckhart Tolle. "I am madly underlining everything," she said. "It's so fabulous. You have to read it."

I trusted my friend's enthusiasm and decided to buy the audiobook to take along on the trip. My first day on the beach, I settled down with my tape player and earphones—and immediately I was hooked. It became my routine, and I looked forward, each day, to hearing the next chapters.

The book was powerful. It wasn't only what the author said, it was also *how* he said it: his voice, his manner of speech, his whole way of being. There wasn't a wasted word; every sentence he spoke went straight to the heart. It felt so inspired.

Early in the book, Tolle relates how, after years of depression, he reached a place of utter despair and said to himself, "I just cannot live with myself any longer." In that moment, on the brink of suicide, he suddenly realized how odd that thought was. His next thought was, "If I cannot live with myself, there must be two of me: the 'I' and the 'self' that 'I' cannot live with."

This intellectual breakthrough led Tolle directly into a radical experience of personal transformation. With the awareness of these two apparent identities—the "I" that was the consciousness *observing* the thoughts, and the "myself" that was *doing* the thinking—he understood for the first time that he was not the content of his mind. When he stopped identifying with those thoughts and could observe them as separate from himself, he found love and joy where before there had been fear and suffering. He writes that from that point on, there was a permanent undercurrent of peace in his life.

Most of us remember hearing the phrase "I think, therefore I am." However, what Tolle says, in effect, is "I am, therefore I think." Tolle's book helped me to understand that no matter what is going on in your mind, it's not really who you are. Your mind is a tool of the self—a part of your being—but not the real you. The real you stands *behind* your mind—and is far greater than the mind itself.

Hearing that, I had a glimpse of true freedom. I saw that I was no longer at the mercy of my mind: Even if fearful thoughts came into my mind, *I* wasn't fearful. I didn't have to be gripped by emotions but could watch them come and go.

I had always been drawn to inspirational books, and I thought that *The Power of Now* was a brilliant synthesis of many others I had read before. What Tolle said wasn't new, but because it was presented in the context of his own life story, it had tremendous clarity and power. It felt almost like a graduate course—as if all the other books I'd read had led me to this one special book. Still, my understanding and experience of Tolle's principles were intellectual, not experiential. It took a personal drama of my own to make his concepts real.

We returned home from our vacation, and for two weeks, everything went along as normal. Then one morning I received the type of call that every parent fears.

"Mrs. Leach?"

"Yes?"

"It's about Patrick."

I felt a sense of dread. It was his high school calling, and I could hear in the principal's tone that the news wasn't good.

"What's happened?" I said.

"Your son has had a seizure. He's on his way to the hospital."

I raced over to the hospital and ran inside. As you can imagine, I was in a state of extreme anxiety and fear. I kept thinking, *What does this mean, a seizure at age seventeen with no outward signs that anything was wrong?*

The doctors performed a battery of tests and, after what seemed like an agonizingly long period of waiting, they informed me of the diagnosis: Patrick had a brain tumor. They said they were uncertain whether it was malignant or benign, and they would have to operate as soon as possible.

My world turned upside down. All my former plans and priorities vanished from my mind, and I could only think over and over again: *What's going to happen to Patrick? How's he going to handle this emotionally? Is it cancer? Does that mean chemo? Does it mean a year from now he could be gone?* I remembered conversations in the past in which people in crisis had talked about looking into the abyss—and now I understood what they had meant. My mind was gripped with the most powerful fear I had ever known. I felt helpless and vulnerable because the situation and outcome were totally out of my control.

So I began doing all the research I could—trying to understand the problem, locate the right surgeon, and so on. My mind was in turmoil, and it was almost impossible for me to sleep. I feared that at any moment, Patrick might have another seizure and need my help. At the same time, I realized that I had to create a feeling of normalcy, not just to keep myself sane but also to help Patrick, who was taking his cues from me. If I appeared upset or fearful, then I would send him a signal that he should be, too.

In the midst of this trauma, I remembered *The Power of Now* and turned to it to help me create the best possible environment for us both. Every night, I listened to the tapes. Freed from the grip of fear by Tolle's words and the sound of his calm, gentle voice, I was able to fall asleep. When I woke in the wee hours of the morning and my mind naturally turned to fearful thoughts, I put the earphones back on and listened again. I found great comfort in Tolle's soothing spirit and in the book's profound message: *All fear comes from living in the past or the future, which are both in our minds—in reality, it is always* now. *As long as we stay with the Now, we have peace. Knowing this, we can choose peace at any moment.*

I began to experience this wisdom at a very deep level. My fear was based on what might happen in the future. It had no reality in the Now. If I stopped and asked myself, *Is anything bad happening right this second?* I realized that the answer was no. Patrick was alive, we were together, and *in this moment*, he was okay. Then I became peaceful, and grateful, and could go back to sleep.

During the month that we were waiting for surgery, I practiced "being in the moment of Now" many times each day. On some level, I was always aware of Tolle's message and the truth it conveyed. The future was too scary to contemplate, and the past was already gone. All we had was the Now. I learned to find peace in that moment and, stringing those moments together, I was able to convey a sense of peace and well-being to Patrick.

And in the end, everything worked out fine. Patrick had no further seizures, the surgery itself went beautifully, with no complications or brain damage, and the tumor was benign.

From my own experience, I think the truth and wisdom that Tolle brings forth can help anyone in a time of crisis, as well as in everyday life.

Emotions come and go, but we are not those emotions; they just pass through us. At any moment, we can choose to participate in fear and doubt, or we can turn to the Now and find peace. Then, from that place of peace, we can continue forward to deal with the situation at hand. Our life situation may be the same, but we can alter our response to it.

After Patrick was given a clean bill of health, I experienced such profound joy and gratitude that everything around me—even life itself—seemed to radiate and sparkle. I found myself living in the Now more and more and feeling increasingly centered and calm. In that state of calm, undistracted by thoughts and concerns about the past and future, I discovered something wonderful: the "I" behind the mind is part of one connected presence. That peace that I found in the moment of Now is at the core of every individual being and also the collective Being of everything that is. I was experiencing what all the great spiritual teachers throughout time have told us: We are all connected; we are all one.

Today, the inspiration and wisdom I received in *The Power of Now* helps guide our work in the Shei'rah Foundation. My partner, Howard Rosenfeld, and I started the foundation to fund and support projects that promote an awareness of unity that celebrates diversity. The foundation works primarily with youth, funding media-based projects. One of our projects, called Chat the Planet, links up kids from all over the world via two-way TV, so they can talk about things important to them. On several occasions, Chat the Planet has connected college-aged kids in Baghdad with college-aged kids in Manhattan. They talked about dating, school, music, the war, and so on, and quickly became real people to one another.

Young people easily see that beneath the variations of language, culture, and religious beliefs, we are more alike than we are different. There is no real separation. What we do to another, we do to ourselves—if we hurt another, we're hurting ourselves. If more people could understand this simple truth, the global situation could change dramatically.

Today I am doing all that I can to further awareness of Eckhart Tolle's central message: that peace can be found in this moment of Now. It is empowering to know that we can rise above our thoughts of fear and doubt to a place of oneness and peace—a place in which we create a new reality, not only for ourselves but also for the world.

Gay Hendricks

Gay Hendricks is one of the major contributors to the fields of relationship transformation and body–mind healing. After a 20-year academic career, he and his wife, Dr. Kathlyn Hendricks, founded the Hendricks Institute, which offers seminars in relationship enhancement and somatic wellness. Gay has published more than 25 books, including best sellers *Conscious Loving*, *The Corporate Mystic*, and *Spirit-Centered Relationships*. He has appeared on more than 500 radio and television shows on various networks, including *Oprah*, CNN, CNBC, and *48 Hours*. ■

For many years now, I've found that some of the deepest shifts in my life have come when I have a book in my hand. When I read, I pause often to let an idea or a phrase resonate within me. Resonance, in this case, means feeling the vibrations of something in the sensitive instrument of the body.

My first clear experience of resonance was on a physical level, during a meditation retreat at a Zen monastery. On the retreat, a gong signaled the beginning and end of the 40-minute meditation period we practiced at dawn and at dusk. The head monk invited us to let the vibrations of the gong resonate within us as long as we could feel them. On the first day or two of the weeklong retreat, I heard the gong as a deep-toned "bong" that quickly faded within seconds. As the week went on, though, something quite remarkable happened. I grew more sensitive in my mind and body, because of the hours of meditative practice, the quiet work of gardening (which was done in silence), and the long strolls in the forest that surrounded the monastery. With my increased sensitivity, I began to notice that I could feel and hear the gong for longer and longer periods of time. By the end of the week I was savoring the subtle vibrations of the "bong" for minutes instead of seconds. I mentioned this awareness to the head monk, and he told me that the meditation hall had been constructed to enhance this experience. Indeed, the very wood used in the building had been carefully chosen by his mentor for its pleasing resonant qualities.

I like to think transformational reading works in the same way. Each one of us can construct a resonant interior that allows us, with practice, to appreciate deeper and deeper levels of connection with the concepts and the music of the words. I believe that our sensitivity to resonance is cultivated simply by pausing as we read, to try on the concept we're reading about in our own body and mind. Once we open to it, this resonance has the power to shake loose old beliefs and stir the deep well of our being. This technique can produce dramatic results—even when reading books you have read before.

I came across the teachings of Epictetus in my twenties. The title of his small book, *The Enchiridion* (Greek for "close to hand"), is often translated as *Manual* or *Handbook*. My own translation of it is *The Book of Life*, because I believe that its wisdom can be applied to everything essential about human existence. Gathered by Epictetus's students 2,000 years ago from his oral teachings, *The Book of Life* is regarded by many as humankind's first self-help book.

I first read *The Book of Life* during an especially cerebral period of my life: as a graduate student. It made tremendous sense to me on an intellectual level, and in the years that followed, I used Epictetus's concepts in my practice and in my own life. It wasn't until much later that I experienced a whole-being shift from reading the same material.

About eight years ago, in a time of deep sadness about the loss of my granddaughter, a child I'd loved and held in my arms nearly every day for the six months she was with us, I felt despair about ever being able to get out from under the cloud of grief that engulfed me. Weeks had gone by, and I couldn't shake the sadness. I'd talked to friends, to counselors, to family, and still the sadness remained. Part of me knew I needed to dispel the fog of grief so I could be present for others who needed me, but knowing this was not enough to make it happen.

I was still in mourning when one day, seeing my ancient, battered edition of Epictetus on the bookshelf, I picked it up and read the first line:

You can be happy if you know this secret:
Some things are within your power to control
and some things are not.

I felt Epictetus speaking directly to me across the centuries and paused and resonated with what he was inviting me to do. I took a few deep breaths and let the wisdom of these simple words suffuse me. I felt a profound shift inside my mind and body. I realized that the fact of my loss was far outside my power to control. I could not control it or change it in any way! As this sank in, I realized where much of my recent stress and suffering had come from: I'd been expending massive energy trying to control the past—attempting to rewrite reality so that my loss had never occurred. I had been attempting to reinvent the past, and the exertion had exhausted me.

Suddenly I saw that I'd been trying with every fiber of my being to control something I could not control. I cannot describe the serenity that rushed over me when I relaxed my attempt to control the uncontrollable.

An even deeper understanding began to sink in. I realized that I had been engaged in a battle to control the emotions of grief and sadness in my own body. I saw that I had been trying to minimize them, to make them not be there, to get over them. Even my family and friends, with the very best of intentions, had been trying to talk me out of my feelings. They had told me that "time would heal me," that "a brighter day would someday come." They had meant well, but underneath their helpful plat-itudes had been the unspoken message: *Don't feel what you're feeling.*

I had been trying to control things that were fundamentally uncon-trollable, and the cost had been the moment-by-moment disruption of my peace of mind. My inner experience since my granddaughter's death had been somewhat like driving a car with one foot on the accelerator and the other on the brakes. I had felt nothing but an unsettling inner shimmy, and the rattle had unnerved my every moment.

But now, with the help of Epictetus, I realized the pointlessness of trying to control my emotions. They have a life of their own, and they will last as long as they last. Applying the wisdom Epictetus conveys in his first sentence, I relaxed my resistance, letting go of my effort to wish my feelings away. A whole-body, whole-being serenity began to spread through me, and it felt very, very good. The clouds of grief began to disperse; I felt life begin to flow in me again. I still felt the sadness, of course, but now I was at peace with it . . . simply letting it be. For me it was the essential first step in moving beyond the devastating experience so I could be there for the other loved ones who were counting on me.

That brief moment in time exerted such a powerful positive influence on me that it has affected the way I live my life and practice my profession ever since. Once I counseled a woman who had left an abusive marriage and a husband who sought to control nearly every move she made. Although she was now out of the marriage, she had taken her own internal control mechanisms with her into her new life. She doubted her every move. *Should I go back to school? Yes, but what if I fail? Should I go out with the man who's been seeking me out at church? No, what if he's just another control freak?* Her control-mind tied her in knots.

I asked her point-blank: "What are you trying to control that's in fact absolutely uncontrollable?" She blinked rapidly as she tried to cogitate the meaning of what I was asking. Suddenly she got it. "I'm trying to control the past *and* the future," she said. "I'm trying to have my marriage turn out differently, to succeed instead of fail. And I'm trying to get hold of the future and make a deal with it so I don't ever feel that kind of pain again. No wonder I'm so wired I can't sleep at night! No wonder I wake up tired."

Tired and wired . . . controlling the universe can definitely make you feel that way. I know, because I've been in exactly that same place. I've gone to bed wired and awakened tired, exhausted by the struggle to change the unchangeable. Thanks to Epictetus, though, I haven't had to stay there as long each time. When I feel the high-wire tension of anxiety or the sluggish muddiness of a depressed mood coming on, I pause and let the first line of Epictetus resonate in me. I ask myself, *What am I trying to control that's not within my power to control?* I reflect on it deeply: *What am I trying to change that's unchangeable by me?*

I pause and ask myself those questions still. Even after so many years of feeling their gentle power in my life, they never, ever fail me.

Pierce O'Donnell

Pierce O'Donnell is one of the leading trial lawyers in the country. A partner in O'Donnell & Mortimer LLP, Pierce has handled many complex cases in a variety of fields, including entertainment, environmental, intellectual property, energy, securities, products liability, toxic tort, real estate, constitutional, and antitrust law. A graduate of Georgetown and Yale Universities, he clerked for Supreme Court Justice Byron R. White and Judge Shirley M. Hufstedler of the U.S. Court of Appeals for the Ninth Circuit and was named one of the 100 Most Influential Lawyers in America by the *National Law Journal*. Pierce is also the author of five books and numerous articles. His most recent book, *In Time of War: Hitler's Terrorist Attack on America*, was published in 2005. ■

In our family, John F. Kennedy was revered—he might not have been the Second Coming, but he was pretty close. My father, one of the few Democrats in our town, was the chairman of the local party for decades. There was a radio on top of our refrigerator, and I remember all of us listening to the election returns in 1956 when Adlai Stevenson, whom my parents also worshipped, lost for the second time by a landslide to Dwight Eisenhower. That was a dismal day for us.

We were very excited about ideas at our house. We talked about issues such as poverty and equal rights, and from an early age I believed that everyone deserved respect and fair treatment. Like most kids, my three sisters and I learned by watching and listening to our parents. They showed us that principles were important, and that there were such things as values: Lead a life of purpose. Don't embarrass yourself or your family. Don't cheat. Turn your homework in on time. Keep your word. In our family, there was definitely the concept that we do the right thing.

So when I read *Profiles in Courage* by John F. Kennedy, I was already wired to appreciate its message. I read it on a spring day in 1962, sitting by Crystal Lake in my hometown of Averill Park, New York. I was 15 years old, a sophomore in high school, and President Kennedy was still in the White House. As I sat there turning the pages, a whole new world opened up to me—one I had never imagined. It was a world of statesmen and of leaders rising above party and politics, and sometimes even the will of their constituents, to do what they thought was right regardless of the personal consequences.

I had always been interested in politics, and as an Eagle Scout had studied local, state, and national government for merit badges. But now, as I read Kennedy's famous book, I saw the moral conflicts behind the decisions and events of history. Written in 1955 while Kennedy was still a freshman U.S. senator from Massachusetts, *Profiles in Courage* contains stories about a number of past U.S. senators and other public servants. I was especially impressed by the story of Edmund G. Ross, a young, newly elected Republican senator from Kansas, who cast the decisive vote in the impeachment trial of Andrew Johnson. Ross's fellow Republicans had engineered the impeachment of the president in order to take over the executive branch. But in an incredible act of political courage—which instantly doomed him to political oblivion—Ross voted for Johnson's acquittal. Despite tremendous political pressure, he did what he thought was right. *What a hard thing to do,* I thought, admiring his bravery.

But the story that had the largest impact on my life is tucked away at the back of the book in the section called "Other Men of Political Courage." There, Kennedy devotes, literally, just four or five paragraphs to John Adams of Massachusetts, the first vice president under George Washington and the second president of the United States. Kennedy begins by describing how, during the Boston Massacre on March 5, 1770, British sentries fired on and killed five Bostonians. In the aftermath, the British captain and seven soldiers were indicted and charged with murder by the colonial government.

At that time, John Adams was in his mid-thirties—an up-and-coming young lawyer, and more importantly, a pre–Revolutionary War patriot—a Son of Liberty. He, his cousin Sam Adams, and John Hancock were the three leading anti-British activists in the Massachusetts Colony. Nonetheless, when no lawyer was willing to defend the British soldiers, John Adams agreed to do it himself, even though those eight men represented everything he despised.

Adams did a brilliant job of defending the soldiers in two trials and proved there was no evidence that his clients had maliciously and without provocation fired on the mob attacking them. He had accepted this unpopular representation—and zealously championed their defense—because he believed in the rule of law. Adams wanted to prove that the people of Massachusetts Colony and the 13 American colonies were capable of honorable self-government, and that meant even detested British soldiers could get a fair trial in hostile Boston. Eventually, the soldiers were acquitted.

Adams won the case but paid a heavy price. He lost most of his law practice and many of his friends and was reviled in the press. Even his cousin ostracized him. From the start, he realized that this would happen, so his defense of the soldiers was an exceptionally noble and courageous act of conscience.

This story opened my eyes to the world outside the little hamlet of Averill Park—a world of big ideas and people willing to take a stand for what's important. I am convinced that I went on to become a lawyer because of this book, and specifically this one-page reference to John Adams's gutsy defense of the Boston soldiers.

Reading *Profiles in Courage* also made me take a harder look at myself. At 15, I was not a popular kid; I was overweight and always the last one picked. To make matters worse, I'd always thought that being "one of the guys" was the most important thing in life. Kennedy's stories and commentary woke me up, helping me to see that popularity was ephemeral and not the true measure of a person's character.

Not long after that, I had a chance to put my new ideals into action. People's defining moments are precipitated in many different ways; for me, it was seeing Billy Norman being teased. Billy, who was mentally handicapped, lived across the street from us. He was a little older than I, and as children, we had played together. He had a great tire swing in his backyard, and his father had an old DeSoto that we used to sit in and pretend we were driving.

The bullies in our public high school liked to make fun of Billy. They'd knock his books down, ruffle his hair, and pull his sweater up over his head—stupid stuff. The worst of them was a guy named George. I always hated the way they treated Billy, but I never did anything about it, maybe because George and the others were older and bigger than I was.

Then, one day I saw George giving Billy a particularly hard time. Acting on impulse, I walked up to him and said, "George, you're a real tough guy picking on Billy. You know, it doesn't take much to make fun of someone who doesn't have all of his faculties." Then I said, "What if Billy was your brother?" I was afraid I might get popped in the nose for that one, but I didn't care. I just had to stand up for what was right. George said something snide, but he and his buddies walked away and let Billy alone.

Kennedy's book influenced me again when I was elected student body president my senior year. As president, I had to appoint someone chief justice of the school's supreme court. I chose my opponent, a senior who was ideally suited for the position, over my campaign manager, a junior, who had worked hard to get me elected. I knew many people would be mad at me, but I didn't feel I had a choice: Again, it was just the right thing to do.

From high school, I went on to college and law school and then had the honor of a lifetime—becoming a U.S. Supreme Court law clerk for Justice Byron White. I clerked for White, who was an extraordinary man, for 13 tumultuous months—from July of 1973 to August of 1974—during the Watergate era. I attended the Senate Watergate hearings and followed the dramatic developments as they unfolded. The Saturday night that Special Prosecutor Archibald Cox was fired, I thought I might hear tanks rumbling down the cobblestone streets of Capitol Hill where I lived. I heard the historic argument in the Supreme Court in which Special Prosecutor Leon Jaworski battled for access to the presidential tapes, and I assisted Justice White in drafting a portion of the Supreme Court's landmark opinion in *United States v. Nixon*, establishing that no person (including the president) is above the law.

Imagine my excitement! I'd come from a small, rural town where my dad (an orphan who grew up in Hell's Kitchen) owned the liquor store, my mom was a librarian, and my aunt was the postmaster. Now, I was at the highest court in the land—the Supreme Court—a witness to history. All this inspired me to run for Congress six years later. I was trounced in the Ronald Reagan landslide in November 1980, and although it was a valuable experience, I ended up with a sour taste in my mouth because of the influence of money and the tremendous amount of fund-raising required for campaigning. Once I had a family, I decided that I'd rather settle down and practice law.

Over the last 25 years, I've handled civil cases ranging from environmental, pharmaceutical, and constitutional law to antitrust, copyright, and securities. Every case gives me an opportunity to learn something new. I have taken on some unpopular causes as well. I've handled civil rights cases, represented maligned journalists who have been fired for doing their job, and just filed a brief in the Supreme Court, advocating the cause of Guantánamo Bay detainees.

Inspired by Senator Ross, who gave the president of the United States he despised a fair trial, and by John Adams, who defended the British soldiers whose presence in Boston he found an abomination, I take on controversial cases because I, too, believe the highest principle in democracy is the rule of law.

The day that President Kennedy was assassinated, I was sitting in biology class when the terrible news was announced. I rode the bus home and walked over to my father's store in the village. I had never seen my father cry before. This war-hardened man, my hero—who was still a six-foot-three, 190-pound specimen of steel—wept and hugged me. "They killed him! They killed him!" my dad kept saying as he sobbed uncontrollably. It felt as though my world was coming unglued, spiraling out of control. It was a very sad time for my family and the country.

Yet today, despite the revelations of the darker side of Kennedy's Camelot, the valuable legacies of his idealistic vision and spirit remain. The remarkable examples of nobility and integrity that Kennedy documented in *Profiles in Courage* have the same power to genuinely inspire that they did 50 years ago. On that long-ago day, my life was lifted to a higher plane, which has guided and directed my actions ever since.

Pat Williams

Pat Williams is the senior vice president of the NBA's Orlando Magic. Previously, he was the general manager of the Philadelphia 76ers for 12 years, including the 1983 season when they were NBA champions. Pat is a highly successful motivational speaker, as well as the author of numerous books, including *Forever Young: Ten Gifts of Faith for the Graduate*, *Go for the Magic*, and *The Paradox of Power: A Transforming View of Leadership*, and he is widely known for his promotional and marketing expertise. Pat and his wife Ruth are the parents of 19 children, 14 of whom are adopted from four foreign countries. ■

I started my sports career as a baseball player. When I graduated from Wake Forest University in June of 1962, although I had plans to go to graduate school in the fall, I also wanted to play baseball. My father and I shared a deep love of the sport, which started for me the day he took me to my first game when I was seven. It had always been my dream to play professionally, and he had encouraged me in that goal. Driving home from my graduation that June, my father had been killed in a car accident. Though deeply saddened, I decided to "take a swing" at that dream anyway. A week later, I signed a contract with the Phillies organization and was promptly sent to play for the Marlins, their minor league team in Miami, Florida.

I hadn't been in Florida long when one afternoon on a day off, I was browsing at Burdine's department store in downtown Miami. I ended up, as usual, in the book section. I'd been spending a lot of my spare time reading baseball books by sports writers and sports historians. That afternoon, my eye was caught by a book lying on a table of new releases. My attention was immediately riveted by the book's cover. It was a photograph of a man with close-cropped, sandy-colored hair sitting in a ballpark, his leg propped on a stadium seat, a cigarette held in one large hand as he stared across the field. The book was titled *Veeck—As In Wreck: The Chaotic Career of Baseball's Incorrigible Maverick* and was written by Bill Veeck himself.

Everyone in the baseball world knew about Bill Veeck. He was the owner of teams in the big leagues—he owned the Cleveland Indians for a while, the St. Louis Browns, and the Chicago White Sox. Yet more than that, he was a legendary sports executive and was known as "baseball's flamboyant promoter." I had been fascinated with Bill Veeck for years, so I paid the $3.95 they were asking for the thick, hardcover book. You can imagine my pleasure when I opened the cover and noticed that it contained Veeck's signature.

Standing in the store, I began reading. The first chapter was about one of baseball's most bizarre moments: the day in St. Louis in 1951 when Bill Veeck, as a publicity stunt, sent a midget named Eddie Gaedel to the plate to lead off in a real game. I remembered opening the newspaper when it happened and seeing the picture of Gaedel standing at home plate, his number 1/8 jersey hanging loosely on his miniature frame, the catcher kneeling behind him and the umpire hunched over in the background. As an 11-year-old, I had been wide-eyed with wonder at the daring of the stunt—Veeck had thrown a cream pie in the face of convention, upsetting my notions about the solemn nature of the sport. I wasn't surprised that the book would start with this famous caper, but I was startled to read that one of Veeck's associates in this stunt was a man named Big Bill Durney. Bill Durney was the general manager of the Miami Marlins, the team I was playing for!

That summer I studied Veeck's book. His ideas and audacity intrigued me. So many things he'd done to promote baseball were outrageous, risky, or just plain silly, but always memorable. Veeck once said, ". . . In baseball, all [the fan] walks away with is an illusion; an ephemeral feeling of having been entertained." He felt his job was to develop and preserve that illusion by giving fans more vivid pictures to carry away in their heads. To that end, he hired the famous midget as well as men in spacesuits, and had live lobster giveaways, lush firework displays, tightrope walkers, flagpole sitters, exploding scoreboards, and more. One of my favorites was Grandstand Managers' Night, in which a thousand fans sitting behind home plate held up *YES* or *NO* signs in response to questions of strategy posed by the team's coaches, while the team's real manager sat back in a rocking chair with a pipe in his mouth and a pair of bedroom slippers on his feet.

Veeck attracted national attention for the novelty and sheer comedy of his gimmicks, but they had a practical side as well. Through his efforts, he took many of his newly acquired teams from the edge of bankruptcy to solid financial success, sometimes doubling game attendance in a single season. And under his management, Veeck's 1948 Cleveland Indians team won the World Series and his 1959 White Sox won the American League pennant.

Veeck was controversial—a lot of the other owners hated him—but as the years have passed, it's become clear that he was unappreciated by the people around him because he was simply ahead of his time. We have Veeck to thank for introducing the use of players' names on the backs of uniforms, and he was one of the first owners to break the racial barrier in baseball. In 1947, Veeck signed African-American player Larry Doby, only weeks after Jackie Robinson was hired by the Brooklyn Dodgers. Veeck's vision changed the face of sports promotion, and he was a pioneer in many areas of baseball finances that are still in practice today. *Veeck—As in Wreck* is still the funniest, liveliest, and most influential sports book I have ever read.

Playing for the Marlins, I saw quite a bit of Bill Durney. I made a point to seek him out and spend time with him. We talked about Veeck often, and at the end of the season, I told him, "More than anything else in the world, I want to meet Bill Veeck."

The summer season had been fascinating. I had thoroughly enjoyed being a professional athlete, learning about the game I loved. I knew my odds of becoming a big-league player were remote, but why not a career in the front office? That week, I drove back to my home in Wilmington, Delaware, unsure of what my future held exactly—though I knew I wanted to be in baseball.

I'd been in Wilmington only a couple of days when I got a call from Bill Durney. "I've spoken to Bill Veeck," he told me, "and he would be pleased to see you. Here's his number."

At the time, Veeck was in retirement, living in Easton, Maryland, which wasn't too far from Wilmington. I picked up the receiver to call him but couldn't bring myself to dial the phone. I did this many times as I tried to master my nerves and shyness. *Bill Veeck.* I was calling *the* Bill Veeck. Finally, I dialed the number Bill Durney had given me—I can still remember it: TA2-4545—and the man himself answered the phone! Startled by the refined quality of his voice—I was expecting something brasher—it took me a minute to respond. I told him who I was, and he said, "I've been expecting your call. When are you coming down?" That was a Monday. He told me to come on Wednesday and gave me directions.

Wednesday arrived—one of those clear, gorgeous September days so characteristic of the middle-Atlantic region of our nation. I took the highway south to Veeck's estate on the Chesapeake Bay and drove up the driveway. There he was, sitting on the porch of the house he called Tranquility, sunning himself as he read a book. I knew that Veeck had lost a leg in World War II while he was in the marines, and wore an artificial leg. That day, his shirt was off, he had on a pair of khaki shorts—and the leg was off. I later came to know that Bill Veeck was never a man to be formal with visitors and that he was voracious reader who always had a book or manuscript in his hand.

I got out of the car and joined him on the porch. Once we shook hands, I was his friend. That was Veeck's way. I expected to stay maybe 15 minutes, just to meet him, but he invited me to stay for lunch. Everything about that day made a deep impression on me. I can even remember the menu—bacon, lettuce, and tomato sandwiches served by his wife, Mary Frances. We talked about a variety of things. Bill Veeck had a remarkable repertoire of interests and a great talent for conversation. At one point I told him I didn't think I was going to make it as a ballplayer and asked his advice. He told me to learn to type, to take classes in advertising, to train myself in bookkeeping and economics. Four and a half hours later, I finally left, little realizing the enormous impact this man was going to have on my life.

For the next 25 years, Bill Veeck was a friend, a mentor, a hero. I never worked for him, but he advised and guided me through the early years of my sports career. It was his creative and original approach to marketing baseball—really to life itself—that shaped my own evolution from player to sports executive and eventually to motivational speaker and author.

When I stopped playing baseball, I did everything he'd told me to do that first day I'd met him (except the bookkeeping; I couldn't make myself stay awake for that one), and by the time I was 24, I was the general manager of my first baseball team, South Carolina's Spartanburg Phillies. In the years that followed, I sought Veeck's counsel on a regular basis, and he was always there for me until his death in 1986. Following his advice brought me national recognition and was the foundation for my career success both in sports and as a speaker. Bill was always talking me up to people. In fact, on two occasions, he even wrote about me in his syndicated column, giving me national exposure. Then, in 1969, he recommended that the owners of the Chicago Bulls hire me as their new general manager, which they did. In the space of 12 months, I went from managing a minor-league baseball team to becoming the general manager of the Bulls! I was only 29 years old. That was the turning point of my professional life—my career literally took off after that.

I cannot count the times I've asked myself, *What would he do? What would he say?* Yet Veeck's influence went far beyond sports and promotion. Being so close to him and seeing his unabashed devotion to his wife and family, his open and friendly attitude to everyone he met—fan, player, reporter, or owner—had a lasting effect on me. I emulated Bill in my marriage, my parenting, and in the open and honest way I try to relate to people. Over the years I have found that although I've emulated Bill, I have become more myself and have found a deep and lasting sense of self-worth.

In 1994, I was asked to address a group of young people interested in sports management careers at a dinner in Miami, Florida, the same place I had started my career 32 years earlier! When I sat down to write my speech, my mind kept returning to Veeck and the myriad ways that he had affected my life. I came up with about seven or eight guiding principles I'd learned from Veeck and wrote them up. The speech was a great success. After that, I continued to add to the list and soon realized the material would make a powerful book.

In 2001, after years of research interviewing the many people whose lives had been touched by Veeck, my book, *Marketing Your Dreams: Business and Life Lessons from Bill Veeck, Baseball's Marketing Genius*, was published. In the book, I listed the qualities of Bill Veeck that had so deeply impacted me: his passion and enthusiasm, his creativity and imagination, his humor, originality, humility, and more. I wrote a chapter on each one of them. It was my tribute to Bill Veeck, allowing me to share with the world the insights I'd gained through my long association with him and also showcase the remarkable traits that had inspired and influenced my achievements and goals. Veeck thought, worked, laughed, and loved like no one else—freely and unconditionally. He taught me by example, and my memories of him continue to guide me today.

Looking back, it is hard to imagine the course my life might have taken if I hadn't gone on that innocent shopping trip and picked up that book in Miami—if my path had not met and become intertwined with Bill Veeck's unique and amazing trajectory.

Lou Holtz

After turning around the fortunes of college football programs at several universities, Lou Holtz landed the top job in his profession in 1986 when he was named head coach at Notre Dame. His 1988 Notre Dame team won the college national championship (a story chronicled in his book, *The Fighting Spirit*), and Lou posted winning seasons until he retired at the end of the 1996 campaign. He came out of retirement in 1999 and returned to South Carolina, where he coached until his second and final retirement in 2004. During his coaching career, Lou was known as an exceptional motivator, and he translated that skill from coaching to professional speaking after his retirement. He is also the author of *Winning Every Day: The Game Plan for Success* and *A Teen's Game Plan for Life*. In 2005, Lou joined ESPN as a college football analyst. ▪

I once found a little bit of "magic" in a book, and it turned my life around. It was in 1966, when I'd gone to the University of South Carolina as a defensive coach under head coach Marvin Bass. My wife, Beth, was eight months pregnant with our third child, Kevin, and we had spent every penny we had in the bank on a down payment for a home. We were in the middle of a spring practice when I woke up one Monday morning to this headline: "Marvin Bass Resigns." I immediately said to my wife, "I wonder if he is related to my head coach." Of course, by the time I was halfway through the story's first paragraph, I knew the subject of the headline was my head coach.

I was flabbergasted. We had no idea Coach Bass was even contemplating resignation. According to the report, he had accepted a position as head coach in the Canadian Football League. That afternoon, the as-sistant coaches met with our university's president, Thomas F. Jones. He told us he was determined to hire the best coach available. President Jones further warned us that whoever that person was, he might very well prefer to bring in his own staff as a condition of his employment. We im-mediately understood that our jobs were in jeopardy.

After an extensive search, President Jones hired Paul Dietzel. An un-derstandable choice. Paul had been an outstanding coach at West Point; he had also coached Lousiana State University to a National Champi-onship. Coach Dietzel and I didn't know each other. Which was not good news for me. Like most head coaches, he wanted his staff to be composed largely of people he had worked with previously. Paul retained only two of Coach Bass's assistant coaches. I wasn't one of them.

I was unemployed for over a month, a long time for someone like me who had worked since he was nine; I felt very defeated. Our savings ac-count was down to four figures: around $10.95. With a growing family to support, I was feeling pressure. It would have been an unbearable period, if not for my wife. She could not have been more supportive or encour-aging. Beth never complained. She went to work as an X-ray technician to help keep us in groceries. She also bought me the motivational book *The Magic of Thinking Big*, by David Schwartz, hoping it would help me feel less depressed.

In his chapter on goals, Schwartz writes that anyone who is bored by life has probably forgotten his or her dreams. He invites readers to get back in touch with them. As a first step, we are asked to list all the things we have ever wanted to accomplish. I had a lot of time on my hands, so I took out a pencil and paper and divided my list into five categories:

1. As a husband/father
2. Spiritually
3. Professionally
4. Financially
5. Simply for excitement

It was with the fifth category that I let my imagination run wild. Here are some of the things I included:

1. Jump out of an airplane
2. Land a jet fighter on an aircraft carrier
3. Travel the ocean in a submarine
4. Go white-water rafting on the Snake River at Hells Canyon
5. Be on the *Tonight Show*, starring Johnny Carson
6. Attend a White House dinner with the president
7. Meet the Pope
8. Go on an African safari
9. Become a scratch golfer and play the top 50 golf courses in the world
10. Run with the bulls in Pamplona (provided I was matched with a much slower person)

And on it went. I had 107 goals on my original list. Suddenly, I was looking at my life differently and was excited about the future. When I told Beth that I was determined we do all of them, she said, "Gee that's great, honey, but why don't you add 'I want to find a job.'" Good note—the list expanded to 108.

So far, we've managed to achieve 102 of those dreams—including dining at the White House and meeting the Pope. We're still working on the others. From the moment I made that list, we became participants, rather than spectators, in our life. You do the same and you'll find you don't want to spend much time sleeping; you'll be afraid you might miss something!

Rudy Ruettiger

Rudy Ruettiger is a motivational speaker best known as the inspiration for the motion picture *Rudy*, the story of a young man who steadfastly pursues his dreams against all odds. He is also the founder of the Rudy Foundation, whose mission is to help children of all ages around the world reach their full potential. Rudy is the author of *Rudy's Insights for Winning in Life: If You Knew You Couldn't Fail, What Would Your Goals Be?* and *Rudy & Friends: Awesome and Inspiring Real Life Stories of Ordinary People Overcoming Extraordinary Odds.* ■

Once, when I was a young man, I set myself a goal and never gave up—ever. Everyone told me I couldn't do it, but in the end, I reached that goal. Although I wasn't a great student—or at five feet six inches and 165 pounds, a great football player—I ended up not only graduating from the University of Notre Dame (my childhood dream) but also making the final tackle as the last game of the season ended! As people chanted "Ru-dy! Ru-dy!" I was carried off the field on the shoulders of my teammates in triumphant glory.

You can rent *Rudy*, the movie based on my life, and see it all in living color. But there's one detail that was left out: At a crucial point in my journey I read a book that accelerated my progress toward my dreams. This is that untold story.

I came from a large blue-collar family in Chicago. I had trouble in school and didn't know until later that I had dyslexia. As a kid, I had visions of being somebody—a police officer, an astronaut—and I'd think, *I could be that.* I'd see myself doing heroic things, such as hitting a home run in Yankee Stadium or going to Notre Dame or, even better, playing football at Notre Dame. One of my favorite visions was being one of the Fighting Irish.

But people would tell me, "You can't do that. You aren't smart enough. You aren't big enough. You aren't strong enough." School was always difficult for me. I wanted to learn, but I couldn't seem to—at least, not in the traditional way. I thought that since I couldn't learn this way, I couldn't learn at all, so I had no hope of getting into any college. No one ever told me there were other ways of getting there besides taking college prep classes and getting high scores on SATs and ACTs.

I got tired of the noise of everyone telling me why I couldn't, and why I shouldn't, and why I wouldn't. I felt like I was living in a box labeled "This is where you belong." Well, that's a self-fulfilling prophecy: if you hear it enough, you start believing it. I knew that if I didn't change my friends or my environment or my circumstances soon, I'd end up somewhere I didn't want to be.

But it sure was hard to break out of that box. After high school, I went to work at a power plant. Most of the time, I wondered, *Why am I doing this? Why am I here, working swing shift? This is not what I want to do. But what else am I going to do?* Finally I thought, *Enough!* and signed up for the Navy. It was during the Vietnam era, and a lot of people were worried about getting drafted, but I said, "Well, I'm going to control this deal by volunteering instead of having someone else tell me what to do."

With that one crucial shift in thinking, my whole attitude began to change. I saw that by taking control of things, you get better options. Military life was good for me, though it certainly was tough. Boot camp was a real eye-opener. I was glad I had good parents who had taught me a lot about character, because that's what kept me going in a tough environment like that. I understood what it took to be part of the team—to play my role and contribute. When I saw that it wasn't about becoming a star but about being part of something bigger than myself, things really began to fall into place.

In the Navy, I'd proved to myself that change was good, and also that I could do something I'd thought was impossible—get out of that box! But when I finished my tour of duty with the Navy, I went right back to work in the same power plant, same swing shift, still thinking, *I don't want to do this, but what else can I do?* Then a good friend I was working with died. He knew my dream was to go to Notre Dame, and he had given me a Notre Dame jacket not long before, saying, "You were born to wear this jacket." Now, with his passing, I understood that life is too short to hold back on your dreams. I knew I had to get on with it.

A few days later I was in a bookstore, looking in the self-help section, when I saw a book called *Psycho-Cybernetics*, by Maxwell Maltz. I pulled it off the shelf, started reading, and found it was easy to read and made a lot of sense. I took the book home and read it cover to cover, and then started again at the beginning. One message stood out for me: You are in control of your destiny. Your mind is very powerful; what you think is your reality.

The book made it clear that I hadn't gotten what I wanted in my life because I didn't believe I could do it. I had never really done the work in school, never buckled down and studied, because I had thought that the fact that it was difficult for me meant I couldn't do it. Now I understood that just because something is a struggle doesn't mean you can't do it. It just means you've got to find a different way of doing it.

With this understanding, I made up my mind, and things started happening—fast. Although I was already 23, I immediately headed for Notre Dame with the attitude, "I'm going to do this, period, end of sentence," and new opportunities were created just by my showing up. I went without a game plan. Maltz said if you take action, the plan will unfold in front of you. You can develop your game plan as you move toward your goal. Sometimes it's better not to have everything all laid out; focusing too much on how you think it should go can cause you to miss opportunities.

It took a lot of courage for me to leave home without my family's approval, to leave my job and move toward the dream. But I packed my bags and showed up in the middle of the night at the University of Notre Dame. I knocked on the door of the faculty residence hall and said, "Now, tell me how to get here."

The man who answered the door was a priest who was the former president of Notre Dame. He was kind to me, as were the two other priests he called in to help, and they set me up in a dormitory for the night. Looking back, I was in what I now call "the God loop," where people come into your life and help you. The priests knew I was distraught, because no reasonable person shows up at the door in the middle of the night, asking how to get into Notre Dame. But once they started talking to me, they knew I wasn't crazy. They saw that I was just a very passionate young man, filled with desire and determination. That got them caught up in my journey and made them want to help me. They told me to start by going to Holy Cross Junior College, which was right across the street. They said, "Doing well at Holy Cross will help you get here."

Finally, instead of people saying I couldn't do it, I had people giving me a positive step I could take. This encouragement made it possible for me to do the hard work I hadn't done before. They weren't guaranteeing anything, but they were making what had been impossible possible. My attitude changed: I knew I could make it happen now. I had hope.

At Holy Cross, I made good progress just by going to class and paying attention, asking a lot of questions and focusing. I had never done that in high school because I didn't believe it would make any difference. People had only told me why I couldn't do it. *Psycho-Cybernetics* cleaned up that area of thinking for me. Now I knew that those people could not determine my reality. Only I could do that—by making sure my thoughts always affirmed my belief in myself.

And it worked. I eventually transferred to Notre Dame and became one of the Fighting Irish, even if my role was mainly to give others someone to practice against. I had a small part to play, but I gave it everything I had, and believed in its value. My moment of glory, when it came, was every bit as fulfilling as I ever imagined it would be, just like in the movie.

Today people look at me and see that they can reach their goal, whatever it is—being a doctor, a lawyer, a good mother or father; being a better writer, actor, or businessperson. In the years since the movie came out, I've gotten countless calls from people saying, "I stuck in there because of your movie. I wanted to quit—it got tough—but I just kept going one more time."

I learned from *Psycho-Cybernetics* that it's all in what you think. I wasn't a great athlete, but I knew I could be part of a great team. To this day, they haven't made a movie about Joe Montana, one of the greatest football players in the world—yet they made a movie about Rudy. Why? Because what people want to see—even more than the greatness in others—is the greatness possible in themselves. Every one of us uses our mind to create our life. My story can be your story—if you are willing to swim against the stream, fight against the odds, and believe you can be whatever you want to be.

Danny Edward Scott Casalenuovo

After a three-year trial and sentencing period, Danny Edward Scott Casalenuovo is now completing a five-year prison sentence. He is a member of the Tutoring Counsel Committee, teaching language and math to fellow inmates. He is employed in the prison's T-shirt factory and working on building his life from the inside out. Danny is a contributing author of the book *Serving Time, Serving Others: Acts of Kindness by Inmates, Prison Staff, Victims, and Volunteers*, by Tom Lagana and Laura Lagana. ∎

In 1997, I was arrested for impersonating a police officer. I wasn't behind the wheel or on a two-wheeler with blue and red flashing lights. Dressed in plain clothes, I flashed a police badge as a disguise to gain access to private homes I was stealing from in broad daylight. Worst of all, I didn't steal because I needed the money. I stole for the sheer thrill of it.

As I entered the Los Angeles County Jail that day, the terrible consequences of my actions came crashing down on me. I was leaving my innocent family behind in a state of devastation. My wife and daughter were forced to move in with my in-laws, and my wife had to stand by and watch our home, our car, and our family life slip out of her grasp. The horrible choices I'd made had destroyed our life together and damaged my child's future. A year and a half would go by before my wife would even write to me.

Those thrills cost me everything that mattered. The four-bedroom house filled with laughter was gone. No more glowing fireplace with crackling logs or inviting aromas of a home-cooked meal; no sweet daughter to tuck in at night and read a bedtime story to. I could no longer sit on the front-porch swing with my wife and have a nightly calm-down talk under a billion brilliant stars. Gone was the bond of trust and the comforting closeness of my wife and daughter—the two people I loved most.

My new home was a musty, square jail cell—a dingy, depressing room with dull gray paint peeling like a bad sunburn, and big brown armor-plated bugs crawling out of every corner. The jail, which felt like a giant concrete tomb, held 350 men, each with an unstable attitude ranging from anger and hate to greed and lack of self-control.

The day I first walked into that stale room, my only possession was tucked under my arm—a blanket. I was wearing the rest of my capital: one pair of socks, a T-shirt, jumpsuit, and one pair of much-too-small boxer shorts because processing wasn't the time to be choosy about sizes.

All the bunks were occupied, so I scouted out a spot on the floor, away from most of the traffic and chaos, and moved in. I rounded up a foam mat and made house with my blanket. Exhausted and emotionally drained, I collapsed onto my bed.

The following day, a short, slight man woke me. "Would you like a book to read?"

Looking up at him, I mumbled, "Sure . . . thanks." To this day, I still don't know his name.

That was the day I was fortunate enough to receive a copy of *Chicken Soup for the Prisoner's Soul.* During the days and weeks that followed, I read it from cover to cover scores of times. I read that book so often that I could recite some of the stories as if they were favorite poems.

One day, a nearby inmate asked me who I was talking to. "Oh, I'm sorry," I said. "I didn't realize I was talking. I guess I was reading out loud."

This old man stared at me with a look of intense interest before he finally said, "Would you start that story over?"

At first I was embarrassed, not knowing how to respond. Suddenly, I heard myself say, "Sure I will." I began to read to the inmate I knew as Old Man Sam.

As I read, I looked up at one point and saw deep emotions reflected in the old man's eyes. A chain reaction occurred, and I found myself crying with him. It was a wonderful release, a tremendous feeling to share so deeply with this stranger who was now my friend. A great change took place in my heart at that moment. I felt a fulfilling happiness, and a kind of peace surrounded my spirit.

Within the hour, Old Man Sam had rounded up seven buddies. Like Sam, they were much older than I. Soon, Sam had me reading stories to them, and within 30 minutes I was crying right along with those men, too.

What's happening? I thought to myself. We were sharing real emotions with one another without judgment. These were tough characters, too—some of the most street-hardened men in that concrete warehouse of 350 souls.

As the days passed, the group, now known as "The Circle," grew from 7 to 15. My readings continued. Every day, the circle of men sat quietly for two full hours. During those readings, we could escape the madness and hatred that seethed around us. Every once in a while I'd look over at Old Man Sam, and he'd flash me a big, beautiful smile.

About a week later, our reading session had to be cut short because of an important announcement. The housing deputy shouted, "Canteen items will be delivered this evening to those who ordered earlier in the week!" (The canteen was where we bought snacks and supplies.) There was an immediate flurry of activity throughout the room. Most of the men I'd been reading to, including Old Man Sam, scattered like giant ants.

I sat back, paying close attention to what was taking place. Every jail or prison has a crowd of bullies. I saw that all of the bullies in the room were conducting serious business with selected inmates. Some of those being bullied were from The Circle—one was Old Man Sam. As I watched, I noticed the bullies were taking the identification wristbands from the older, defenseless guys—some of whom were mentally or physically challenged.

As The Circle members regrouped, I realized what was happening. Their heads hung low. Sam and the other bare-wristed men stared at the floor, withdrawn—some crying silently. Sensing fear and tension, I waited for a few moments before asking, "Where are your wristbands?" I looked at Sam, waiting for an answer to confirm what I had pieced together. Then I noticed a red hand-shaped mark on his left cheek.

"Who slapped you, Sam?" Sam raised his left hand to cover the welt on his face. In tears, he looked at me and said, "Don't ask!" Then he rose and walked off, followed by half of The Circle. Filled with anger, I planned my next move.

When the canteen supplies arrived, Old Man Sam's last name was called, but he didn't move from his bunk. Instead, the bully who had stolen his wristband answered to Sam's name, made his way to the front of the crowd, showed the wristband, and collected two plastic trash bags full of supplies. Then he casually walked away.

Passing by without a word, this giant of a guy dropped the wristband on Sam's bunk. Sam slipped the tattered band back over his bony hand and then rolled over and faced the wall. In that moment I realized what an awful time the people I'd robbed must have had—their homes invaded, their personal belongings stolen. Seeing Sam's anguish, the full extent of what I'd done hit me for the first time.

I couldn't watch any longer. Running to the front of the dorm, where a deputy stood observing the canteen distribution, I let the cat out of the bag. As the next bully approached, I tipped off the deputy as to what was taking place. When the man advanced to the front to collect what was not his, he was checked, busted, and taken away. After an emergency count, the deputy knew that what I'd told him was true. Each member of The Circle was reassigned to a safer housing unit. At least three dozen men moved out—including Old Man Sam.

Late that night, nine thugs had a "talk" with me about my ending their "Fund Circus." When they were done, I reported to the front of the dorm in dire need of medical attention. X-rays showed a broken right hand, fractured right wrist, shattered right cheekbone, and broken nose. What the X-rays couldn't find, my nerve endings pointed out. But through all the pain, I felt a huge smile in my heart.

Soon after I was taped and bandaged and my hand set in a cast, I, too, was reassigned. The first face I saw was Old Man Sam's. He and most of The Circle couldn't believe my condition—neither could I. But what upset me most was that I'd lost my book. *Chicken Soup for the Prisoner's Soul* had helped me spiritually and had been the catalyst for the true rehabilitation I'd experienced.

Old Man Sam knew how I felt but suggested that I wing it. So from my memory, I recited some of the stories that had touched me deeply. The Circle grew quickly to 20.

One day, all of us in The Circle were sitting together. We had just started to tell personal stories about our lives when we were interrupted by a stir at the front of the dorm. "Someone just moved in," we heard. Suddenly I recognized a familiar face—it was the leader of the gang of thugs who had broken my bones and blackened my eyes.

"Oh God!" I yelled. Reaching into my locker, I grabbed a razor and concealed it in my left hand. It wasn't much, but it was all I had to protect myself through a second round. The mountain of a man walked right up to our circle and looked into my eyes. He stood in front of me for what seemed like forever. Finally I said, "What? What do you want?"

"It took a lot of courage to do what you did," he said to me.

"No," I said, "what I did was the right thing. It had to do with being a good man. Have you come to beat on me some more?"

Staring down at me with unreadable eyes, he reached behind his back. I tensed, but when he brought his hand back into view, it held a book. He said, "This belongs to you. I saw you reading it. I found it the night I hurt you, and now I want to give it back."

Handing me my book, this giant man apologized for beating me up. We stood there in silence for a few seconds, and then he continued, "Do you mind if I join The Circle? I'd like to listen to you read."

I was shocked—not only because he wanted to join us but also because I was willing to let him!

The 10 minutes that followed were the strangest of my life. As I sat there, dumbfounded, with blackened eyes, my hand in a cast and a nose that throbbed with every beat of my heart, I opened my book to the story "My Bag Lady Friend and Me" and began to read aloud. The opening quote by Hubert Humphrey was exactly what I needed to hear at that moment: "The greatest healing therapy is friendship and love."

As I read, I noticed a change taking place in the newcomer's features and posture. Something seemed to be causing pain in his heart. With a sad, worried look, he slumped forward in his seat. I continued to read. Then abruptly, he stood up and interrupted me. "Name's Allen. . . . I'm sorry for hurting all of you . . . and stealing from you," he said.

It was he who showed courage that evening, apologizing personally to each man he had abused. Allen even gave each of them a hug. The way he stood up and said he was sorry helped all of us, especially me. In the months that followed, I began mailing apology letters to my victims. In those letters I wrote a little about what had happened in the Los Angeles County Jail and how Allen's words led me to send my apologies.

Two days after Allen's courageous act, I was transferred to the prison where I would serve out my sentence. The Circle had become so addicted to hearing stories from *Chicken Soup for the Prisoner's Soul* every day that I decided to leave the book behind. I felt it was intended to be read daily, to those without hope. I chose Allen to be the book's keeper. When I handed it to him, he vowed he'd read it himself, and find someone who would read it out loud to the group.

Before I left, Allen was already at work making a protective cover for the book. *He'll take care of it,* I thought. *And he'll take care of the guys around him, too.* I don't know what more you could say than that about the power of a book.

Farrah Gray

Farrah Gray, now 21 years old, started life on public assistance in Chicago's inner city. He was a card-carrying businessman at age 6, and at 8, he formed a business club that financed his neighborhood ventures. By age 14, he had an office on Wall Street and was a millionaire. Today Farrah, now a multimillionaire, is the spokesman for the National Coalition for the Homeless and the founder of the Farrah Gray Foundation, which focuses on inner-city community-based entrepreneurship education and provides scholarships and grants. Farrah is the author of the best-selling book *Reallionaire: Nine Steps to Becoming Rich from the Inside Out.* ▪

By the time I read Deepak Chopra's *The Seven Spiritual Laws of Success*, I had already created a lot of success in my life: I was the cohost of a nationally syndicated talk show and had my own venture capital business—and I was only 11 years old. Still, I wasn't where I wanted to be.

I didn't understand how the whole "success thing" worked. It seemed so unreliable. I saw so many good people who worked hard and didn't get anywhere. I wondered if there were any rules you could follow to guarantee success. My own achievements had come from a combination of creative ideas and a lot of hard work, but I wanted to go further.

Starting out, I had a lot of things going against me: I grew up in a South Chicago housing project. My mother had left my father and was working at three jobs to support herself and her five kids, despite being sick a lot of the time. We were very, very poor and also on public assistance.

By the time I was six years old, my mom had had two heart attacks. Even though I was just a kid, I wanted to help her not have to work so hard. So I went out, found oversized rocks, and painted them. Then I went around knocking on people's doors and selling them as paperweights, bookends, and door stoppers. I went all over the neighborhood, finding as many doors as I could to knock on, and I ended up making $50. It was the first money I had ever earned. I felt so rich. I remember taking my mom out to a sit-down restaurant to eat.

That was my first business. The next year I started another: selling homemade lotions door to door. Being in business, I thought I should have a business card, so I cut out a piece of cardboard and wrote my name on it. I started to write that I was the president of my company, but I thought people would get me confused with the president of the United States. Then I heard someone introduced on TV as "the twentieth-century CEO." I didn't know what a CEO was, but the man looked important and successful, so I wrote down *21st Century CEO* because I'd be doing business in the twenty-first century.

Not long after I made my cards—I was around eight years old—I met a businessman who worked with my mother. When I gave him my card, he laughed and said, "I can see you want to go into business." He told me he had a think tank that came up with ideas for businesses and the government, and he suggested I start a similar group with my friends to get some businesses started ourselves.

I liked that idea a lot, so I created a club called UNEEC, which stood for *Urban Neighborhood Economic Enterprise Club*. I got about 15 of my friends, all around 8 to 12 years old, to say they'd join. I called around and got the Ramada Inn on the south side of Chicago to give us a free meeting room. I also arranged with someone to provide transportation for us. Then I started inviting local business professionals to talk to us about business, kind of like a career day.

We met so many wonderful people who gave us great business advice. We called it our Business 101 class, and it made us really want to start a business. We were ready, except for one thing—we had no money. So I went out and started raising money. I talked to the same people who had come to give us advice and asked them to introduce us to others who might make small, not donations, but investments.

I'd say, "We're going to offer you an ROI, or a return on your investment." A lot of people laughed, but there were others who really believed in us. That was the beautiful thing. Eventually we were able to raise $15,000. We knew people in our neighborhood who sold drugs and made a lot of money, but I explained why this wasn't a good idea in the business terms I'd learned. I said that drugs give you a lot on the front end but not a lot on the back end. They understood what I meant right away. Our business club started companies like lemonade stands, cookie companies, comic book companies, and roving mini-marts, which did really well. My friends ran most of them, while I continued to raise money for new businesses.

Then, when I was nine, my oldest brother, Andre, got a job in Las Vegas. Since my mom was always working, he took me there to live with him. I kept working on the club back in Chicago, raising money over the phone. I had been doing that for two years when one day, at some event we were at, I met a lady who was the producer of a live radio and TV show called *Backstage Live* that reached more than 12 million people every week. I walked up to her and said, "Hello, ma'am, how are you?" and I gave her my little spiel about our business club.

She told me they usually interviewed celebrities, but she wanted to have me as a guest on the show because she liked me. So she and her partner interviewed me on *Backstage Live*. In the days following the interview, they received such a great response that they asked me to be a regular guest cohost. Because of my age, the Las Vegas media began to notice me. I was even interviewed about my business club on NBC during the Olympics.

On one hand, I loved being a host on the show, but on the other, I was frustrated because the businesses weren't taking off the way I wanted them to. They were growing slowly, but I wasn't sure if I was on the right track. I wondered about what more I could do to be a success—what was it that made one person succeed while another person failed? Soon, I felt restless all the time and began thinking, *Why can't I feel happy and calm?* I felt stuck and wasn't sure where to turn. Then one day I saw a book Andre had brought home: *The Seven Spiritual Laws of Success*. I grabbed it and started reading.

In the book, Chopra writes about the importance of harmony and being in tune with the laws of the universe and of nature. That made

sense to me. Most of the people I knew who grew up poor didn't understand what they were doing wrong. If you're a good person, you think,
"Isn't that enough to make me successful?" But you can be doing a lot of
negative things that are self-sabotage tactics and not even know it.

I learned from Chopra that there are laws governing life and the universe, and that you have to cooperate with them to be successful. Take the
law of gravity—it doesn't matter if you're wonderful, beautiful, smart, or
positive, if you walk off the roof of a building, you're going to go down.
Or if you put your finger in an electric socket, it doesn't matter if you know
the laws governing electricity or even believe in them; you're going to get a
shock. If you don't know those laws, it can be difficult to get ahead.

For me, the most important law Chopra wrote about was the "Law of
Least Effort," which says it's not just about hard work; it's about finding
your true purpose and your true area of excellence. I was actually of-
fended when I first read about this law. I said, "He's a fool! I saw my
mother work so hard. How dare he say it's not about hard work!" But it
was when I followed the Law of Least Effort that my real success began.

The book said that the Law of Least Effort works when you follow
your own nature—what is natural for you. If you know and follow those
things, it becomes easy to live your life's purpose. I thought about that
and came up with a few questions that helped me figure it out: What
comes easy to me but harder to others? What would I want to work on
for a long time—even if I was never paid for it? And on the basis of those
answers, what I could do to help the people around me?"

When I asked myself these questions, the idea for my next business
came easily. I started Farr-Out Foods, a food company for kids. Our first
product was syrup. I used the same recipe my grandmother made for us
on the stovetop back in Chicago, when we hadn't been able to afford to
buy syrup. This business fit the three criteria perfectly: It was easy for me
because first of all, it was targeted to kids, and I knew what kids liked and
what attracted them to buy things. Plus, I liked to cook, so coming up
with food products came naturally to me. Second, it was really interesting and enjoyable for me to work on, and third, it definitely helped kids,
who always love syrup! And sure enough, it was a great success. I ended
up doing $1.5 million in sales with the company and then selling it for
over a million dollars, which made me a millionaire by the age of 14.

I got so excited seeing that the law worked. Before I read Chopra's book and learned about that law, I had tried so many other things that I put a lot more effort into that didn't gel. Now I had a formula I could count on.

Many times over the past 10 years, I have used the Law of Least Effort and the other spiritual laws that Chopra wrote about—through all my business ventures, from Kidztel, which sold prepaid calling cards for kids, and *Innercity Magazine*, which I owned, to a show I produced on the Vegas strip and the new real estate brokerage I just opened in Las Vegas. In fact, my own book, *Reallionaire: Nine Steps to Becoming Rich from the Inside Out*, was inspired by many of Chopra's ideas.

The term *reallionaire* means someone who has real wealth—the kind that is more than money. For years, it confused me to see all the people on television who were famous, who had all the money in the world, who lived in mansions. One day you'd see them on *Lifestyles of the Rich and Famous*—and then you'd see them the next day on *Access Hollywood* or *Extra* going into rehab, committing suicide, or getting arrested for something crazy. Reading Chopra's book, I realized that those people had built more in their outer world—money and popularity—than what they had built for themselves in their inner world, so it had created a lopsided success.

Today, at 21, I am trying to teach others what I've learned: that it's important to be rich from the inside out. For that you need to follow the law—the laws of the land *and* the laws of the universe. This is what has made me happy and peaceful, which is what I call real success.

Louise Hay

Louise Hay is known as one of the founders of the self-help movement. Her first book, *Heal Your Body*, was published in 1976, long before it was fashionable to discuss the connection between the mind and body. In 1984, *You Can Heal Your Life* was published and soon became a *New York Times* best seller. More than 30 million copies have been sold, introducing Louise's concepts to people in 33 different countries. Louise now heads Hay House, a successful publishing company. In addition, the Hay Foundation and the Louise L. Hay Charitable Fund are two nonprofit organizations established by Louise that support many diverse organizations, including those dealing with AIDS, battered women, and other challenged individuals in our society. ■

I began with parking spaces and green lights. Back when I was just starting to understand that we create our reality with our thoughts, I thought, *Well, let's put this into practice.* And silly as it sounds, I found that if I really put my attention on getting a parking space or a green light when I needed one, I would get one! It blew my mind.

When I saw that you could literally change your life if you were willing to change your thinking, the idea just exploded within me. I had had a rough upbringing and was somebody who had never gone to school much. In fact, I was a high school dropout and had never really studied anything—but when this concept was presented to me, I just had to learn more about it.

So I began to take classes in manifesting what you want in your life at the Church of Religious Science. In the course of my studies there, I came across a little book that has meant so much to me. *The Game of Life and How to Play It*, by Florence Scovel Shinn, helped me crystallize my own thinking and moved me forward on the path to where I am today.

Florence began teaching in 1926, the year I was born. A real pioneer, she was a powerful woman who put herself out there in a bold way that was very unusual for women of that era. But she was absolutely committed to the teachings. Although her ideas were still totally unknown to the general population, Florence was strong and confident about them. She made declarative statements with great power and understanding. All the way back in 1926, she was saying, "If you don't realize that thoughts create things, you are behind the times." I read that, and I thought, *Oh yes, yes, yes*. I wanted to emulate her, gain the insights she had, and understand where she was coming from.

The many biblical references in her writings didn't mean a whole lot to me because I've never been a Bible person, but I got past those by using the word *universe* or *life* instead. As I practiced speaking these new beliefs and using spoken affirmations to influence what was happening in the world, I saw that "demonstrations," as we called them, happened, and life started to shift a little bit this way, and a little bit that way.

Gradually, I formed an understanding of how affirmations work, and how our mental beliefs affect our physical bodies, and I began to practice and teach what I had learned. My first book, *Heal Your Body*, written in 1976, was a tiny 12-page pamphlet of healing affirmations for a wide range of ailments. My second, more detailed book, *You Can Heal Your Life*, was published in 1984. I've heard from thousands of people who have used this knowledge for good in their lives. And I've benefited tremendously myself. For example, when my cancer was diagnosed years ago, I considered all the treatment options and decided to develop my own intensive program of affirmations, visualization, nutritional cleansing, and psychotherapy instead. Within six months, I was completely healed.

From the very start, Florence inspired me by demonstrating the power of thought and word to manifest what people desired. She used to say she would "speak the word" for them. If a woman needed an apartment, she'd say, "Infinite Spirit, open the way for the right apartment." That would be literally all she said. And if the woman was smart, she would go away and repeat that over and over again. And doors opened miraculously for people.

Yet Florence was always working for harmony. She would often speak the word for harmonious relationships for people, but the results she sought would always be good for all the parties concerned, not just the person asking for help. If somebody wanted to get married to a certain person, Florence wouldn't ask for that specific outcome; she would simply ask for the perfect relationship for the person who wanted to get married.

Florence's books are very much like mine in that she gives lots and lots of examples, so there is something for everyone. You can find yourself in her books and then find an answer just for you. What more could you want? I also love the fact that she was simple, because I've always been a simple person, too. Intellectuals have a terrible time with me because they say, "Oh, she's so silly; it's so simple." But simple works!

I've always been for the beginner, for the ordinary person. That's where I come from. To this day, all I want to do is improve the quality of people's lives. How can I help you make a better life? Let's do it simply, and easily.

I'm almost 80 now and have been sharing these ideas for a long time. From the moment I set my foot on the spiritual pathway, my life has never been the same. Life has decided what it wants me to do, and I've done it. I take action, but really I have the sense that life is living me. What I notice these days is that if I need something, it just comes to me, and often in the most mysterious—or as Florence would say, magical—ways.

The Game of Life and How to Play It started me off in the right direction. I never had a chance to meet Florence, as she was gone before I began to study. But she taught me that you have to jump in with both feet and trust in these truths and practice using them. I believed and I trusted, and now I know—it works! It doesn't matter where I go or what happens; I'm not concerned about life because I know that whatever lies before me is good.

Rhonda Byrne

Rhonda Byrne is the creator of the worldwide film phenomenon *The Secret*, a feature-length film on DVD, seen by hundreds of millions of people in its first year of release. She also wrote the companion book, *The Secret*, which sold more than one million copies in its first three months in print and is now a *New York Times* and *USA Today* bestseller. The DVD and book have been featured on numerous television shows, including *Oprah*, *The Ellen DeGeneres Show*, and *Larry King Live*, and in newspapers and magazines all over the world. Rhonda launched her production company, Prime Time Productions, in 1994 after 20 years' experience as a senior producer for Australia's Nine Network, where she was involved in the creation of many award-winning programs. As Prime Time's executive producer, Rhonda has remained the key force behind the company's television production success within Australia and throughout the world. Since being sparked into action by the words of Wallace Wattles in the *Science of Getting Rich*, her life's passion has been to bring joy to billions. ▪

For most of my life, I've considered myself a happy person; I've always had a loving family, wonderful friends, good health, and creative work that I enjoy. Yet one night in October 2004, I found myself in a state of total and utter despair.

Over the course of the previous 12 months, I had worked incredibly hard making six movie-length television specials and I was totally exhausted. On this particular night, I had just hung up the phone after talking to my mother, and I was deeply concerned by her emotional state. My father had died six months earlier. My mother and father had had the most beautiful love affair that I'd ever seen, and now my mother had basically collapsed to her knees with grief. She was feeling terribly alone in the world. She hadn't seen anyone in days and was so lonely she didn't want to go on. I had been trying to make her feel better, but nothing I said seemed to help her at all. I was a long way away, so I couldn't be with her and was terrified that she wouldn't be alive in the morning. I had never felt so completely powerless.

I was in a really bad way. My daughter, who was 23 at the time, came to me and asked me what was wrong. When I told her, she said, "You really need to read something that I have." She went off and came back with this old, tattered book. It was *The Science of Getting Rich*, by Wallace Wattles. Handing it to me, she said, "The last page of it is missing, but you'll get the idea." I couldn't imagine how this book could help: What did getting rich have to do with helping my mother?

Although I could barely see the words for the tears in my eyes, I began reading. With each sentence I read, my eyes widened. I had never read anything like this before.

The book, as it turns out, *is* about getting rich—not only in terms of money but in every possible way, including relationships and health. As I read, it became clear to me that what Wattles was presenting was actually the science of life. He wrote *The Science of Getting Rich* in 1910 for the coal miners in his area, so the book is quite short and the language is simple. He doesn't get into philosophies or theories. He doesn't explain why or how it works. He just says, "Do what I say and your life will completely change."

I was barely breathing as I turned the pages. Deep within, I knew that every single thing he said was true: This was the Truth, with a capital *T*.

The next morning—after I checked on my mother, who, though still miserable, seemed to be slightly better than the night before—I began doing research on Wallace Wattles. I read about his life and every single thing he had ever written. Then I wanted to find out who his mentor was. My research led me back through history, century after century, reading book after book after book. Within just a few weeks, I read dozens of books. What I discovered in my search was the secret to having everything I wanted in life: money, health, love, success. When I applied this knowledge that I now call "The Secret" to every single aspect of my life, my life was completely transformed.

The longest chapter in Wattles's book is on gratitude, and it's also the chapter that had the most impact on me. Wattles writes that gratitude enables us to create more of what we want in our lives. He says you must focus on all of the wonderful things you have in your life and not on the things that you don't have, and then practice being grateful for all those wonderful things.

It sounds simple, but I realized I had been doing the opposite in my life. I didn't spend much energy on the things that were going well. Instead, I focused on my problems: not having enough money, not having enough time, being under stress. After reading Wattles's book, I completely changed my thinking habits. In the area of finances, instead of worrying about the money that I didn't have, I was grateful for the money that I did have. I also imagined the money that I wanted to have—another important component in creating wealth.

If my goal was to have more and more money, I knew I had to experience—in my mind, body and heart—what it felt like to have a lot of money as though I had it already. For me, that would mean feeling that I could give money away. As a test of this theory, I decided to draw some money out of my not-very-big account to give away.

I withdrew $500 in 50-dollar bills and walked down the street, looking for total strangers to give money to. As I walked, I looked at each person I passed, thinking, "Who am I going to give it to?" The funny thing was that I wanted to give it to everybody!

I gave away the first 50-dollar bill in a department store. I was going down an escalator and overheard the conversation of the couple behind me. The girl was saying that she really wanted to buy an outfit. Her boyfriend said, "Why don't you buy it? It will look great on you." She said, "Oh, I can't afford it. It's too much money." Just as we reached the bottom of the escalator, I turned around, handed her the 50-dollar bill, and said, "Yes, you can."

You should have seen their faces. The two of them froze. The girl was the first to recover, and giving me back the bill, withdrew her hand quickly, saying, "Oh my gosh, I can't."

I said to her, "Yes, you can, because you really deserve it," and I put the note back in her hand and walked away.

I can tell you that the person who received the most from that experience was me. I felt so wonderful. When I finished giving away the rest of the 50-dollar bills, I had never felt so wealthy in my life. Do you know, within 24 hours, $25,000 came into my life in a way I could never, ever have dreamed? All from doing the exercise of giving away $500, which had been inspired by Wallace Wattles. Since then, money has continued to flow into my life in a way that I can only describe as miraculous. And being grateful for the riches in my life has become automatic.

Using my new insights about life, I immediately worked out a way to help my mother. I knew I couldn't teach her all of this—she was in such grief and despair, she couldn't have heard the words. Instead, I asked her to do something very simple. I asked that every time she felt that awful fear and despair inside her, she immediately stop whatever she was doing, go find her little dogs—we called them the puppies—and pat them. I instructed her to pat the puppies for at least one minute. "Could you do that?" I asked. She said yes, she could definitely do that.

Less than two days later, she called, saying she couldn't believe what was happening. When the fear came, she told me, she remembered she had to go to the puppies. And every time she patted the puppies, that feeling, that horrible despair and grief, left her. Now, she said, just beginning to walk to the puppies was enough to make the fear go away. Within a couple of days, just from doing that, she was feeling happier. And of course, as she began to feel happier, people started coming into her life.

Within two weeks her house was full of people. Her friends were calling her all the time, bringing her flowers and presents, taking her out here and there. It worked, because she had stopped focusing on the negative and had begun focusing on the good things in her life. The only thing I had been able to think of that always made my mother feel good were the puppies. I knew that when my mother was patting the puppies she was thinking about the puppies and nothing else; she was simply enjoying the puppies. So this was the perfect healing tool for her. Within one to two weeks, my mother's life had totally turned around, just from patting these puppies.

Seeing the power of this knowledge, I decided I wanted to share it with the world. Drawing on my experience in television and film production, I began putting all the elements together to create a full-length film on DVD called *The Secret*. Wattles's book tells you how you can live the life that you want, without any limits, no matter who you are and no matter where you are now. *The Secret* encompasses all of the power of that knowledge and brings it to the screen in the simplest and clearest form. It is "The Secret" to whatever you want and tells you how you can be, do, or have anything.

I know that Wattles's message can change people's lives for the better. It certainly changed mine. Reading *The Science of Getting Rich* was the start of a huge shift in me. I have come to realize that I am so much more than this little physical body. I have control over everything in my life, and there is a power within me that can create whatever I want. All I have to do is to change how I think and feel, and the whole of my life, in every single area, will change—and that's exactly what I've done. In every single area of life, I decided what I wanted, and that's what I've gotten.

The Secret, which launched in 2006, has been a phenomenal success! The DVD was translated into nine languages and was seen by hundreds of millions of people within the first year of its release. Shows about *The Secret* appeared on television—Oprah featured it twice!—and articles were printed in newspapers and magazines everywhere. I ended up writing a companion book, also called *The Secret*, which sold more than a million copies in its first three months in print and topped bestseller lists all over the world. *The Secret* spread like wildfire because it strikes a deep chord in so many people.

Today, my whole life is so magnificent. The happiness I felt before has been multiplied many times over: I am surrounded by people I love, I have more than enough money, and my work is fascinating and fulfilling. The joy I have in just being alive and being able to be on this marvelous planet one day after another is incredible. Feeling this way—and knowing how simple it is to create the life you want—how could I not share "The Secret" with everyone?

Mark Victor Hansen

Mark Victor Hansen is the cocreator of the biggest-selling book series in history, *Chicken Soup for the Soul*, with more than 100 million copies and more than 100 different titles in print. Mark has been a public speaker for 31 years, entertaining and enlightening audiences worldwide, and is the author of seven additional books and several popular audio programs. He is the recipient of numerous honorary degrees and awards, including the prestigious Horatio Alger Award. ■

Today, it's become second nature for me to think big—really, really big! I have an attitude of abundance, and as a result, I enjoy a lot of prosperity in my life. But it wasn't always this way. In 1974, I was bankrupt and upside down. Then I read a book that totally changed how I looked at life and money.

My parents came to this country as immigrants from Denmark. Because they lost everything in the Depression, while I was growing up I often heard them say, "Do you think I'm made of money? Money doesn't grow on trees!" and other things like that. When a person has had those kinds of statements branded into their brain and etched into the fabric of their being, they start to buy into the idea that there's a shortage in the universe. As a result, I created that shortage in my own life on a catastrophic level. After my bankruptcy, to get moral support I started driving from Long Island into Manhattan on Sundays to meet some friends and hear Dr. Norman Vincent Peale preach at his church on Fifth Avenue. Dr. Peale delivered a message of hope; something I needed badly at that time.

One week, after hearing Dr. Peale, my friends suggested we go up to Harlem to hear a minister named Reverend Ike. Reverend Ike was called the "money minister" because he talked a lot about financial abundance and had a flamboyant lifestyle. But what really got my attention was his claim that everything he had—his giant church with 5,000 people in the congregation each week, and his radio show with its huge audience—had come because it was exactly what he had visualized as a poor kid growing up in South Carolina.

We drove to Harlem and went to his church. During his sermon, Reverend Ike talked about using your consciousness to create what you want in life. His message was really about abundance of all kinds, not just financial. He hit right on my spark plugs, and I started attending his church regularly. One Sunday soon after my first visit, Reverend Ike recommended a book that had been pivotal for him: *Resurrection*, written by Neville Goddard, better known as just Neville. I bought the book at church that Sunday and started devouring it that very night. I knew that if this book had changed Reverend Ike's life, it could change mine, too.

Since that first time, I've read *Resurrection* again and again. I've gotten hundreds of people to read it, and talked it through with lots of different people. Over the past 31 years, I've taken ownership of the principles and have achieved all the results that I wanted back then, and much, much more.

Neville taught that you should "start at the end and go forward." That is, think of what you want to create in your life and start from there. Imagine that goal, focus on it, keep it clearly in view—and you will achieve it. Stephen Covey recently popularized a related concept—"Begin with the end in mind"—but Neville's teachings are more spiritual in nature. He wrote about what he called "The Law: Imagining Creates Reality."

Neville learned The Law from his own experience. He grew up in Barbados during the Depression. As an adult, he lived in New York and worked as an actor. Years before he wrote *Resurrection*, he began to get glimpses of the power of his mind. At one point, he really wanted to go back to Barbados to see his family, so every night before he went to sleep, he visualized the drops of sea spray on the boat as he was arriving in Barbados on a beautiful, sunny day.

Every night he visualized those drops, shining in the sun. A week later, he had the money for a round-trip, fully paid ticket to travel back to see his family. It came to him effortlessly, through what he called "mystical means."

When I read that, I said to myself, *I can do that. I can visualize having best-selling books. I can visualize being happily married and having great kids.* I visualized all of that, and over the years, that's exactly what I've achieved.

I started using Neville's suggestion right away. Back then, I was giving sales training talks in small insurance offices, ideally four times a day. To get back on my feet financially, it was important to have a full schedule of talks, so I started imagining my calendar filled with appointments. I practiced seeing and holding that vision.

I had a very specific procedure. I'd put on some soothing music, like Pachelbel's Canon in D. Then I would close my eyes and take ownership of the concept. By that, I mean I just went over the concept again and again until it became a part of my belief system. At night I'd lull myself to sleep with the thoughts such as *I am going to have absolute prosperity. I am going to have a great day selling tomorrow. I am going to earn my way forward and get out of the depression I am in. I am going to wake up optimistic, positive, hopeful, and helpful and make a difference in the lives of people around me.*

After a few days of doing this, I had the idea to print out a little postcard with my picture on the front and the message that I was giving sales training talks to insurance agencies and a list of the companies I was talking to. I sent it out to every insurance agency in Long Island, Manhattan, New Jersey, and Pennsylvania.

Over the next two weeks, my calendar got booked up for the rest of the year. I saw that it really did work; my calendar was full, and I wasn't depressed anymore. While holding the image of the end result I had wanted, I had acted on the ideas that came. I just held to what Neville says: "You've got to affix to your thought to transform," which has always reminded me of something Einstein once said: "Imagination is more important than knowledge."

Before I learned about the power of the imagination, my method of operating was basically to struggle and barely get along. I thought that politics, the economy, and the media controlled the world. What I came to understand is that what really controls even those huge institutions is the collective imagination of individuals. Imagination is the imprint of the individual mind on the formless intelligence that brings what we desire into being. It is a form of spirit or God in action.

Neville writes that resurrection isn't just what happened to Jesus; it's the resurrection of Christ's consciousness within each and every one of us to enable us to manifest what we desire. It's about changing reality, changing every circumstance for the better. When I read Neville's book, I was introduced to an entirely new concept: having an idea permeate, penetrate, and fill the inner spaces of my mind, then go out into the universe and bring back the exact result that I keep sending it out after. I've proven again and again that it works.

In fact, I've had to increase my imagining ability to keep ahead of the achievements in my life. And I find that the bigger I think, the more effective the imagining becomes. Today, I'm working on changing the financial consciousness of the world. One of my personal goals is to help create a million millionaires who will each give $1 million back to their religious organization, charity, or nonprofit. My students have donated hundreds of millions of dollars so far, and very soon may blow past a billion. At this rate, within 10 years my students could give away over $1 trillion.

Neville inspired me to find abundance in every part of life and to keep that abundance flowing. For example, if you breathe in all that you can breathe in right now, that's abundance. But if you hold it, you lose it. That's why you've got to keep giving it away, so you can make room for more, because there's always more coming in to inundate you. One of the most ancient texts in the world, the Upanishads, says this: "Out of abundance they took abundance, and still abundance remained."

This idea of "circulating one's good" is the basis of tithing. Tithing 10% of your income to the source of your spiritual inspiration is something both my wife Patty and I believe in. About six years after I first read Neville, we were refinancing a piece of real estate and taking $60,000 out of the new loan amount. We asked ourselves, "Is that income? According to the IRS, if it's a loan, technically it isn't income—but are we using it as income?"

We decided that the answer was yes, so we tithed on the full $60,000. That meant we had to write a check instantly for $6,000. Oh man, I was breathing hard as I wrote out that check! Tithing is so counterintuitive—how can giving away money create more abundance in your life? I was almost hyperventilating as I thought, *I could go buy more real estate. I could do all these wonderful things with this.*

Remembering Neville's words, I visualized writing big, powerful checks and having plenty of money, so I could do it with no concern. But as I walked out to the driveway and put the letter in the mailbox, I still felt the resistance. I can remember opening the mailbox and thinking, *I don't want to do this. I don't want to do this. I'm giving away six grand to the church. What am I, nuts?*

But I did it, and just a few minutes later, the phone rang. It was the bank, calling to say they were giving us 2% off the interest rate on our loan. We were in shock. This would save us $2,000 a year, which on a 30-year fixed loan meant we'd get back $60,000—a tenfold return of our tithe.

There was no apparent reason why the bank decided to give us the 2% rate reduction. But they gave it. I can only believe it happened because, as I had learned from Neville, imagination is spirit in action, and the spirit in me had moved.

Since that time, I've relied on this powerful law many times, and as a result I've filled my wallet, filled my future, and have had a fulfilling life and career. I never lost touch with the law, and today I feel that much of my success can be traced to Neville's book. *Resurrection* contained the revelation that resurrected my life: You create abundance—on all levels—with your own wonderful imagination.

Michael E. Gerber

Michael E. Gerber is an entrepreneur, small-business guru, and the best-selling author of seven books, including his latest, *E-Myth Mastery* (*E* stands for *entrepreneurial*). He is the founder and chairman of E-Myth Worldwide, which since its inception in 1977 has worked with more than 50,000 individual companies and is the leading coaching, training, and educational firm in the world focused specifically on Michael's vision: to transform the lives of small-business owners worldwide. ■

At the beginning of each of the chapters in my books, there is a quote that captures the chapter's message in seed form. If anyone went through and looked at those quotes, they would instantly know a lot about me. The cited books and authors—including Robert Pirsig's *Zen and the Art of Motorcycle Maintenance*, Fritjof Capra's *The Turning Point*, Theodore Levitt's *Marketing for Business Growth*, and Roberto Assagioli's *The Act of Will*—tell the story of the many and varied literary influences in my life. But it is the quote from *100 Selected Poems* by E.E. Cummings at the beginning of chapter three of my first book, *The E-Myth*, which reveals the book and author that had the most impact on me.

I first read Cummings in 1955, when I was 19. After graduating from high school, I wasn't sure what I wanted to do, so I volunteered for military service. This was just on the heels of the Korean War. Assigned by the army to be a company clerk, I was being trained at Fort Ord in Monterey, California. In my barracks, I met a guy named Pat, who, before he'd been drafted, was in a Ph.D. program in Romance languages. We often had long philosophical conversations—not a common activity in army life—and it was Pat who introduced me to E.E. Cummings.

I had read poetry before. At synagogue school, I remember reading outrageous stuff from Allen Ginsberg and upsetting everybody—the rabbi, the kids, their mothers—but I had never been really moved by poetry the way I was when I first read E.E. Cummings.

It was on one of my days off, when I'd left the base and was lying on the beach in neighboring Carmel, that I first opened a volume of Cummings's collected poems. I was immediately struck by the completely original way Cummings used language. All at once, I saw that words could be organized differently on the page than they normally were. And the way in which Cummings moved the words added layers of extraordinary meaning—most of which I couldn't discern, but all of which stirred me. The way the words were framed on the page, coupled with the fact that he didn't use capital letters, suddenly showed me that you can shape what you say, the words you use, and perhaps the life you live *any way at all*. And there are so many original ways to do that. I felt breathless, inspired—dazzled by this sudden vision of possibilities.

I studied the poem on the page in front of me. How had Cummings conceptualized that? It came to me that I didn't think he had. It wasn't an artifice; it wasn't something that he had done to be clever. It was simply his inspiration using the shape, texture, sound, and juxtaposition of words to express a reality.

Lying there on the sand, I began to think about my own reality. I was just on the cusp between being an adolescent and being a young man. It had become increasingly clear to me that being in the army was so completely the opposite of what I wanted to do and be, of who I was. Suddenly, reading Cummings, experiencing this whole new vivid way of expressing oneself and being in the world, I knew that I wanted to be a poet.

Before entering the army, I had wanted to be a musician. I'd been studying and practicing music since I was 10 and was a *very* good saxophone player. But when it was time to stop practicing and go to work—when it was time to be a musician—I couldn't do it. I felt so ordinary compared with the remarkable musicians I idolized, who were icons of music. Technically I was good enough, but I'd set my standard as breaking through, breaking out of the box—breaking out of my ordinariness. I felt too confined in my own imagination; I always had the feeling that there was something, just there, waiting, but I couldn't get to it. My belief was that musicians such as Charlie Parker and Sonny Rollins got to it. I was no Charlie or Sonny, so I'd given up trying to be a professional musician, and because I didn't know what else to do, I'd ended up in the army.

Once I read Cummings, I saw that he had gotten to it, too, but through poetry. Cummings's poetry gave me a glimpse of the unlimited potential to create and express oneself freely—at a time when I had absolutely no possibility of directing my own life. In the army, I was completely under the control of the powers that be. To my surprise, instead of being unhappy with this limitation, there was a sense of surrendering to that, and in the months following my epiphany on the beach, I experienced myself as I was, right there in each moment. And because I couldn't choose any *one* of the possibilities, they all remained open to me.

In that state of surrender, I felt vibrant and alive; I felt a light shining on my days, on my minutes, my hours. The light was a feeling of intense presence, and I couldn't tell what the presence was. There was no "mentalizing" it. Even looking back now, I can't say it was God, because that would just be my fanciful imagining of it.

Reading Cummings had opened a door, and I had stepped through it. Although my choices were limited to almost zero in the army, there was at least one level at which I felt the infinite options available to me. I could create something as small as a tiny poem without any rules whatsoever, just as Cummings did. I could do that anywhere—stealing a few minutes for myself—and something magical would happen.

So I wrote poems, but over time, the same thing happened that had happened with my music: I fell back into my old habit of feeling inadequate and ordinary. Despite the light I was experiencing inside when I wrote the poems, when I looked at them again, I didn't believe that my poetry could have the heft, the weight, the brilliance of Cummings's work. To produce poetry like Cummings's, you had to be some amazing, unique, rare human being, and I knew in my soul that I wasn't. I wasn't strange enough, deep enough—whatever enough.

When I finished my training in California, I was shipped off to Korea, and when I came home after the army, I entered what I call my wandering Jew period. Although I was now in charge of my own destiny, I didn't seem able to settle into any of the many paths open to me but went from one thing to another without any coherent plan for the future. My first job after the army was selling shoes in a women's shoe store. Then I sold encyclopedias. Next I sold photographs door to door. In 1960, I went to Europe with the woman who was going to be my first wife. I took my saxophone and played in Paris, Holland, Spain—all over Europe. After about a year, we ran out of money. Returning to New York City, we somehow managed to buy an old yellow taxi, which we drove from New York to California. I was a beatnik with a beard and saxophone; driving through the South and through Texas, I often got stopped by cops. They'd say, "Boy, where are you going in this taxicab?" And I'd say, "I have no idea."

For many years, that was the story of my life. You could call me a free spirit. That sounds romantic, but mostly I felt I was a failure. Yet even though I was always lost—I was also always inspired by something. Inside there was a light, but there was darkness, too. I can still remember my first conscious experience of that light: the extraordinary sunlight on the beach in Carmel, the luminosity of Cummings's poem, the richness and excitement of my imagination welling up and beginning to create poetry, only to eventually crash into the other part of me: the dark part I call the critic, who knew I wasn't "enough." This continuous alternation between the light and the dark has followed me throughout my life.

When I was 50, I wrote *The E-Myth: Why Most Small Businesses Don't Work and What to Do About It*, which became an international best seller. Like the rest of my life up until that point, the whole E-Myth phenomenon came about by chance—a happy accident. Almost 10 years earlier, I'd been visiting my brother-in-law. One day, he brought me with him to call on a client of his who was having trouble generating leads from the ads my brother-in-law had done for him. Listening to their discussion, I started thinking about what I would suggest the client do. I discovered that I had a talent for seeing the causes of the problems small businesses faced—and the solutions to those problems! The many different jobs I'd held had given me a unique perspective on the ways that human beings produced results, whether playing the saxophone or running a business. I saw the need for fail-safe systems in order to master whatever one does.

For two years I worked with my brother-in-law, and in 1977, I started my own consulting practice. Over the next seven years, I developed a theory I called the Entrepreneurial Myth, or E-Myth, and the practices to apply it. In 1985, my book was published, and after that, my career took off. Over the last 20 years, I have written six more books about the E-Myth and created an international consulting company: E-Myth Worldwide. I have achieved a great deal of success by any standard—except perhaps my own.

Anyone who sees what I've done would say, "That's silly, Michael. Look what you've accomplished," but inside my heart, inside my mind, inside my body, I am still that teenager, still that wandering Jew. I feel I have never been brave, daring, or bold enough. I have never been *outrageous* enough. Now, though, at the age of 69, I am finally getting over it.

A year and a half ago, I hired a CEO to manage E-Myth Worldwide, and I've been free to do whatever I want. I'm creating a brand-new company called Infinite Options. Our mission statement is to create new ventures that transform the lives of people worldwide.

One of the ventures I'm in the process of inventing is called Intense Experiences. IE creates two-and-a-half-day intense experiences. The first is on creativity; the second is on will; the third is on intention, and so on. These are productions unlike anything that's ever been done. They are to personal growth what Cirque du Soliel is to a circus.

Another of these ventures is designed to revolutionize the lives of entry-level employees in the food industry. Two hundred and fifty thousand people leave the food industry every week; replacements have to be hired week after week after week. These are dead-end jobs for people with limited futures—and nobody cares. I am creating a venture that transforms that reality. And I absolutely know it can be done.

These are just two of the daring things I have in mind. Through Infinite Options, I'm finally going to be outrageous. When people tell me, "Yes, but . . . ," I don't even want to listen to them, because at my age, what's left but to be brave enough, bold enough, daring enough—outrageous enough?

Looking back 50 years to the book that transformed my life, I see that my life has come full circle since that day on the beach when I first read E.E. Cummings and glimpsed the passion, the extraordinary excitement, of being able to create whatever, whenever, and however I am moved to. Infinite Options is the fulfillment of that vision.

Tim Ferriss

Tim Ferriss is an accelerated-learning researcher, world traveler, and guest lecturer at Princeton University. He is fluent in Japanese, Mandarin Chinese, German, and Spanish. He holds national titles in Chinese kickboxing (International Kickboxing Federation), is the first American to hold a Guinness world record in tango, and has worked with more than 80 world-champion athletes as director of research at BrainQUICKEN LLC Research and Technologies. Tim is the author of *The 4-Hour Workweek: Escape 9-5, Live Anywhere, and Join the New Rich* (www.timferriss.com). ∎

I grew up in Springs, New York, a town on the easternmost tip of Long Island, separated from most of the rest of the world by the vast expanse of the Atlantic Ocean. Maybe it was the feeling of living on the edge of the world that sparked my desire to explore and learn what lay beyond the infinitely stretching horizon. Or it might have been my job as a "test reader" for our next-door neighbor, Ed Packard, who was the cocreator and author of the wildly popular Choose Your Own Adventure book series for children. Each book, after an introduction to the story, gives the reader choices of how the story—which usually involves exciting adventures in exotic locales—should progress. Depending on the reader's choice, the plot unfolds in different ways and eventually leads to one of a variety of possible endings. As a reward for my feedback on his books in progress, Mr. Packard sometimes gave one of the books' characters my name. I remember fantasizing for hours about the adventures described in those books!

Whatever its source, this childhood longing to travel and experience the unknown made me particularly receptive to the two books that would later transform my life. Those books—*How to Make Millions with Your Ideas*, by Dan Kennedy, and *Vagabonding*, by Rolf Potts—have completely changed the way I think about work and enabled me to create a life of adventure and meaning that I had only imagined was possible.

Even as a kid, I questioned the assumptions about life that most people around me seemed to accept without thinking: You go to school, get a 9-to-5 job, get married, have kids, buy the house with a white picket fence, work 50 weeks a year for 30 years, and then retire. I don't think there's anything wrong with that, but I wanted something different. I knew I wouldn't find it in Springs, so I asked my parents if I could go to private boarding school. We definitely weren't wealthy, so paying for private school was a stretch—but all through my childhood my parents had told me they could always find the money for education or books. They agreed to send me.

At 15, I left Springs and the ocean behind and went to St. Paul's School in the middle of the New Hampshire woods. It felt as though all the options in the world had opened to me. At East Hampton High School, for a foreign language I'd had the choice of taking Spanish . . . or Spanish. At St. Paul's, I could choose from 15 different languages. I had been involved in martial arts for years, and so I began studying Japanese.

I almost quit only one week later! It turned out that "conversational" Japanese also contained a healthy dose of reading and writing with ideograms, or "characters," which gave me flashbacks of struggling through the alphabet with mild dyslexia as a child. After a sit-down pep talk with my teacher and six months of study, I landed in Japan through an exchange program and never looked back. It was my first time out of the country, and my introduction to Asia was nothing short of life-changing. I experienced an entirely different culture, deepening my conviction that there were many other ways of living and enjoying life. I was excited and awed at the possibility of following my own interests and tendencies—though I knew it might be difficult and even scary at times.

Back in Concord, I was browsing through a bookstore one day and noticed a little blue paperback face out on the shelf. The title, *How to Make Millions with Your Ideas*, caught my attention. *Well*, I thought, *if someone can tell me how to make millions with my ideas—which definitely aren't going to fit well into the conventional jigsaw puzzle—the book will need some real plot twists.* I opened the book and read a few pages. It wasn't your typical get-rich-quick material: how to make a lot of money in any specific way, such as with the stock market or real estate. Instead, Kennedy outlines concepts that involve creativity and out-of-the-box thinking to produce success with any product or service. His ideas and examples really grabbed me—I had never realized that entrepreneurship could be so inventive and daringly unconventional. One concept stood out immediately: informational marketing, or taking expertise and turning it into product. I shelled out the $15 they were asking for the book—at age 16 that was a lot of money for me—and took the book back to my dormitory. I read the whole thing in one sitting and dog-eared nearly every page. I was excited by the concepts but wouldn't do anything with them until a few years later, when I was in college.

I had managed to get accepted to Princeton University. Although I didn't have the usual perfect SAT scores (I never even finished the test), I'd packaged myself in a way that appealed to the admissions office, and my parents, with the help of our extended family, had scraped together the funds to supplement the partial scholarships I received for tuition. To help cover my expenses, I got an $8-per-hour job working at the East Asian Library, which was basically an attic with zero ventilation and no air-conditioning. It was like working in a sauna but without the relaxation. I started looking around for alternative ways to make money.

Remembering Kennedy's book, I tried to think of an expertise I had that would be valuable to someone else. I came up with the idea to write a little book titled *How I Beat the Ivy League*. I planned to market it through guidance counselors all over the United States to the large number of college-bound high school students I thought would be interested in the topic. I ended up making an audiotape program from the book and spent a few hundred dollars—the last of my savings—to have it produced. I didn't sell more than a handful. There I was with boxes of audiotapes that no one wanted to buy. *Well*, I thought, that *didn't work*. But my years in competitive sports had made me philosophical about mistakes and failure: Getting your face put in the dirt was just part of the game.

Once again, I looked around for something I knew that others could benefit from. I inventoried my skills: good at languages, wrestler, kickboxer, captain of the judo team, knowledgeable about marine biology, could speed-read . . . speed-reading! That was it! My roommates and buddies were always asking me how I spent less than an hour on reading each night when they usually spent three to four hours. As a child, I'd had not only dyslexia but also dysgraphia (writing letters incorrectly), which had made school a challenge. When I transferred to St. Paul's at 15, I knew immediately that I wouldn't make it through the school's extremely rigorous academic program if I didn't learn how to read faster. So I went to the library and devoured everything I could find about how eyes actually take in and process visual information. It wasn't hard to understand the mechanics, and when I analyzed how my own eyes moved across the page, I realized that my eyes were jumping around too much as I read. I developed exercises to smooth out the jumpiness and practiced them regularly. Within weeks, I could read significantly faster than 99% of the population and still absorb the information.

I decided to give a three-hour speed-reading seminar on the technique I'd devised, which I named the PX Method: $50 per person and a money-back guarantee. I made up flyers and posters and put them everywhere. Thirty-two people showed up for the course and not one asked for their money back. I made $1,600 in three hours—a definite improvement over my job at the East Asian Library! It was the first successful test of the principles I learned in Kennedy's book.

I turned to Kennedy's book again a few years later. After college, I took a job in Silicon Valley during the dot-com boom—and lost it a year later, when the boom went bust. Once more, I was looking for a way to make a living and began thinking of a product I could create and sell. Drawing on my experience in sports, I worked with biochemistry Ph.D.s from top Ivy League universities to develop a nutritional product for athletes that I could package and ship. The beauty of this plan was that unlike my speed-reading seminars, the profits didn't solely depend on my direct involvement—another key element of Kennedy's formula. The product could be manufactured and then shipped automatically.

My business took off. Within a year, I was making more money per month than I had been making per year at my Silicon Valley job! Before I knew it, BrainQUICKEN had a client roster of over 80 world title holders in professional and Olympic sports, all swearing by our products. There was only one problem: I was miserable. I had fallen into a common entrepreneurial trap: I was working 12-hour days and felt chained to my business. I'd started the business as a means to an end—a vehicle for doing other things, which in my case meant traveling and learning languages—but now the business was running me instead of the other way around.

I started looking for answers. I read and researched business books and systems. I stumbled onto economist Vilfredo Pareto's 80/20 principle—80% of the output comes from 20% of the input. In other words, 80% or more of the results come from 20% or less of the efforts. After a very detailed analysis, I realized that more than 95% of my revenue was coming from fewer than 10% of my accounts. I looked at where I was spending my time: I was running after the other 90% of the people who were only contributing marginally to the bottom line. When I stopped doing that, my workday immediately shrank from 12 hours to 6.

I continued to streamline my business further. Soon I was down to two hours per day, and the time required of me was falling fast. I figured that if my goal was to travel extensively, I needed to make the company self-sufficient enough for me to be gone as often as I wanted. Long-term travel would be the "final exam" for my business, so I began looking for books on the subject.

Most of the books I found were travel guides—listing places to stay and eat and sights to see on vacation. They were aimed at people who worked regular jobs and took a week or two off at a time. Then I found a book that made me look at my life, work, and goals in an entirely new way—*Vagabonding: An Uncommon Guide to the Art of Long-Term World Travel*, by Rolf Potts.

Potts has crafted a book that is specific in its recommendations but still flexible enough to apply to a wide range of travel experiences—vacations, sabbaticals, or indefinite forays. Potts gives many practical pointers for all aspects of adventuring long term, including picking a destination, financing travel time, and working and volunteering overseas, as well as readjusting to ordinary life. His idea that you don't have to wait for retirement to start doing what you've always dreamed just made sense. I'd finally found another person who thought the way I did.

But more than that, *Vagabonding* presents a philosophy about travel, which Potts says isn't about escaping ordinary life for a period of time but about discovering your life. It's a lifestyle choice that may require a major shift in one's priorities. I found Potts's concept of voluntary poverty and simplification very interesting. It made me realize how much stuff I had accumulated that I just didn't need—so many things I had were just taking up space on my "mental plate." I ended up going through all of my earthly belongings and getting rid of 80% of them. As soon as I did that, it became easier to prioritize everything I did and enjoy everything I had. This process of simplifying my life was exhilarating—but was still only a warm-up for the big experiment.

In 2003, taking only a small backpack—with Potts's book in it—I bought a one-way ticket to Europe and left with no timetable for my return and no clear itinerary beyond my first stop: a friend's apartment in London. The morning after I arrived, my friend left for work and I woke up at 10:00 AM in the empty apartment and . . . had a quasi–nervous breakdown! I literally bolted upright in bed and shouted out loud, "What the $%&@ am I going to *do* today?!" Although there was a whole city for me to explore, I felt completely lost without the routine of work—and thinking about work—to give my life structure and meaning. Removing myself from my deeply engrained work habit forced me to take a long look at my values and priorities. Although I'd always worked, I'd never stopped to ask myself what I was working for: How much money did I need? What was I trying to accomplish? With this new opportunity to reflect on these questions, it became clear that (1) I hadn't defined my goals clearly, (2) I often worked out of guilt—so I wouldn't appear "unproductive" to others, and (3) I had actually become overly regimented and fearful of the unknown. My habits, designed to help me succeed by brute force, were killing me spiritually and emotionally.

Over the course of the trip, living life as a vagabond helped me to tackle all these issues and jump directly into self-knowledge and self-development without the distraction of working for work's sake. At first, I acted the part of tourist because I didn't know what else to do—visiting museums, parks, landmarks—but it got boring quickly. Everything changed when I shifted from "seeing" things—simply logging away memories—to doing things and learning things. By the time I left

London, the trip had taken on a life of its own. I had figured I'd be gone for 8 weeks, but I ended up visiting 16 countries over the course of almost 18 months.

The trip was a rediscovery process—working the way I had up until then, I'd let nearly all of my passions and interests atrophy. Traveling, I was able to revive old interests and create new ones: I trained with champion fighters in Oslo, learned to tango in Argentina, and snorkeled in Panama. What enabled me to do all of this was applying the principles in *Vagabonding*. And my business, set up along the lines recommended by Dan Kennedy's book, functioned beautifully without me and continues to provide me the freedom to do what I really want to do. Using the information in these books has allowed me to fulfill my childhood dream of "choosing my own adventure" and has put a 24-hour smile on my face.

Christiane Northrup, M.D.

Christiane Northrup, M.D., trained at Dartmouth Medical School and Tufts New England Medical Center before cofounding the Women to Women health care center in Yarmouth, Maine, which became a model for women's clinics nationwide. Board certified in obstetrics and gynecology, she is past president of the American Holistic Medical Association and an internationally recognized authority on women's health and healing. Dr. Northrup is the author of three books, including the number-one *New York Times* best seller *The Wisdom of Menopause*. Her latest book, *Mother-Daughter Wisdom: Creating a Legacy of Physical and Emotional Health*, was nominated for the Quill Award, and in March 2005, Dr. Northrup hosted a PBS special on the same topic. She currently writes a monthly print and electronic newsletter: *Women's Wisdom for Optimal Health and Healing.* ∎

I have always been interested in the study of life—in all its forms. I grew up on a farm and constantly wandered around our pond, collecting salamanders and pollywogs, examining seed pods and plants. I was Artemis, the goddess of wild things, roaming the fields and observing life. In junior high biology class, when I saw my first time-lapse photography of the pollination of a flower, I was absolutely fascinated. I wanted to be a biologist, but I also had a deep appreciation of the magic inherent in nature, in addition to the science. I was the type of kid who drew paper-doll fairies and sat all day in the lilac bushes with them, immersed in a fantasy world, making up stories of fairies and nature sprites.

In my family, religion was a relaxed affair. My mother was raised Catholic but had bad experiences with the Church as a teenager. When I was growing up, she told me that Nature was her church and she preferred to spend her Sunday mornings taking long walks in the woods around our home. My father, who attended the local Episcopal church every week, did so more from tradition and a sense of community than from any deep feelings of piety. I was given my choice of churches, and it was perfectly acceptable if I didn't attend either. Religion was a personal matter in our household.

When I was 13 years old, I often babysat to earn money. One day, a friend of my parents asked me to babysit for her grandchildren. I appeared at the requested time, said good-bye to the departing adults, and began the usual child care routine. As I walked past a table in the hallway, I noticed a cardboard box lying on top of it. The unopened box was addressed to my parents' friend, Mrs. Gretchen Carroll, and the words *"Natives of Eternity* by Flower Newhouse" were printed clearly on its side. Something about the box called out to me, but I kept moving. I put the kids to bed, and probably did the dishes—my mother had drummed it into me that I should leave any place I babysat in better shape than when I'd found it. At 13, I was the poster child for obedience, for minding my manners and being studious; I did not open other people's mail. So you will understand how intense the call of that box must have been, for once the kids were sleeping and the kitchen was clean, I put aside my scruples and tore open the box to get to the book I knew was inside.

When I saw the cover of the book, I literally stopped breathing for a moment. It was the most beautiful, most exquisite, most *arresting* thing I had ever seen. It was a painting of an angel, but it wasn't like any angel I had ever seen before. It was a male angel with an amazing depth and strength in his face. He radiated such power and goodness that I felt I was looking at a divine being for the first time.

Flower Newhouse, of the Christward Ministry in Escondido, California, was a Christian mystic, and the book I held was a catalogue of celestial beings from the angelic realms, their portraits drawn from her direct experience. She could actually *see* the angels that inhabit our world and guide every facet of human existence. In her book, she describes the angels of the elements, of the directions, of birth and death, of everything you can imagine. I sat for two hours, looking at every page, drinking in the pictures and devouring the information about a realm that I had only imagined and hoped might exist. And on some level I recognized those beings; I had no doubt that Flower Newhouse's pictures and descriptions were accurate.

I could hardly contain myself. My heart was racing and I wanted to talk to someone about what this book meant to me. My whole world had shifted. Suddenly, I had language and pictures—evidence of a reality that I always felt was too good to be true—and I knew that life was not the way the adults thought it was. Clearly, there was a whole unacknowledged dimension underlying our everyday physical existence. I had always believed this; now I saw that fairy tales were as real as the "real" world I was trying to fit myself into.

When it was time to go home, I put the book back into the box and set it on the table. As soon as I got home, I told my mother what I had done and then told her all about the book. Seeing how profoundly moved I had been by reading it, she didn't scold me, and said she would let Mrs. Carroll know what had happened. She told her friend, who apparently didn't mind that I had opened her mail, because a week later, Mrs. Carroll gave me my own copy of *Natives of Eternity*, which I still have today.

It was the beginning of an important relationship for me. Mrs. Carroll, in her fifties at the time, took me under her wing. For the next five years, she invited me over every week for a visit and a metaphysical chat. She fed me wonderful breakfasts and treated me as a special guest. Our conversations, which ranged over a wide variety of esoteric topics, were nourishing to me as well. These discussions laid the foundation for many things that happened later in my life. They were the underpinnings of my whole spiritual approach to life and medicine, instilling in me the understanding that consciousness, other beings, other worlds—things we can't see with the five senses—are in fact a living, breathing reality.

Becoming a doctor had never crossed my mind, but when I finished college with a degree in biology, I very quickly realized that getting an advanced degree in that field, which would lead to a life in research, was not what I wanted after all. After graduation, I spent a year at home, working at an office job and fretting about what do next. Finally a professor of mine advised me to go to medical school.

One of my early rotations as an intern was the maternity ward. The first time I saw a baby being born, I nearly fell to my knees in awe. I'd never had anything affect me that deeply. It was like the night I first read *Natives of Eternity*; I could hardly contain myself. When it came time to specialize, on one level I knew that I wanted to be an obstetrician and gynecologist, but my intellect kicked in immediately, saying, "Why would you want to do that? It has the worst liability insurance and the most night calls on the planet!" But as time passed, I realized that, for me, being with women in labor was like breathing. Sitting with women who were pregnant or had premenstrual syndrome or who had just miscarried—all of it felt so natural. It was just what I was born to do.

I received standard Western obstetrical and gynecological training and began to practice, but as time passed, because of my exposure to spiritual ideas at a young age, I began to see my role as being a midwife not only for physical birth but also for the birth of who a person really is, in the greater sense. I felt that I could provide support in the process of the soul becoming embodied more fully. The biological way that spirit comes into matter is through conception, gestation, labor, and birth, but that is also a metaphor for the way that everything—whether ideas, novels, gardens, or relationships—is conceived, gestates, goes through labor, and is born.

To give birth to anything, you must die to other things. And everyone goes through a kind of labor when they are shedding an old skin and becoming something else. There's always a time when a person wants to say, "I'm not doing this. This is too hard." I've seen it countless times with women in childbirth: Just when they are fully dilated and ready to push, they've had it. "Okay, I'm done. I'm not doing this anymore." That's when someone has to be there to help them through the process, and that's true whether a woman is birthing a baby or a deeper understanding of who she is.

In my work, I often think of the angels of transition that I saw in Flower Newhouse's book. It's not hard to feel the presence of angels when a baby is being born. It's enormously helpful to remember they are also present when someone is dying. The energy of death is very much the same as the energy of birth. Understanding that there are spiritual beings helping on a deeper level is enormously comforting and calming in all transitions.

I learned all this on a physical level up close and personal in the delivery room, and now, instead of midwifing one woman in labor at a time, I can use that same knowledge to "spiritually midwife" women in a much more collective way, through my books, my PBS specials, my lectures and newsletters.

My message to women about the wisdom in their bodies is grounded in my belief that the body and the spirit are intimately connected. Many people have come to believe that their spirit or soul is one thing and their body is something else—something that needs to be taken care of by doctors. I've come to see that the place where women miss the connection of spirit and body most is in menopause. Hormonal shifts are nothing but boosts to your own soul's labor and birth process. We say things such as "Your hormones are making you feel this or do that," but that's not it. It's just your soul using the hormones to direct you to become more of who you are. The soul may use the irritability of too much estrogen relative to progesterone, but these hormones are in service to something much bigger, and that's the part that people don't get. Menopause is another birth canal—a big one. It can be one of the healthiest and most wonderful times in life—if you don't fall prey to the mind viruses that tell you that everything disintegrates after 50. It's just not true.

Flower Newhouse's book and the relationship it inspired with Mrs. Carroll, a wise woman going through menopause, were major influences in my life. They enabled me to see through the illusion of the enormous mind–body split that's embedded in us, starting almost before birth. Today, my job is to put those two things back together. My background on the farm, with all the earthiness and common sense that imparts, combined with my study of the realm beyond our senses, starting with *Natives of Eternity*, has made me what you might call a practical mystic— well suited for the work I have chosen to do.

Doreen Virtue

Doreen Virtue, Ph.D., holds three university degrees in counseling psychology. A former psychotherapist, Doreen teaches metaphysics, psychic development, and angel therapy classes worldwide and is the author of more than 25 books, including *Angel Therapy*, *Healing with the Angels*, and *Archangels and Ascended Masters*. She has appeared on *Oprah*, CNN's *Talk Back Live*, *The View*, *Good Morning America*, and *Coast-to-Coast Radio*, among other programs. ∎

For many years, I was a closet spiritual person. As a child raised by two metaphysicians, it was my experience that being spiritual was something to hide: It made you different, strange, even weird. Although my parents looked normal—they always dressed in J.C. Penney clothes—they were completely New Age. My mom was a professional spiritual healer and my dad an aerospace engineer who quit his job to write about his passion: model airplanes. They decided they could just pray for everything they needed. They were firm believers in the power of affirmations and visualizations.

One year, when we needed a new family car, my parents bought a little model car and put it on the dining-room table. My younger brother and I were four and six at the time, and my parents had us all sit in front of the little car and visualize it being full size in the driveway. And darned if they didn't get it! Still, I resented time spent visualizing; I just wanted to watch *Batman* on TV.

In the mid-1960s when I was growing up, New Age thinking wasn't widespread. The other kids in the neighborhood made fun of me because

I used words like *manifest* and *Divine timing*—common expressions in our household. They'd laugh and roll their eyes, and wouldn't let me play in their games.

All this left me pretty confused. On the one hand, I believed in what my parents were doing—I couldn't help it: I'd seen miracles. But I didn't like being ostracized for being different. So as I grew older, I shunned anything "spiritual." When I was in my twenties and most of my friends were rebelling against their Catholic or Baptist parents to embrace New Age beliefs, I rebelled against my New Age parents and became a Methodist!

My life was pretty rocky at that point. I had gotten married very young and had two kids by the time I was 22. I had been attending college off and on since high school, trying out different majors—music, accounting, journalism—but nothing stuck. I decided to give college one last shot, this time trying a psychology major and philosophy minor.

These classes were different; they felt like therapy for me. And when the professors talked about existentialism, the study of the meaning of life, I knew that I had found my place. I read everything they suggested: Martin Buber, Soren Kierkegaard, Nietzsche, everything. Then one of my professors recommended Viktor Frankl's book, *Man's Search for Meaning*. It turned out to be a true eye-opener for me.

An Austrian-born psychiatrist, Frankl was captured during World War II and sent to the Auschwitz concentration camp. Although he lost everything—his family, his home, a manuscript he was writing, and his freedom—he found that there was one thing that no one could take away from him: his right to choose happiness at any given moment. Frankl learned to extract happiness from the smallest things: a bird's song, a sunset, a small flower growing next to the camp's barbed wire fence. No matter how grim his situation, he learned to stay in charge of his emotions. He was actually happy much of the time, and this was possible only because he understood that our happiness isn't contingent on outside circumstances. It's a matter of choice.

I remember very clearly the day I first read Frankl. There was something about the energy of the book when I first saw it that magically attracted me, and I couldn't wait to read it. I sat under a tree on the campus of Palomar College in San Marcos, California. As I read, I remember feeling my stomach unclench and become relaxed for the first time in a long time. Even though I was reading about really difficult, even horrifying, situations, there was something about Frankl's overarching attitude of optimism that gave me hope for myself and my children—and for the world's future.

I'd been living much of my life with an anxiety that went deeper than my superficial problems. For a long time I had been fighting an inner knowledge that my life's purpose involved spiritual teaching. I had inherited my parents' metaphysical gifts, but I had been rejecting them because I thought I'd be ridiculed if I openly taught spirituality. Keeping my life purpose at arm's length had led to the same sort of anxiety that Viktor Frankl and other existentialists discuss. Yet I didn't come to terms with that issue till some years later.

The immediate influence of the book was to change my outlook on my current situation. My husband and I had divorced. I was working to rebuild my life as a single mother, and I felt very alone. Reading about Frankl's experiences in the concentration camp humbled me and helped me put my issues into perspective. *If he could survive life-and-death struggles with grace*, I thought, *then I can certainly walk through my issues of single motherhood in a peaceful way*.

When I faced a child custody battle, I clung to Frankl's words as a way of staying positive. I knew that my thoughts would make a huge difference in the outcome, so I refused to even imagine losing custody. I kept a positive outlook, and eventually won the case.

I often thought of Frankl when life seemed difficult. To this day, his ability to feel peaceful and happy while doing slave labor or sleeping on a cold, dirty cot helps me to locate an inner reserve of contentment. And like him, I've found that doing this always has some healing effect and improves the external situation, too.

Another aspect of *Man's Search for Meaning* that significantly changed my life was contained in a story Frankl tells about hiding in a building as part of an attempt to escape from the concentration camp. As he hid, he suddenly had a strong gut feeling to run—to get out of the building. To do so would ruin the escape and expose him to grave danger, but he followed his intuition—which was very fortunate, because moments later the building exploded. Reading this strengthened my belief that, in addition to choosing happiness, what we need to do to prevail in life is to notice our intuitive impressions and follow them.

This story eventually prompted me to come out of the spiritual closet—though in a roundabout way. For many years after college, my inner guidance had been urging me in this direction, but I was still resisting. By that time I was a well-respected psychotherapist and had published a couple of successful books on eating disorders. I was afraid of losing everything, as I had lost my friendships as a child, if I appeared to be too odd to people. But then, on July 15, 1995, I had a brush with death myself that reinforced the message of Frankl's story.

I was all alone one day in an empty parking lot in the most dangerous part of Anaheim when two men accosted me. One of them pointed a gun at me and they told me they wanted my car and my purse. As I stood, frozen with fear, I suddenly heard a voice in my right ear telling me to scream with all my might. There was no one there, and I knew immediately that it was an angel. For a split second, I hesitated. Common wisdom says that you shouldn't scream if someone is holding a gun on you—plus there was no one to hear me; the area seemed deserted. But I listened to the voice and to my gut feeling—just as Frankl had when he ran from that building—and I screamed. The noise attracted the attention of a woman I hadn't seen, sitting in her car on the other side of the parking lot. She leaned on her horn, and people rushed out of a nearby church and scared off the two men. Afterward, I got down on my knees in the parking lot and thanked God for saving my life. I said to God, "What can I do to repay you?" I received the same guidance I'd been hearing within for so long, which was to teach the things that I'd been raised with. I knew I was supposed to tell people about the power of the mind and spirit to heal us and to create the life of our dreams. The days of renouncing my spirituality were over.

That night I went home and immediately called Unity Prayer Service, a religious science prayer service, to ask others to join me in praying that I would forgive the men. I didn't want to hold any fear in my heart. It worked. I love them now and believe they were the best thing that ever happened to me.

After that experience, I began to teach about the power of visualization, of affirmation, and of intuition. Today my motto is "Follow your inner guidance at any cost." I tell this to all my clients, because as Frankl experienced and as I've seen countless times myself, it saves your life in little and big ways.

John Gray

John Gray, Ph.D., is the author of 15 best-selling books, including *Men Are from Mars, Women Are from Venus*, the number one best-selling relationship book of the last decade. More than 30 million Mars and Venus books have been sold in more than 40 languages throughout the world. An expert in the field of communication, John's focus is to help men and women understand, respect, and appreciate their differences in both personal and professional relationships. John has appeared on numerous television programs, including *Oprah*, the *Today Show*, *CBS Morning Show*, *Good Morning America*, and *Larry King Live*, and has been featured in *Newsweek*, *Time*, *Forbes*, *USA Today*, *TV Guide*, and *People*, among others. ▪

We humans use only a small percentage of our full potential. The amazing achievements of geniuses such as Einstein, Mozart, and da Vinci give us a tantalizing glimpse of our own capabilities. Can you imagine what it would it be like to fully use our intelligence, creativity, and energy? As a teenager, I read a book that introduced me to this concept, changing my life forever.

I grew up in Texas in the 1950s. My parents were eclectic, highly spiritual people, and they pursued their spirituality in ways that were definitely unusual for the time and place we lived in. My dad, an oil executive, was always studying spiritual things. When I was four years old, he taught me yoga. There were seven children in our family, and my dad would have us all on the mat doing yoga with him every morning.

My mother was ahead of her time, too. When I was 14, she opened a spiritual bookstore, in Houston of all places, very much like the well-known esoteric bookstore the Bodhi Tree in Los Angeles. Although my parents shared their enthusiasm about the spiritual realm with us kids, they were wise enough to never force their spirituality on us.

In the late 1960s, like most teenagers at that time, my bedroom was a black-lit lair, with incense burning and walls covered with posters of my favorite bands—the Beatles, Jimi Hendrix, the Doors, and so on. When I was almost 18, the Moody Blues album *In Search of the Lost Chord* came out, and one of the songs featured the sacred sound "om." One day, when I was playing that particular track, my mother walked into my room and was instantly enthralled. She said, "Oh, what beautiful music! Can I listen?" And I said, "Sure." She sat down and very quickly became completely still, a blissful expression on her face. I had never seen her do this before but assumed she was meditating. I felt a connection to her, and like a contact high, a calm contentment soon come over me as well. I closed my eyes and let myself float, hearing the music and being with the peace I felt inside.

When I asked her about it afterward, she described her meditation as "going up into the light." This experience made a deep impression on me. I thought, *Wow, this is very cool. What other people are trying to achieve through drugs, Mom can do by just closing her eyes.*

While in my room, she noticed a Beatles poster of the *Magical Mystery Tour* album on my wall, and she said, "Did you hear that the Beatles went to India to visit a man named Maharishi?"

I said, "No; who's that?"

She replied, "Oh, you should find out about him. The Beatles spent time with him, and it had a huge impact on their lives and changed their music."

That was all she said—just a little hint and a suggestion to pique my interest.

Then a few weeks later, I went to the bowling alley to pick up my brother, and a friend said, "There's a samurai giving a presentation in the meeting room upstairs. You should check it out." I went, but my friend had got it wrong. Instead of finding some far-out *samurai* warrior, I walked in on a *seminar* about Maharishi Mahesh Yogi and Transcendental

Meditation (TM). I remembered what my mother had said, and I was very intrigued. I listened to the whole talk and stayed for a while afterward. When I arrived home late, my parents thought I had been off getting into trouble somewhere. I said, "No, I went to this seminar on Transcendental Meditation."

My father was skeptical and said, "Yeah, sure, what did you hear?"

I told him all that I'd heard—practically the whole 30-minute talk. He was satisfied that I had really been at the seminar and both my parents were pleased that I was so excited about something spiritual like meditation.

Next, I read Maharishi's book, *The Science of Being and Art of Living*. In it, Maharishi explains that we are using only 10% of our potential, but through meditation we can change this. We can develop an open mind, an open heart, and a healthy body. TM, he says, enables us to make a conscious connection to the Source that created us all, which allows us to use more of our inner potential and create our lives as we want them to be. It was the most thrilling thing I'd ever read.

I began meditating right away and soon became fully involved in teaching TM. Eventually, I became Maharishi's personal assistant and traveled with him for nine years. In that time, I began to experience everything that Maharishi wrote about in his book: a state of continuous blissfulness, more energy, and unbounded awareness. I felt one with the Source of the universe, with that which permeates all. I would spend as many as 10 hours in blissful meditation, sometimes having all kinds of insights and illuminating experiences, and sometimes just luxuriating in long, deep, silent states.

Then, at a certain point, I began to wonder, *What are all these experiences for? I have found my source, but now what?* I realized that the purpose of my life was not just to find the source of love and creativity within myself but also to go back into the world from that inner place and bring peace, happiness, and fulfillment to others. The big questions became: What are my special gifts and talents? How can I make a difference? The last thing that I would have ever imagined is that I would become an expert on relationships.

I knew I wanted to teach, but I didn't want to simply teach what Maharishi taught any longer. I wanted to find my own unique contribution.

The problem was that Maharishi taught the whole gamut, the whole range of spiritual information. However, there was one exception. He always made it very clear that he had no expertise in the area of sex and relationships. So that was the place where I could step out of his shadow and offer something new.

Once out on my own, I started dating and soon got married. Having been a celibate monk for nine years, it was a giant leap for me, but love, sex, and marriage became the arenas in which I found my own individual form of expression and began to achieve mastery. All my years of meditating and searching for the perfect relationship to God had trained me to look at relationships in an expanded, more spiritual way.

Looking back, I would say that those nine years with Maharishi were about becoming proficient in the "science of being"—meditating to develop my full potential—whereas my life since then has been about the "art of living"—applying that potential in all areas of my life. My spiritual journey has brought me to a place where I use the insights I've gained to help millions of people love their partners more completely.

Today, I tell my students that—just as in most areas of our life—we achieve only a tiny percentage of our potential in our relationships, too. We resign ourselves to experiencing just a few years of romantic passion—if that—before it fizzles out. But I've learned it doesn't have to be that way; we can enjoy something so much more magnificent. Everything I teach is intended to help people return to the Source, to the place of continuous creation and love, so we can maintain the romance in our lives indefinitely as we love each other fully.

Philip Goldberg

Philip Goldberg is a spiritual counselor, meditation teacher, and ordained inter-faith minister who has a private practice in Los Angeles and offers lectures and workshops throughout the country. Phil has written 1 novel and 16 nonfiction books, including *The Intuitive Edge: Understanding and Developing Intuition*; *Making Peace with God*, about overcoming the psychospiritual obstacles to intimacy with the Divine; and *Roadsigns: Navigating Your Path to Spiritual Happiness*, which addresses the challenge of integrating deep spirituality with everyday life. His column, "Spiritual Wellness," appears monthly in the e-newsletter *Healthy Update*. Phil is a founding director of the Forge Institute and the director of the Forge Guild, a consortium of spiritual leaders and teach-ers from all paths and traditions. His Web site is at www.philipgoldberg.com. ▪

It had been a bitter New England winter, both inside and out. In the pre-ceding months, as antiwar fury rose with the death toll in Vietnam, the state of my soul grew as tumultuous as the state of the world around me. Beginning with my mother's death two years earlier, through college graduation and relocation, falling in love and suffering heartbreak, at-tending civil rights marches and peace rallies, I had desperately sought answers to the Big Questions. I wanted to know about the purpose of life, about death, about injustice and human suffering—and especially about the chances of finding lasting happiness or anything resembling fulfill-ment. One by one, every purported source of truth and meaning had left me disillusioned. Not even the counterculture trinity of sex, drugs, and rock 'n' roll had met my expectations. They had teased me with brief interludes of ecstasy and transcendence—opening the door a crack to what might be possible before slamming it shut.

A larger and far more promising door had recently been opened by friends who squeezed words such as *meditation* and *enlightenment* into their sentences next to *groovy* and other sixties jargon. Eastern philosophy instantly resonated with me. Unlike religion as I knew it, it seemed to favor experience over belief and faith. A turning point came one day at the Museum of Fine Arts, in Boston, when I found myself in a gallery filled with Buddhist statuary. Alone inside the elegantly simple space, I gazed at the faces of the buddhas. They were stone and wood, but their wisdom, compassion, and unshakable serenity were palpable. *Whatever those guys had,* I thought, *I want it.*

I plunged into the pursuit of nirvana with all the zeal and naïveté of youth, seeking teachings that promised tangible results. Each discovery was as exhilarating as listening to the Beatles' *Sgt. Pepper* album for the first time, but those glimpses of radiant light only made the darkness seem bleaker. Ordinary life seemed, in Shakespeare's words, "weary, stale, flat, and unprofitable," and I had become an insomniac trying to figure out my place in it. Slamming into a dead end, I sank into a cavernous despair.

If I really want what those buddhas had, I concluded, *I'll have to renounce the mundane world.* Claiming I had a personal emergency— which, in a sense, I did—I got someone to cover the classes I taught, stocked up on canned tuna, coffee, and Grape-Nuts, and holed up in my tiny apartment with a handful of borrowed books. I might as well have posted a sign on my door: "God or bust!"

In my do-it-yourself retreat, I pondered the mysteries in books such as *Vedanta for Modern Man* and *The Idea of the Holy*. I tried my hand at one meditative practice after another. When I wasn't doing those things, I plotted my escape from what I derisively called "real life," with all its illusions and false gods. I imagined a Thoreau-like existence in a cabin in the woods, or perhaps in a monastery.

After a few nights of disciplined solitude, frustrated because my third eye hadn't opened and I was still at *two* with the universe, I reached again for the borrowed books. I rejected one, then another, then came upon J.D. Salinger's *Franny and Zooey*. I assumed this work of fiction had been included either by mistake or as my friend's way of giving me some entertainment. I opened the slim paperback with its identical front and back covers—title, author, and two horizontal green lines; no endorsements, no description. I did not put it down until the morning sun lit the snow on my windowsill. I read it twice that night, once purely transfixed and once to study and underline.

The saying "When the student is ready, the teacher will appear" applies to books as well as human beings. This one taught me by upsetting my naïve assumptions and turning my search for wisdom on its head.

The youngest of seven siblings, Franny and Zooey Glass were, like Salinger's Holden Caulfield in *The Catcher in the Rye*, highly intelligent, overly sensitive, uncannily perceptive youngsters who couldn't stand phonies and longed to make sense of existence. In "Franny," the first of the two stories that comprise the book, the 20-year-old heroine is in a deep funk. "I'm just sick of ego, ego, ego. My own and everybody else's," she says, summing up the eternal spiritual dilemma for her boyfriend, a pompous Ivy Leaguer named Lane. An apparently talented actress, she announces that she's quit the theater department at her college, appalled by her own ambition. "Just because I like applause and people to rave about me doesn't make it right," she says.

Like me, Franny was disgusted by society's rampant materialism and superficial values. Her ticket to transcendence, she hopes, is a thin book called *The Way of a Pilgrim*, about a Russian peasant who sets out to discover what it means to pray unceasingly, as the Bible implores. The pilgrim discovers what has come to be called the Jesus Prayer. Franny's description of it made me sit bolt upright, for it paralleled what I'd just read about mantras, a term that had recently been introduced to Western ears when the Beatles journeyed to India. "You get to see God," Franny says of the practice. "Something happens in some absolutely nonphysical part of the heart—where the Hindus say that Atman resides." Lane, of course, thinks she's losing it. The story ends with Franny lying on her back, mouthing the pilgrim's incantation.

Finding words such as *karma* and *chakras* and quotes from *The Upanishads* in a best seller was eye-opening. I felt that Franny's alienation justified my own and that I was on the right track—until I read "Zooey." The message in this story was more disturbing and, as a consequence, more transformative. Franny's dark night of the soul continues in her parents' New York apartment, where, like me, she has holed up with her book and her despair and her sacred yearning. Unlike me, she has company: her mother, Bessie, who is worried sick about her, and her slightly older, equally gifted and spiritually informed brother, Zooey.

In "Zooey," the Glass kids are exposed as smug, condescending smart-asses—and so was I. Their disdain for the shortcomings of ordinary human beings is revealed for what it is: an ego trip, the antithesis of the compassion extolled by the holy books they revere. "You're not kind," Bessie flatly tells her son. Annoyed by her meddling and her offerings of hot chicken broth, Zooey calls his mother stupid, but even he sees the wisdom in her observation: "I don't know what good it is to know so much and be as smart as a whip and all, if it doesn't make you happy."

In declaring the dignity of the ordinary, Salinger smacked me in the face with my own hypocrisy. Like Franny and Zooey, I was egomaniacal in my hatred of egomaniacs, arrogant in my scorn of arrogance, pretentious in my disdain for pretension. I began to question the authenticity of my quest. Was I, like Franny—in sixties parlance—really tuning in, or were we both merely dropping out? Was my meditation, like Franny's prayer practice, "a substitute for doing whatever the hell your duty is in life"? How was our lust for enlightenment any different from material cravings? Was it really necessary—or even desirable—for a seeker of the Divine to renounce "the world"? These disturbing questions were like a whack on the head from a Zen master, a cosmic wake-up call: *Snap out of it!*

In the final section of the story, Zooey scolds Franny for giving up acting—an obvious allusion to *all* worldly action. "The only thing you can do now, the only *religious* thing you can do is *act*," he says. "Act for God, if you want to," but act. He continues, recalling the time that he, at age five, was about to appear on a radio quiz show for child prodigies, and their late brother, Seymour, the family guru, told him to shine his shoes. Zooey balked: Not only could no one see the damn shoes but the audience and everyone associated with the show were morons. Shine your shoes anyway, insisted Seymour. Do it for the Fat Lady. Now Zooey tells Franny, "There isn't anyone out there who isn't Seymour's Fat Lady." And who is this Fat Lady? "It's Christ Himself."

I reflected deeply on this passage, taking from it the understanding that all beings are holy and ought to be treated as such. It reminded me of a precept I'd read, that one should perform even minor household tasks as if the Buddha himself was one's guest.

At the end of the story, Franny "lay quiet, smiling at the ceiling." I put the book down and did the same. I finally knew that whatever life decisions I might make, I would not be a hermit or a monk. Salinger's bottom-line message echoes that of many sages: Ours is not to turn our backs on worldly life but to lift the veil that keeps us from seeing it—all of it—as sacred.

From that day forward, my life's work has been to live an authentic spiritual life while remaining fully in this wacky, seemingly inhospitable world. To enjoy its pleasures, endure its pains, laugh at its absurdities, weep over its tragedies, and always do whatever my duty may be, however senseless it might seem, as if the world depended on it. It's a challenge that never ends, no matter how much I learn, no matter how much I help others to do it, too. I still can't think of anything more meaningful.

The same copy of *Franny and Zooey* is on my bookshelf to this day, with its yellow pages, its stained cover, and its quaint 95-cent price sticker. As I perused my ancient underlinings before writing this story, I was struck by how few I would erase. What were revelations all those years ago are valuable reminders now. In fact, I think I'll go back and give this one more polish—to make it shine. I owe it to the Fat Lady.

Bernie Siegel, M.D.

Bernie Siegel, M.D., is a retired pediatric and general surgeon and the author of several books on healing. His first book, *Love, Medicine & Miracles*, published in 1986, is considered a landmark commentary on the process of inner and outer healing. A former president of the American Holistic Medical Association, he is the founder of ECaP (Exceptional Cancer Patients), a form of individual and group therapy for recovering patients, using patients' dreams, drawings, and images. A tireless advocate of the healing potential within each of us, Bernie lectures extensively at conferences and medical schools on the mind–body connection. ■

To be honest, I really don't believe any book can change your life—only *you* can. Look, two people read the same book: One is inspired, while the other is bored. It's the person—not the book—that creates the transformation. That power lies within each of us. That said, I do believe that an author's insights, when combined with the reader's inspiration and desire to change, can lead to a new life for the reader.

The book that did that for me was *The Human Comedy*, by William Saroyan. I discovered Saroyan's work at a point in my career when, as a physician caring for and counseling people with life-threatening illnesses, I was struggling with many issues. The wisdom so beautifully expressed in Saroyan's writing helped me realize that to successfully treat my patients, I had to help them live—and not just prevent them from dying.

It was 1978. I had been practicing medicine for about 15 years—and burying my own pain about the chasm that I felt existed between what I was doing for my patients and what they truly needed. Once at a workshop I attended, I met a patient of mine who had breast cancer. I was there, unhappy as a doctor; she was there, unhappy as a person with cancer, but we were sharing our pain. She said, "I need to know how to live between office visits." I didn't know how to respond. My problem was that I wanted to care for my patients on all levels, but my training had been more mechanical; I didn't know how to deal with their feelings—or my own.

As a physician, you tend to bury your emotions. I painted a self-portrait around that time that is very revealing. In the painting, I am completely hidden behind a cap, mask, and gown. I felt as though I had post-traumatic stress disorder. I knew if I kept everything locked up in me, it would cause me to become sick, so I was keeping journals to try to deal with it. I also had a lot of questions about death: Why would God make a world like this? What does it all mean? Why all the pain and the suffering? I was searching for answers.

During that period, I read "The Daring Young Man on the Flying Trapeze," a short story by Saroyan about an impoverished young man who dies of hunger. At the very end of the story, the young man lies down on his bed to die, and as his life slips away, he sees death as a trapeze to God. The Earth circles away, and he becomes airborne. Saroyan describes the young man's death with three astounding words. He says, "he became un-alive, dreamless, perfect." Boom! It hit me—maybe death wasn't the worst thing that could happen to someone.

Think about it. Noah didn't argue with God about all the other nice people who maybe ought to get on the boat. My sense was that Noah knew he was the one who had the tough deal: everybody else was being recycled and getting a chance to start again, while he had to continue on. When I accepted the premise that dying wasn't the worst thing that could happen, something important changed about the way I looked at death— and life—and it affected how I did my job as a doctor.

After that short story, I read every book I could find by Saroyan. When I read *The Human Comedy*, everything turned around. The book opened me to death, life, and at last, to my own feelings—it helped take the lid off all the things I was holding inside.

In *The Human Comedy*, a coming-of-age tale set in California during World War II, Saroyan portrays life as a human comedy. We're here, he tells us, to enjoy, to laugh, and to use our experience for growth, and for good. Most of us don't see life that way, but Saroyan uses the various elements of his story—the war, the death of a parent and a brother, the way people help one another in times of need, the discussion a schoolteacher has with her students about leading a meaningful life—to help us see that while life has tragedy in it, it isn't tragic. Through his characters, he tells us that death is not the end of life if we recognize that the love we give and receive is immortal.

Saroyan says this beautifully in what to me are perhaps the most important words in his book: "But try to remember that a good man can never die. . . . The person of a man may leave—or be taken away—but the best part of a good man stays. It stays forever. Love is immortal and makes all things immortal. But hate dies every minute." These words—plus the idea I took from the trapeze story that when we leave our bodies we become perfect again—have sustained me through many years of dealing with death and loss on a regular basis.

Another of my favorite quotes from the book is about doctors. The main character, a young teenager named Homer, tells his elderly friend and coworker, "Doctors don't know everything, Willie. They understand matter, not spirit, and you and I live in the spirit." That quote really struck me because I'd been facing that dilemma every day. My medical education had trained me to treat diseases and the body, and to write prescriptions—not to care for people's spirits or get to know about their lives and their experiences. These Saroyan-inspired insights changed not only my thinking but also my practical approach to being a doctor. I started asking my patients about their lives, not just their symptoms. And I began forming support groups for people with life-threatening diseases, something that is common nowadays but up until that time simply hadn't been done.

The amazing result I found as a physician was that when you help people really live, it's good for their health. They don't die as predicted. When my patients began focusing on enjoying their lives and the time they had left, suddenly, I began to see what doctors call spontaneous remissions. The thing is, they're not really spontaneous; they're usually the result of somebody doing something different. But doctors who don't ask for the story don't understand what's going on in their patients' lives.

That human story is what Saroyan is talking about. I began asking patients, "What are you experiencing?" and then helping them deal with their experience. What I found was that if you did this, it made a difference in a person's ability to fight his or her disease.

When people can deal with the experiences they're having, they can live their lives fully. And that often has a miraculous effect on their health. My favorite example of this was with a patient of mine named John. A landscaper all his life, he was nearing retirement and was very depressed about it. He had developed an ulcer, which some people thought was caused by his depression.

I removed the ulcerlike part of the tumor, but when the pathology report came back, it showed there was cancer at the margins of resection. I told John that he had a cancer that we couldn't cure through surgery; he needed more treatment.

John said, "You forgot something." (That was always his line.)

I said, "What did I forget?"

He said, "It's springtime. I'm going to go and make the world beautiful. When I die, I'll leave a beautiful world."

John left the hospital saying he didn't want chemotherapy or radiation. He didn't show up in the office again until four years later, at which time he said, "I have a hernia from lifting boulders in my landscape business."

When he hadn't come back to the office, I had assumed he was dead. Instead, his depression had gone away, because he had started living again. He didn't go home to deny death; he'd gone home and fully embraced life. When we tested him again, he showed no sign of cancer. To make a very long story short, John died more than 20 years later, at age 94. He spent the rest of his life making the world beautiful. I've seen it in many cases since then: When you start loving your life, your body chemistry changes.

As my work with support groups grew, I began practicing medicine less and speaking and writing more. And as health care professionals began to listen to what I had to say, I stopped practicing altogether so that I could talk to them and help more patients that way. I am especially happy to lecture at medical schools. It's like spreading seeds. Almost 30 years later, I'm still running support groups for people with cancer and others, with any afflictions, who want to come.

One of the questions that always comes up in our groups is why bad things—such as diseases—happen to people. Why isn't the world perfect? I once wrote something called *Understand Why* because I had those questions, too. At the time, I wondered, why do kids die, why do kids have cancer, why, why, why? I wanted the world to be perfect. Then I came across a story that helped me tremendously: A rabbi, called the Baal Shem Tov, is watching Jews being slaughtered in Russia. He is heard to say, "I wish I were God."

A student turns to him and says, "You'd stop all this?"

He replies, "No, I wouldn't stop or change anything, but I'd understand why."

Over the years, I have come to believe that a perfect world would be meaningless. We're here to love and learn. That's what this wisdom is about. Saroyan writes, ". . . And the world is full of people and full of wonderful life. All things are part of us. We have come here to enjoy them and to thank God for them."

When we do this—even if we are dealing with a life-threatening disease—the things we face become opportunities rather than problems. Though we know eventually all lives end, it makes our acts meaningful when we choose to experience life and love fully.

I have learned to accept mortality. I will love this life until my tired body dies; then, as Saroyan says, I will leave that love behind in every life I have touched—an immortal part of me still on Earth.

Dave Barry

Dave Barry is a best-selling author and Pulitzer Prize–winning humor columnist. Dave has written a total of 25 books, including *Dave Barry's Money Secrets*, *Dave Barry Turns 50*, *Dave Barry Is from Mars AND Venus*, *Dave Barry in Cyberspace*, and *Dave Barry's Complete Guide to Guys*. He also plays lead guitar in a literary rock band called the Rock Bottom Remainders, whose other members include Stephen King, Amy Tan, Ridley Pearson, and Mitch Albom and who, though not musically skilled, are extremely loud. Dave lives in Miami, Florida, with his wife, Michelle, a sportswriter, and his children, Rob and Sophie, neither of whom thinks he's funny. ■

The book that had the most influence on me as a writer—and maybe as a person—was a book called *Inside Benchley*, by humorist Robert Benchley. Humor was greatly valued in my family. Other families competed on the basis of academic achievement; in ours, it was whether you could make other people laugh. As a kid, I was what you'd call a wise-ass little twerp. At school, I distinguished myself by not getting in nearly as much trouble as I would have if the authorities had been aware of everything I was up to, and was eventually elected class clown at Pleasantville High, class of 1965.

Growing up, I was an avid reader and especially loved to read humor, but until I was 10 years old, I'd never found anything that really slayed me. That summer, my father, who was a big Benchley fan, gave me *Inside Benchley*. I immediately devoured it. As soon as I finished it, I sat down and read straight through the rest of my father's Benchley collection, probably half a dozen books. Because it was summer, I could spend all day just reading one after another of the short humor essays he had written, mostly for *Life* magazine and the *New Yorker*.

I just could not believe how funny they were. How could any grown-up have been that silly and gotten away with it? It was a wonderful epiphany for me. What really struck me was that Benchley was so silly and yet at the same time so obviously smart.

You could tell Benchley was a very well educated guy. I found out later that he went to Harvard and was also a widely respected theater critic whose reviews showed incredible erudition. In addition, he often wrote about events in the news. I was reading essays in the '50s that had been written in the '30s for the most part, so there were topics he wrote about that I wasn't familiar with, yet I still loved his writing. He also wrote parodies of operas, of classical literature, of science—things that I recognized required knowledge and education, but he was making fun of them. He took a learned, adult world and turned it on its head. I thought that was so wonderful—and so funny.

I probably didn't get half the jokes, but I think kids' sense of humor is underrated. They can get what's supposed to be funny and even a sense of why it's funny, even if they don't actually recognize the allusion that's being made. Sometimes when I go to a book signing, little kids will come up and tell me they've read a column of mine and I'll think, "Oh my God, that wasn't intended for you!" But clearly they got something out of it.

Even at the age of 10 I understood enough to decide that if I could be like anybody, I wanted to be like Robert Benchley. Up to that point, and for some time after that point, I didn't really write a lot of humor because you don't write much of anything when you're a kid—except for what you have to write, which is mainly book reports about books you haven't really read. But when I finally reached the point where I wanted to write and I could choose what I wanted to write about, there was no question in my mind but that it was going to be short humor essays.

I was very inspired by Benchley's writing. He proved that humor didn't have to be the stupid, Three Stooges type of comedy; it could be much more sophisticated. When I set about writing humor—starting in high school for the high school paper, and then in college for the college paper—I admired Art Buchwald and Russell Baker and later Erma Bombeck and folks like that. I thought they were funny, but the person I wanted to write like was Robert Benchley.

So when I picked targets, I tended not to write classic political humor or classic household humor, but just silly humor. I'd take a topic that is ordinarily addressed in a dry and serious manner, like science or something like that, and just go for it, which is what Benchley did so well. To me, his best voice was the voice of false authority: "Today, we're going to explain how chemistry works." Because he'd read a lot of authorities, he could mimic them beautifully, but everything he'd say would be absurd. That is my favorite voice to write in, and it's definitely Robert Benchley's voice.

Today I have a whole bookshelf full of Benchley books. Like the Beach Boys, whose 25 best songs are continually repackaged—there are probably 78 *Best of the Beach Boys* albums—many of Benchley's books contain a lot of the same stories. Though I don't have all his theater reviews, I have most of his humor writing that was ever anthologized. I've collected Benchley's books for years, and now my wife seeks them out and buys them for me when she can find them. At this point, I think I have pretty much every book he's ever written.

There are a lot of really great humorists out there. But to this day, when I don't want to be funny—when I don't want to be the guy who's thinking of a joke—and I want somebody to amuse me, the person I'm still most likely to pick is Robert Benchley.

Sue Ellen Cooper

Sue Ellen Cooper is the founder and Exalted Queen Mother of the Red Hat Society, an enormous "nurturing network" for women over 50 that hopes to gain higher visibility for women in that age group and to reshape the way they are viewed by today's culture. Sue Ellen has devoted much of her adult life to family and to a part-time career as a commercial artist. Her first book, *The Red Hat Society: Friendship and Fun After Fifty*, was published in April 2004. ■

Considering that I am a "woman of a certain age" who frequently wears conspicuous cherry-red hats with vivid purple party dresses, it is surprising that as a child, I wasn't very childish. I was the eldest in a very serious family; we were very German in our thinking. Growing up, I was always concerned about responsibility, careful behavior, and doing what was right and proper—*what would people think?*

In the mid-sixties, when I was in college, I found myself floundering as I tried to choose a major. According to my parents' rock-solid traditional views, certain fields were more suitable for girls than others, and the premier career goal in their eyes would be teaching. But my natural bent was for the arts. I knew I had some aptitude in two areas: visual arts—particularly drawing and painting—and writing. Which should I choose?

Ultimately, I compromised. I listened to my parents' warnings that I was unlikely to build a secure career by drawing and painting, and chose to major in English, dreaming not of teaching, as my parents assumed, but of writing.

After settling on my major, I cast about for a minor. I chose philosophy—partly to confound my parents, who would view philosophy as no more practical than fine art. To me, it sounded so delightfully esoteric, so sublimely nonutilitarian! This would be the perfect way to indulge in an (exceedingly mild) rebellion! As it turned out, however, the exposure to the history of thought fueled my hunger to understand the nature of humanity and the meaning of life. It also introduced me to an author who would have an enormous influence on my life.

In philosophy class we read widely, and I discovered C.S. Lewis. I enjoyed his famous Space Trilogy, which includes *Out of the Silent Planet*, *Perelandra*, and *That Hideous Strength*, both as great science fiction/fantasy and as an allegory of one man's journey to know the basic truth underlying all of life. On my own, I read more of Lewis's work, and I grew to respect him as both a wonderful writer and a wise man. Then, a few years after leaving school, I discovered another of his allegorical novels, *The Great Divorce*. This book came to mean more to me than anything I had ever read.

After graduating from college, I ended up in the most traditional career of all: that of a stay-at-home mom. This was entirely natural in those days, and I loved the life I had with my new family. But inside I was still seeking the truth about the meaning of life. *The Great Divorce* began to give me some answers.

The premise of the book is deceptively simple. The story follows a motley group of travelers, first encountered as they are lined up at a bus stop in a dreary, gray town (later revealed to be Hell) awaiting the arrival of a magical bus. After a period of waiting, punctuated by arguments and physical altercations, some of them manage to board the bus. To everyone's surprise, it soon becomes airborne and heads upward to an unidentified destination, a place eventually revealed to be Heaven.

Over the course of the narrative, each of these travelers has the freedom to make an amazing choice: He can choose to extend his visit to Heaven for eternity—or he can return to Hell on the next bus. Each traveler encounters a spirit, sent to meet him, who engages him in intimate conversation regarding his life on Earth and his imminent choice.

Though each encounter is different, the truth that is revealed in all of them is disturbingly honest and provocative. Each person is forced to make a choice and, more importantly, to justify that choice.

The fascinating thing is that not everyone chooses Heaven! And the reasons why shed so much light on human nature. In the space of a startlingly few pages, this book examines the best and worst characteristics of human love, the true nature and power of individual choice, and the eternal, irreversible effects resulting from the exercise of free will. Via the unexpected vehicle of fantasy, Heaven is rendered real and infinitely desirable. Hell is seen as a dreary, yet safe, refuge from the soul-stretching demands (and potential liberation) of Heaven.

Whenever I read *The Great Divorce* (and I've read it many times), two particular characters always stand out for me. The angelic messenger offers both of them Heaven, saying, "You can have eternal joy in the most beautiful place in the world. All you have to do is let it happen." But in order to remain in Heaven, there are things these characters would have to let go of—petty, foolish resentments and prideful feelings—and they don't want to. So they refuse. They just can't accept Heaven because it would require them to release something they are holding onto—even though it is only harming them!

Shocking as it was to read this, I could see the same tendencies operating in my own life. If confronted with that choice, would I be able to let go of my need to control everything and everybody? Much as I wished the answer would be a resounding yes, I couldn't be sure. I saw how difficult it is to let go of any mode of behavior you've lived with all your life, even though it can mean the difference between happiness and misery, freedom and feeling burdened, love and loneliness. I decided I didn't want to end up in a "jail cell," imprisoned by my own smallness yet holding the key in my hand. Over the years, this awareness has positively affected many of the decisions I've made.

Along with letting go of control, I knew I needed to lighten up. Lewis helped me have a better understanding of Christianity. I've always gone to church regularly and read the Bible, but the playfulness and the fantasy element he uses helped me to explore my faith from a different angle. It was a revelation to me that you could lighten up and investigate things from a less somber perspective. The fate of one's immortal soul is dreadfully serious, yet you can read *The Great Divorce* on other levels and be quite amused and entertained.

The playful aspect of the book especially spoke to me because for years I had been trying to work my way back to the best parts of childhood—those lighthearted, carefree parts I'd missed the first time around. I thought of this often and looked for ways to bring more fun into my still quite serious life. But it wasn't until my daughter and son were grown and I was heading into middle age that this desire blossomed, leading me to found the Red Hat Society. Who would ever have thought that super-responsible me would inspire thousands of middle-aged women to wear mismatched clothes and be silly together!

Like *The Great Divorce*, the Red Hat Society is actually about much deeper things, such as love and acceptance and joy and mutual support—important, weighty things. When we started, it was a lark, pretending to be royalty and playing dress-up—rediscovering joys last known in childhood—but it wasn't long before we realized we were also developing a powerful sisterhood with a huge capacity for support and caring.

Now I see that for most of my adult life, in my post-stay-at-home career as an artist and now with the Red Hat Society, I have simply been trying to play. The society's message is: Just lay that burden down and come play! Have a wonderful day and let it be. If you loosen up and stop worrying about everything so much, who knows what glorious things will happen? Take some time for yourself with your friends, and rediscover the joy of plain old silliness and laughter. And if you do this with the same people several times, you are going to bond through that shared happiness and find you have a terrific support group. Those people will be the ones who will be there when you need them.

I think Lewis titled his book *The Great Divorce* because there is a certain line of demarcation in life, and you have to decide whether you will step on one side or the other. You have to make a choice. And that choice might require a divorce from whatever is keeping you on the wrong side. In my case, I got a divorce from my controlling side.

I marked this event in a small way that was very big for me. When the Red Hat Society began to grow, I said that if we ever grew to 10,000 chapters, I would get a tattoo. I never believed it would happen, so I thought I was safe! But within a very short time, it did happen, and everyone around me started reminding me of my promise. They always said it in a teasing way and assured me I didn't really have to do it. But I kept thinking, *But I said I would*. Besides which, it was a silly thing to do. The perfect way to celebrate my new approach to life. Though I wouldn't necessarily advise others to emulate this, on our very next business trip, my Vice-Mother—my right-hand woman and second in command—accompanied me to a tattoo parlor where we each got a tattoo on our hip. What design did we choose? Matching red hats, of course!

EllynAnne Geisel

EllynAnne Geisel is the writer and apron curator of *Apron Chronicles: A Patchwork of American Recollections*, a traveling exhibit of photographic portraits, 200 vintage aprons, and the stories of the people who wore them (www.apronchronicles.com). Artifact guardian to more than 300 aprons, EllynAnne has also created her own collection of apron designs (www.apron memories.com) and is the author of *The Apron Book: Making, Wearing, and Sharing a Bit of Cloth and Comfort* (Andrews McMeel, September 2006). ▪

In 1958, I was 11 years old and my Southern-girl heart fell in love with my future husband. As things turned out, the hours spent practicing my signature as Mrs. Elvis Presley could have been put to better use.

On a muggy summer day a year later, I stepped aboard the bookmobile—a traveling library in the back of a truck—and checked out the week's reading. Settling into the cool grass underneath a shade tree, I picked up the thickest book, turned to the first page, read the first sentence, and fell head over heels. Today, over four and a half decades later, I'm still in love with *Gone with the Wind*.

At the time, I was a preteen GRITS (Girl Raised In The South), belle-in-training, and shallow thinker. I was not particularly interested in the whole War-Between-the-States-historical-background thing against which the novel was set. Instead, I was enamored of the story for its romance (especially when it involved Rhett Butler) and Scarlett O'Hara, the coquettish main character. Both spoke to me in a way that girl sleuth Nancy Drew and nurse Cherry Ames did not.

Raised to be a Scarlett-like confection—sweet, stylish, coy, and coiffed—with a man-pleasing disposition, I was wide-eyed at the discovery that Scarlett was actually an actress playing the part expected of her. By doing so, she could have her cake and eat it, too. Using her exterior to bedazzle the people around her, she was free to be a different kind of girl inside, an independent and strong-minded girl—a lot like the girl inside of me. Deep down, I wanted desperately to someday be a published writer. I had always loved to tell stories to anyone who would listen and spent hours writing gossipy diary entries, drippy fan missives to movie stars, and chatty correspondence with pen pals. But I kept this desire a secret, feeling sure I wasn't really smart enough.

In any case, the writer thing was piddlin' next to my passionate interest in all things romantic and domestic. I was already in serious preparation mode for homemaking and motherhood. My role model for those vocations was not Scarlett, who spent scant time or thought on such things, but Harriet Nelson, star of the weekly TV show the *Adventures of Ozzie and Harriet*. From Harriet, I learned an apron need not match one's dress color (except on holidays, when a theme apron was appropriate), and that housewifery could be a rewarding career choice.

My own mama hadn't taken that path. A college graduate, she was a full-time bookkeeper for my father's business and was the mother of six children. What she *wasn't* was at home, like all the other mothers in the neighborhood. She wasn't at home like Harriett, wearing a darling, freshly ironed apron and greeting us after school with a plate of pimento sandwiches on white bread that she'd sliced into crustless triangles, and, on a tray, tall glasses of cold chocolate milk. Never mind that if Mama had been home, I'd have ignored her or that her skills were needed in Daddy's business or that she was a happier person working outside the home. She wasn't where I wanted her to be, and that's all that mattered to me. Studying Harriet, I was preparing myself to be the stay-at-home mother I'd longed for.

In *Gone with the Wind*, I learned from Scarlett that it was possible to be someone other than the person people assumed I was. Harriet provided an additional flash of epiphany: As long as there was food on the table and clean laundry in dresser drawers, Harriet's day was a mystery to her family. Harriet was free to do what she liked. If I could combine the lessons of my two mentors, I could find love and romance and be a wife, homemaker, and mama, yet secretly pursue my goal to become a writer. But for any of this to be possible, I'd first need the ideal husband. So I turned to Scarlett for direction.

With Scarlett (was there ever a more beautiful name?) as the quintessence of my social aspirations, I spent junior high and high school honing my Southern belle skills in the finer arts of small talk, flirting, and backstabbing. I dismissed math as too difficult to deal with and biology as unnecessary to my goals, which freed up considerable time to prepare for marriage to a well-heeled guy. According to my Dear Diary entries during those years, I was busily walking around the house balancing a book on my head; performing a specific isometric exercise while chanting, "I must, I must, I must increase my bust"; and practicing *American Bandstand* dance moves while clasping my closet door handle. I read movie magazines and my mother's *Cosmopolitan* (*Cosmo* to those in the know) and bought makeup at Woolworth's—but only when the counter ladies were handing out free samples of Evening in Paris perfume. I spent hours talking on the phone to girls I wasn't at the moment gossiping about (see Southern belle skills, above). I watched the movie *Gone with the Wind* a million times, which helped me fine-tune my impersonation of Scarlett and confirmed what I'd suspected: Scarlett was indeed smarter than most men (excluding my daddy, of course).

Even so, seven years of emulating Miss Scarlett did little to prepare me for college admission, except to an institution of minimal higher learning, which was fine by me. Enrolled in the two-year "Mrs." Degree program at the "University of Southern Hospitality," my mission was to find my future children a daddy who could help them with their math homework. I was doing some serious heart-breaking and husband-hunting when I got wind that outside the South, the times for women were a-changin'.

Not certain what that meant, I was nonetheless certain I needed to investigate. Using award-winning theatrics and a river of tears, I convinced my parents I should put my matrimony major on hiatus and transfer to an art school in New York City, where I would study fashion illustration and learn to shop wholesale. They finally said yes, but only if I promised to return to USH to complete my degree.Feeling a flicker of guilt—which I shooed like a bothersome gnat—I crossed my fingers behind my back and agreed.

Up North, with my honeyed accent and fluttering lashes, I was a royal success with the men of Yankee-land, especially since my competition for beaux were braless women with no fashion sense at all, marching around demanding the same pay as the guys who were holding identical jobs. They were members of the new Women's Liberation Movement and called their notion Equal Opportunity. The Scarlett in me called it Spinsterville, and as to their chanting for changes that might affect the wages of *my* future meal ticket . . . well, fiddle-dee-dee! to that.

Although I was living at the epicenter of a man-eating movement that was fast becoming a national and political voice, I just shook my curls at the libbers' rhetoric. What in the world were they thinking, embracing some crazy idea that kicked the guys who were going to be our husbands below the belt? Remembering *Gone with the Wind* during those years upheld my confidence that like Scarlett, who single-handedly pursued her goal of getting the money to pay the taxes on her beloved Tara, I didn't need an organization to show me the way or to be my voice. I was the one in charge of my destiny: Anything I dreamed was possible, and if I just stayed positive and on course, I would be successful.

So I kept my eye on the gold (forget brass) ring, which was to marry a man with a good job, so I could quit mine and become a full-time homemaker and mother. I was a woman on a mission when I met the father of my future children. I knew he was "the one" on our first date, when he figured the tip for our dinner in his head.

Three years later, I sashayed down the aisle, tiny-waisted (like Scarlett!) in a size 2 Priscilla of Boston wedding gown, cheeks pinched to the perfect hue of Blushing Bride Pink, and married my Prince Charming. With the arrival of a baby boy, and then 20 months later, the birth of our second bundle of boy, I recreated Harriet Nelson's household in which to raise my family. Never mind that the year was 1975. I loved tending to the nutrition, laundry, and upbringing of my family and considered it my career.

Fulfilled at home, I knew I was the antithesis of women's liberation. But since I wasn't protesting other women's choices, nor asking anyone to make mine, I hadn't anticipated the denouncing of my career by many of my own gender. So when women's lib dared to label my happy home-making a giant step backward for womankind, I argued back that feminism was about women having the right to do whatever they wanted—including staying at home and burning dinner, not their bras! Still, ostracism hurt.

So while other women broke glass ceilings, I did what I always did when overwhelmed with too many responsibilities or feeling blue, I mentally escaped to the calming familiarity of *Gone with the Wind*. The rereading of my favorite book was always comforting—its prose a re-minder of languid summer days, cool grass under the shade of a tree, and the girl I once was. Within the solace of its pages, I spent time with trea-sured and nonjudgmental friends and often learned something new about the history of the period, but as I grew older and more mature, I also detected flaws in previously flawless characters, especially that of my beloved mentor.

Scarlett was often deceitful, sometimes morally reprehensible, and always a shameful parent. Yet she was the only figure among her surviv-ing family and friends who could see the solution for saving Tara and act on it. She did this by resurrecting within herself ancient skills of survival—skills that had been bred out of her pampered sort. While the society in which she'd been raised collapsed, and the people within it lit-erally died from their inability to save themselves, Scarlett's gumption and vision alone saved her family's future. Those same qualities were mine to resurrect, and I felt them stirring within me.

Then one day, though I had never given much consideration to the woman whose imagination produced my favorite book, the author's bio on the jacket cover suddenly intrigued me, sending me straight to my husband's ancient set of *Encyclopedia Britannica* to learn more.

Looking up Margaret Mitchell, I read she'd been a storyteller and writer her entire life (like me!). She wasn't a student of note, and mathe-matics were her undoing (mine, too!). She was spirited, flirtatious, and charming (me, me, me again!). Excited by our similarities, I continued reading. Divorced after a brief unhappy first marriage, I learned, she was a devoted wife to her second husband. When she was forced to endure a long convalescence after breaking her ankle, husband number 2 brought her piles of library books. Then, tiring of lugging books home, he pre-sented Margaret with a typewriter, saying if she were to have anything new to read, she'd have to write it herself. So in 1926, Margaret began *Gone with the Wind*. She completed the book 10 years later, but it languished in boxes because Margaret had so little confidence in her writing and wouldn't show it to anyone, including a visiting New York publisher who was seeking new material to publish. Only when peeved by a catty remark made in her presence—"Margaret just isn't the type to be able to write a successful book"—did Margaret retrieve her manuscript and give it to the editor to read. He was immediately smitten, and *Gone with the Wind* was published.

Scarlett O'Hara's creator became my new role model. Although I'd continued to write through my busy homemaking days, hardly a soul had ever read anything I'd penned, except those who received my annual family tell-all holiday letter. In 1995, that changed. I began entering writing contests. I wrote essays and a prize-winning children's book and even had a short story published. When Noah, our firstborn, and then two years later, Gideon, our younger son, departed for college, I mourned. Our wholly emptied nest signified that their childhoods, as well as my career as a full-time mom, were truly over. Kissing my first career goodbye, I seized the opportunity to pursue a second career, that of a bona fide writer.

So it was in 1999 that I purchased several old aprons to inspire me as I wrote an article about a piece of classic vintage clothing. I discovered I wasn't the only one who felt a connection to this universal symbol for mothering. This revelation evolved into *Apron Chronicles*, a traveling exhibition of stories, portraits, and more than 200 vintage aprons. Every stage of this project has brought me unexpected joy and countless discoveries. It has changed my life—connecting me with a national community of people, each dear and precious, with an apron story to share.

Today I am a vintage coquette, still married to Prince Charming, and a published author. My life has turned out to be everything I dreamed, and I've accomplished so much more than anyone, including me, expected. If a successful marriage, happy homemaking, and devoted motherhood had been my only achievements, I'd have called my life purposeful and well lived. Yet it is my accomplishments in my second career as a writer that make me believe that when it comes to my potential, there is no limit.

I owe the attainment of my life's goals, and the pursuit of those still to be envisioned, to the serenely clever Harriet Nelson, and to *Gone with the Wind*'s two strong women, Margaret Mitchell and, of course, Scarlett O'Hara, that belle with balls, who taught me that anything is possible, because, after all . . . tomorrow is another day.

Earl Hamner

Earl Hamner is best known as the creator and producer of the Emmy Award–winning series *The Waltons*. The producer of *Falcon Crest* and other television series, he has also written for *The Twilight Zone*, *CBS Playhouse*, and *Theater Guild on the Air*. His seven best-selling books include *Spencer's Mountain*, *The Homecoming*, *You Can't Get There from Here*, and *The Avocado Drive Zoo*. Of his theatrical films Earl is most proud of his adaptation of the E.B. White classic *Charlotte's Web*. ■

Many people think the Waltons of television fame are fictional characters, but in fact they are as real as you or I. I would know—I'm one of them. I recreated my own family—my brothers and sisters, parents and grandparents, just as we were in the Depression years of the 1930s—in my books and eventually on the television series that became so popular all over the world. As a boy growing up in the Blue Ridge Mountains of Virginia, it seemed to me, and still does, that we had quite a good life.

John-Boy, the aspiring writer of the Walton clan, was me. More than anything, I wanted to write books that people everywhere would read and enjoy. It began when I was six. My mother sent a poem I'd written to the Children's Page of the *Richmond Times-Dispatch*, and they published it. My fate was sealed; writing was all that ever interested me from that day forth.

In Schuyler, the mill town where we lived, there was no library. It was a community of working-class people who couldn't afford luxuries like books—especially during those years of the Great Depression.

Nevertheless, our family loved reading. We had two cherished volumes: *A History of Beekeeping*, which my father studied because he kept honeybees as a little sideline to supplement his salary, and the King James version of the Bible, which I read every chance I got. I loved the majesty of the language and the stories, which transported me out of the hills of Virginia to Jerusalem, Galilee, or Rome.

When I was 13, Sister Sherman, a lay preacher from the Episcopal church, came to Schuyler. The first thing she noted was the absence of books, and so she persuaded the owners of the mill—they quarried and processed soapstone there—to set up a library for the town. The owners made available a small cottage next to the mill. Sister Sherman put up shelves and wrote to friends and churches in Richmond, Washington, D.C., and New York, asking them for books.

When the boxes arrived, Sister Sherman allowed me to unpack them and put the books on the shelves. You can imagine the variety of books that came in: travel, fiction, poetry, reference. I was like a drunkard in a liquor store. I would take home stacks of books and consume them, everything from the Hardy Boys and the Bobbsey Twins to authors such as Henry James and Willa Cather. Each book I read changed my life to some degree, but it wasn't until years later that I came across the one book that I feel has had the most profound impact on me.

By then I was a young man of 26, living in New York City. I had taken the long way round to get there. Once I'd finished high school, I had been conscripted into the service during World War II and spent two years in Paris. Before the army, I had never traveled far from home—except of course in my imagination—and so in Paris, I had my first cosmopolitan experience of life. I learned to speak French and even saw the great writer Gertrude Stein on the street. I was in the audience for Edith Piaf's first concert after the end of the war. Her costar was Yves Montand! There was no keeping me down on the farm after that. When I returned to the States, I went to college and then to Manhattan, where I joined the writing staff at NBC (it was still the days of radio, before television). We wrote various things, including dramas for a show called *The NBC Radio Theater*.

One day, the editor of the show assigned me a book to dramatize: *The Time of Man*, by Elizabeth Madox Roberts, published in 1926. The first thing that caught my attention was that Elizabeth Madox Roberts had moved to New York from Kentucky and had written the book in a basement apartment on West 96th Street. I, too, was a transplanted Southerner, living on 87th Street, practically in a basement, so I felt an immediate kinship with her.

When I began reading the novel, I discovered something wondrous and, for me, completely life-changing. Roberts's characters spoke in a way that, while totally unique, was exactly what I had heard as a boy in Virginia. Something along the lines of "All my enduring life I've yearned to be in such a place as this." It was the language of the mountain people: overtones of Elizabethan speech combined with the cadence of African-American speech, which has contributed so beautifully to the Southern accent. The novel's language resonated with me and inspired me to later use the same linguistic style in my own work.

I was also fascinated by the characters themselves. The central character in *The Time of Man* is a 13-year-old girl named Ellen Chesser, who lives in a family of itinerant workers. When we first meet her, she's working with her mother and father, planting tobacco seedlings. I was immediately struck by Ellen's marvelous imagination and sense of wonder. Ellen's mother is a character of great strength and perseverance. Many times throughout the story, she says, "We've got to keep moving on." Moving on becomes a theme in the book—moving to some better place, finding some better life.

At one point, Ellen comes under the influence of a carnival woman named Tessy, who tells her all these wonderful stories about her travels, and Ellen eats them up. I knew that eagerness. Like Ellen, I had been curious about the world. In that makeshift library of my youth, I sometimes found a *National Geographic* magazine mixed in with the books. Reading it, I wanted more than ever to see what was beyond the mountain I called home.

Then, when I was in basic training in Louisville, Kentucky, I met my own equivalent of Tessy. He was a fellow soldier who realized that I was not very knowledgeable about music and good books, so he took me under his wing. He was appalled that I had never heard really good music—I was used to fiddle pickin', what he called hillbilly music. One day he took me to a music store and asked them to play a recording of the second movement of a Tchaikovsky symphony so I could hear it. It was the start of a different kind of education from the one I'd received in the Blue Ridge. Yet the solid foundation of my country upbringing kept me true to the values I cherished as I moved into this exciting and sometimes complicated new world.

The Time of Man simply delighted me. It embodied the nobility I had always perceived in so-called common, ordinary people. I was elated by this newfound style and deep connection with another Southern writer. Roberts gave me permission to write in my own vernacular. Finally, I had found my voice—and my subject matter. Not long after reading her book, I wrote and published my first novel, *Fifty Roads to Town*.

I was floating on air for months after that. My career had been launched. After *Fifty Roads to Town*, I wrote *Spencer's Mountain* and its sequel, *The Homecoming*, which is the book that *The Waltons* is based on. If I hadn't come upon Elizabeth Madox Roberts's novel, *The Waltons* would probably never have happened. Her work helped me portray the hill people, not as thick-browed, shaggy rednecks and hillbillies, but as the courageous, self-reliant, and honorable people I knew so well.

Borrowing Roberts's "pencil," I was able to create a "real" fictional place. Faulkner had Yoknapatawpha County; I had Jefferson County. I knew that area and those people, and had such respect and love for them that I was able to come up with something universal; my stories seem to cross international, ethnic, and geographic lines.

Over the years, I've found that people all over the globe relate to the Waltons and claim them as their own. I was in Vienna once and was interviewed by a Viennese journalist who told me he had been puzzled about where Austrian kids thought Walton's Mountain was located. When he asked some schoolchildren, they said, "Oh, it's in the Black Forest."

The Waltons is still being shown in syndication. I sometimes get mail from people who say, "Thank you for the lesson you taught us last night." I think, "My God, I didn't mean to teach anybody." I wasn't trying to get a message across; as Samuel Goldwyn once said, "Messages are for Western Union." Then I realize that because I have written about such good, decent people, there are messages inherent in the stories that touch the viewer deeply. I suppose, like Ellen Chesser in *The Time of Man*, the Waltons simply appeal to the best in all of us.

N ancy Pearl

The book's cover read *Space Cadet*, by Robert Heinlein. *What's a space cadet?* I thought. I was 10 years old, sitting on the floor in the Parkman Branch Library in Detroit, Michigan, looking at the books that were waiting to be reshelved. I picked up Heinlein's book and started reading it. It's the story of a group of boys, teenagers from Earth, Venus, and other planets, who want to join the Solar Patrol, a peacekeeping body for the whole galaxy.

I was fascinated. It was the first time I truly understood that books can take you to other worlds. Up until then, the books I read were rooted in the everyday world I knew: dog and horse stories, stories about families and people just like me in one way or another. Though I didn't have a horse—I was a city kid—I certainly had a dog, so those worlds were familiar, unlike this vision of an interplanetary Patrol that helped people all over the universe get along. *Space Cadet* introduced me to a whole new type of fiction—and to the experience of how life-changing good fiction could be.

As an urban child growing up in a family that was not particularly happy, I spent most of my time at the library. Reading was an escape for me. The children's librarians were always recommending books to me, and I spent many hours in my favorite spot on the window seats in the children's room with my nose buried in book after book. Those wonderful librarians cultivated my early love of books and showed me that books and libraries can open doors to other ways of being and thinking. I decided early on that being a librarian was the best thing I could ever do; I absolutely wanted to give that same gift to other children—and adults, too.

I also observed the benefits of a reading life in my own family. My father was orphaned early in the Depression and never went beyond the sixth grade in school. Yet he continued to read. As an adult, he ended up selling home improvements in Detroit, but his real love was American history. He was politically active and especially enjoyed reading the kinds of books that describe the way a country is created. Looking back, I can see that it was reading that made up for the formal education he'd missed and that truly defined who he became in his life.

Reading was certainly an important element in the formation of my own values and character. In *Space Cadet*, Heinlein introduced me to the notion of honor and doing the honorable thing. At one point in the book, the main character, a boy named Matt Dodson, is taking a variety of tests that will determine whether he can become a member of the Solar Patrol. In one test, each candidate is given a milk bottle, a blindfold, and some beans. They are instructed to go into a room by themselves, cover their eyes with the blindfold and drop the beans into the bottle.

When Matt is finished, he uncovers his eyes and is horrified to find that only one of his beans has gone into the bottle. He is terribly afraid it will disqualify him; still, despite the temptation to lie about his score, he reports his poor performance honestly. Matt asks the supervisor what prevents someone from uncovering his eyes and dropping the beans in. The supervisor says that nothing prevents it—a clue that things aren't always what they appear to be. Matt realizes (and I did, too) that what was actually being tested was his honor! And so he had done very well. I found that little incident so interesting that I've remembered it all these years. Indeed, the whole concept of honor, plus the idea that we don't always know what we are being tested for, made a deep impression on me.

Space Cadet also provided a vision of world peace I had never imagined possible. I read it in 1958 at the height of the Cold War, when we were all feeling a deep anxiety about the threat of war. The idea in the book of people very different from one another—Martians and people from Earth and Venus—all trying to make one peaceful world was very appealing to me. I felt that no matter what someone looked like, everyone is part of the world and part of civilization and deserves respect and equality.

These ideas, plus the notion of honor and doing the honorable thing, led me to be involved in many of the protest movements of my time. My first civil rights involvement was in 1960, picketing the Woolworth's in Detroit in support of the early civil rights sit-ins in Greensboro, North Carolina. Woolworth's wouldn't serve blacks at the lunch counter, so four brave black men in Greensboro had sat down at the counter and refused to move. They were arrested, of course, but then others came and sat at the counter, too. Like many around the country, we were doing a sympathy protest/picket line at a local Woolworth's. This happened only two years after I read *Space Cadet*. I was probably 12. I didn't go with my parents, but with a group of other teenagers—it was a little bit like the Solar Patrol. Although it was scary to go against authority, I felt empowered by my actions and felt that the protest was the way to help the world be a better place. It was my small contribution to intergalactic harmony.

I've explored so many worlds through reading since those days. After *Space Cadet*, I soon branched out from science fiction to fantasy. I read *The Hobbit* and then *The Lord of the Rings*. I was hooked. Today I still enjoy the genre—among many others, of course.

Initially, reading was a way for me to hide from a reality I didn't like, but it quickly became a vehicle enabling me to know and embrace many different visions of reality. Over the years, books have taken me to cities, countries—even planets!—I could never have traveled to on my own. I became a librarian so that I could share the gift of reading and inspire others to open books—to begin their own journeys of discovery and enrichment.

ally Amos

Wally Amos is an author, lecturer, and entrepreneur. He is best known as the founder of the Famous Amos Cookie Company, which pioneered the gourmet cookie industry. Wally is the author of five books on positive thinking and motivation; he holds an honorary doctorate in education from Johnson & Wales University, has received countless national awards and honors—including the Horatio Alger Award—and has been lauded on the Senate floor. He has appeared on numerous radio and television interviews and programs and, a champion of community service, sits on the board of many charitable causes for literacy and education. Wally's latest project, Chip & Cookie (www.chipandcookie.com), features fresh baked cookies and two chocolate-chip cookie character plush dolls that are used to promote reading aloud. ■

In 1978, I was at the top of my game: Famous Amos cookies were selling "famously" and I had just moved to Hawaii. It seemed that the struggles of my past were over—or at least on vacation. I lived in the most beautiful place in the world and was just beginning an inner spiritual transformation that I hoped would match the great progress I'd made outwardly.

I had spent my childhood living in poverty. When I was 12, my parents divorced and I was sent from Tallahassee, Florida, to New York City to live with my aunt and uncle. Five years later, I dropped out of high school and joined the Air Force. When I left the service, I was hired to work in the mailroom at the William Morris Agency. Within a year, I'd become their first African-American theatrical agent, but life was still a struggle. I never seemed to have enough money to make ends meet.

All that changed when I started making a living baking chocolate-chip cookies—a product I was introduced to as a teenager in my Aunt Della's kitchen. Everyone who tasted my cookies loved them, and before long, I'd opened several dozen Famous Amos cookie outlets across the country. By 1978, business was booming.

Yet even though things were going well, I didn't feel I was really in control of my life. I had money, but something was still missing. Like most people, I'd been raised believing that I was at the mercy of other people and a victim of my outer circumstances.

Soon after I moved to Hawaii, I heard Gerald Jampolsky speak at the Unity church I'd started attending. Then I read his book, *Love Is Letting Go of Fear*. It totally changed my belief system. Jerry showed me that everything really happens on the inside. He taught me that I'm solely responsible for how I feel and how I process experiences. In other words, he put me in charge of my own life, really for the first time.

In *Love Is Letting Go of Fear*, he explains that we can't be loving and fearful at the same time. In any given instant, we can be either in a state of love or a state of fear, and we get to choose which one. Well, if we have a choice, why in heaven's name would we ever choose fear? Since our attitudes and beliefs are directly related to the results we get in life, why would we ever want to be negative? It was the great "aha" moment in my life: Once I understood this—and began living this way—my spirit blossomed.

I began to process things in a completely different way. Whatever the experience and whatever the situation I was involved in, I knew that if I was fearful, it was because I was not loving myself, not loving the situation, and not loving life. Fear comes from forgetting that God—Love—is the source of everything and that in the bigger picture, there is truly nothing to be afraid of.

Today, even though I've been in the cookie business for 30 years, I still get challenged. For example, in August 2005, I opened a new cookie store here in Hawaii. We had some difficulties at the beginning and I started to worry that we might run out of operating capital. I found myself replaying all the old negative thoughts: *What are we going to do if we run out of money? What are the investors going to say?*

With this negativity about the store running through my mind, I sat in a comfortable place and prayed. I asked to be reminded that God is all there is, that He is love and that He is the source of everything. I immediately felt the peace and the comfort of "coming home." It's a practice I have—to align myself with love every day. I use love as a repellant, as a shield that deflects all that is not like love. Once I shift my attention away from the outside struggle and back to love, the outer situation usually soon clears up, as it did with the problems at the Hawaii store.

There is no doubt in my mind that our attitudes and belief systems create the results we see in our lives. Not long after I met Jerry Jampolsky, he introduced me to a boy named Kerry, who was 9 or 10 years old and had sickle cell anemia. The doctors told him he'd never live to see his thirteenth birthday. But Kerry didn't become fearful. He said to me, "I think life is like checking a book out of a library. When you're born, you borrow your body. There's a due date, but you don't know when it is. Once the due date arrives, you just return the body."

It was an amazing experience to meet someone that young with such a powerful attitude. Kerry is 38 years old now. He's still living with sickle cell anemia, but he's not dying from it. He went to college, got married, and has two beautiful young boys. Kerry survived because he knew instinctively to live life from a place of love.

Jerry taught me that we have the power to let go of fear and choose love. We have the power to let go of anxiety and limitation and instead choose a life filled with peace and freedom. But it's one thing to know this, and quite another thing to live it in the midst of a storm. People say knowledge is power—I disagree. It isn't power until you use it, just as an automobile is not transportation until you drive it.

I've learned that letting go of fear is just a decision I have to make again and again: Choose love. Choose love. Choose love. It's what carries me through each and every day with a smile on my face and peace in my heart.

Jack Canfield

Jack Canfield is the cocreator of the bestselling *Chicken Soup for the Soul* series, which currently has 115 titles with more than 100 million copies in print in 47 languages around the world. He is also the coauthor of *The Success Principles™: How to Get from Where You Are to Where You Want to Be* and is one of the teachers featured in the worldwide film phenomenon *The Secret.* For 35 years Jack has conducted seminars in personal transformation for corporations, universities, nonprofit organizations, and the general public in more than 20 countries. He has been a high school teacher, a university instructor, a psychotherapist, and a success coach. Jack has shared his groundbreaking ideas on more than 150 television shows, including *Larry King Live* and *Oprah,* and on 600 radio shows. ■

I spent the first 30 years of my life "in my head." Eight years in military school, four years at Harvard, and two years at the University of Chicago had made me intellectually astute, but at the cost of separating me from my body, my emotions, and my spirit. Military school and Harvard had been all about thinking and logic. My body was simply a container for my brain—and a vehicle to vanquish opponents on the sports field. Feelings, sexuality, and pleasure were to be repressed in the name of academic and athletic achievement. And forget fatigue, pain, loneliness, fear, and anger: One had to rise above all that.

By the time I was a doctoral student in education at the University of Massachusetts Amherst in the mid-seventies, I knew something was missing from my life. Although I had done well, nothing was that rewarding, and I wasn't very happy. It was a great relief to find that many of my courses were focused on deepening one's self-awareness, owning disowned parts of the self, and discovering more authentic ways of being. I attended exciting courses with titles such as Values Clarification, Assertiveness Training, Communication Skills, and Gestalt Awareness, as well as the usual history and philosophy of education courses. As a result, I began rediscovering my previously buried feelings, learning how to pursue my true heart's desires, and connecting more deeply with people and with nature. I also began to explore my emotions and my spirituality through participation in a variety of self-help and human potential groups.

I had been feeling disconnected from my spiritual self and from religion for many years. My mother had been a Catholic but had left the church after divorcing my father when I was six. Because my stepfather was Presbyterian, I had grown up in the Presbyterian Church. Then, in high school, I'd had a deeply disturbing experience that had made me withdraw from religion altogether.

Once a year, our community had Ecumenical Day, in which church members were encouraged to attend the services of a different denomination. When our minister asked me which church I was thinking of attending, I said I was planning to go to a Catholic Mass. I had never attended Mass with my mother and I had always been curious about it—the chanting in Latin, the incense, the weekly confession, and communion. My minister's reaction to this was intensely negative—you'd have thought I had said I was going to defect from the Presbyterian Church and go join up with the Antichrist.

He took me into his office and launched into a 20-minute presentation about how Protestants were better people than Catholics and, because of the superiority of their doctrine, were rewarded more favorably by God. He even brought out a map of Europe that showed the gross national products and average per capita incomes of each country, and pointed out that all the predominantly Protestant countries such as Germany and Great Britain had much higher numbers than the Catholic countries such as Spain and Italy. He concluded by telling me that I would be much more successful in life if I were a Protestant and advised me to visit a Methodist or Lutheran church instead.

I remember leaving that meeting completely turned off by the petty competitiveness, bigotry, and arrogance he had displayed. After that I no longer trusted the messages of love, tolerance, and compassion that were the standard fare of Sunday sermons. By the time I had finished studying the history of religions at Harvard, I had pretty much become an agnostic. I was no longer sure if there really was a God. I began to wonder if Karl Marx was correct when he had proclaimed religion was simply the opiate of the masses. As long as people had God and a promise of a better life in the hereafter, they would put up with anything in this life.

Looking back, I believe the fundamental problem was that my religious education, like most people's, had been strong on dogma and non-existent on how to create and experience a personal connection to a living God. No wonder I was spiritually shut down.

During this period, a professor of mine lent me a book to read: *Life After Life*, by Raymond Moody, M.D. He told me he had read it in one sitting and it had profoundly affected him. I took the book home and read it that night. The book is about Dr. Moody's personal research into clinical near-death experiences. A medical doctor, Moody had become fascinated with people who had clinically died but who had been revived several minutes later and could remember what they had experienced while they were "dead."

From his interviews Moody was able to discern a clear pattern to those experiences. After people died, they left their bodies, floated upward, and were able to look down on their "dead" bodies. They were then transported through a dark tunnel (often while hearing a high-pitched sound) toward a being of light that loved them unconditionally. Many Christians identified this being as Christ, many Buddhists as Buddha, while agnostics and atheists simply saw it as a being of light. Next, in the presence of this being, the "dead" would often review their life with the purpose of seeing what lessons they could learn from it. Inevitably, these people were told they had to return to their bodies, which they did, though reluctantly.

What struck me most was a single comment from one of Dr. Moody's interview subjects. He said that the being of light had asked him two questions before showing him a review of his life. The first was "What wisdom have you gained from this life?" The second was "How have you expanded your capacity to love?" Those two questions, more than anything else in the book, deeply affected me. Rereading the book recently, I was shocked to discover that these questions—which I had remembered as the main premise of the book—were simply two sentences in the middle of a paragraph. They weren't even a major theme that Dr. Moody was presenting, yet they have stuck with me and directed my life for over 30 years.

Reading that section of Moody's book, I came to the conclusion that we are indeed spirits that transcend the flesh, that in fact there is life after this life on Earth, and that the main purpose of our lives on Earth is to deepen our wisdom and to expand our capacity to love. I remember thinking—probably because I was studying education at the time—*Hey, there really* is *a final exam. There are two questions, and it's a take-home test!*

That night, doing the best I could to review my own life, I saw that I had certainly not been focused on becoming wiser or more loving. My life up to that point had been about learning, but not about love and wisdom. I realized, as we say in the education field, that nobody was "teaching for the test." There were very few classes in any school or university called Extracting Wisdom from Your Experience or Learning How to Love Unconditionally. Instead, I had been mostly studying history, geography, mathematics, and biology—all useful, but not critical to the love, joy, and inner peace that had eluded me for so long. And while the churches were exhorting us to be more loving, kind, compassionate, and forgiving, nobody seemed to have an effective curriculum for teaching us how.

As I reflected on what I had read in *Life After Life*, I just knew in my heart of hearts that there was indeed a spirit we call God, and that this force was not punitive but compassionate and loving. I understood that in a sense, we were all in school; we were all learning through our experiences. Dr. Moody's research (and later Dr. Kenneth Ring's and Dr. Elisabeth Kübler-Ross's research on clinical near-death experiences) had given us academic validation for what the mystics and the saints had been telling us throughout the ages.

This profound little book literally changed the course of my life. After that night, I began to deeply pursue my spiritual practices of meditation, prayer, reading, and service to others. I dedicated my life to learning—and teaching others—about love and wisdom. First I did it through my workshops on self-esteem, relationships, and the principles of success. Then I started gathering stories that I felt contained messages of love and wisdom that would inspire and enlighten others. These stories later formed the basis of the *Chicken Soup for the Soul* books.

In my seminars, I often talk about my transformational experience reading *Life After Life* and the lessons I've taken from it. One night after I had spoken at a church, a man from the audience came up to me and told me about his near-death experience after a serious car accident. He said that before the accident, he had been a Christian in terms of going to Sunday services but had never felt very deeply connected to God or his church. A real estate agent, he had spent his life ruthlessly pursuing monetary success. After his near-death experience, although he had remained a real estate agent, he said that he now saw his clients as people he was serving rather than people he was trying to make money from.

He then shared something I thought was very illuminating. "You know," he said, "even though I am a Christian, I don't know for sure if there is a heaven or a hell like the ones they describe in church. I wasn't there long enough to discover that. But I will tell you what I think hell is. Hell is standing next to Jesus Christ *and having him watch you* as you watch the review of your life go by, both of you seeing every incident in your life where you withheld love from another person. You can really feel the pain—yours and theirs—each time you withheld love or compassion from another person."

When I shared that story in a later speech, a man who had graduated from the University of Southern California (USC) came up to me crying. He said he had told his daughter he'd disinherit her if she married her boyfriend, who was attending USC's archrival, the University of California, Los Angeles. He admitted to not having spoken to his daughter for more than a year. Stories like these make it clear how much unnecessary pain we inflict on ourselves and each other when we withhold our love and acceptance.

Today, because of *Life After Life* and the experiences that have flowed from it, I constantly strive to let people be who they are, believe what they believe, and pursue happiness in their own unique ways. This alone has removed a lot of stress from my life. In addition, I have great compassion for myself, my family, and my friends. I am far from perfect, but I keep coming back to the two questions I learned that night in a dimly lit apartment in Amherst, Massachusetts: "How can I be more loving in this situation?" and "What wisdom can I learn from this experience?" The simple act of asking myself these questions, as well as my continued dedication to answering them, have made my journey infinitely more rewarding than I could ever have imagined.

Jim McCann

Jim McCann, CEO of 1-800-FLOWERS.COM, is a man with a knack for making things grow. Starting with a single flower shop in Manhattan, he has grown his company into an international business with 3,500 employees and annual sales of $650 million. His entrepreneurial acumen and vision have been widely recognized in the business community. Among his many honors are Entrepreneur of the Year awards by Merrill Lynch and *Inc.* Magazine. Jim is the author of *Stop and Sell the Roses: Lessons from Business & Life.* ■

I went to John Jay College of Criminal Justice for two reasons: one, because I wanted to become a New York City police officer, and two, because they let me in. I wasn't much of a student, and to this Irish Catholic kid growing up in a blue-collar neighborhood in Queens, becoming a cop was something special. The "men in blue" were like the sheriffs and marshals in the Westerns I watched on TV.

At John Jay, which was then part of the New York Police Academy, I studied psychology and was fortunate to have an inspiring linguistics professor—smart, cultured, and kind. He introduced me to Claude Steiner's work and lent me *Scripts People Live*, a groundbreaking book about Transactional Analysis, which is the study of how individuals interact. It is a complex book with many advanced psychological concepts, but its underlying message—that the quality of our lives is based on our relationships—had a huge impact on me.

As time passed, I realized I no longer wanted to be a police officer. Instead, I decided to devote myself to what had been my part-time job, which was working in a home for troubled teenage boys. Although I loved the job, I wasn't very good at it. For one thing, I was shy—hardly a qualification for working with tough, court-referred teenagers who were only a few years younger than I!

Fortunately, my boss, a member of the Marianist Order named Brother Tom, was a terrific man and a wonderful mentor. I went to him one day and said, "I'm not the right person for this job. Things can get ugly quickly around here, and I'm not very good at controlling the situation. I think I should leave before things get out of hand and someone gets hurt." But Brother Tom wouldn't let me quit. He told me he saw my passion for the job and my big heart, and he said he'd work with me.

As a result, I found myself talking to Brother Tom a lot. The first thing he did was to help me get over my shyness. He suggested I act like a host at a party. When you're a host, he explained, you're not thinking about your own needs and feelings; you're concerned with how everyone else is doing. And when you're giving to people in this way, the amazing thing is that not only are they happier but you're happier, too.

Claude Steiner had come to a similar conclusion. He found that the more a person creates social intimacy in his life, the more content he is. Brother Tom and I spent many hours discussing Transactional Analysis and *Scripts People Live*. I told him that reading Steiner had helped me recognize a fundamental truth about myself—that I am happiest when I am giving and receiving love. We talked about how this truth might apply to others, including the young men in my care. Suddenly the light went on: In spite of all their bluster and denial, every last one of these young men was the same as me; they just wanted to love and be loved. From that moment on, I knew how to handle them.

At the time, there was a teenager living at the home named Joe. He was a quiet kid, but he had a volatile temper. He was a tough guy, as well as a disruptive influence in the house, and I had to go out of my way to find ways to connect with him. One of Joe's quirks was that you could not touch him. If you even brushed up against him, he'd go wild. I had been reading about progressive desensitization in Steiner's books, and I decided to apply this process to Joe. I made it a point to touch Joe all the time, almost imperceptibly at first, until he was used to it, and then gradually more and more strongly until I could pat him on the shoulder or even grab his arm. I would say, "Hello, Tough Joe," and we'd make a joke about it.

Joe had a beautiful head of hair, which he spent a lot of time combing. Eventually, Joe and I reached a point of connection where I could even mess up his hair. He'd yell, "Oh, dang, dude! Again?" and then storm off to the bathroom to look in the mirror and make himself presentable again. He made believe it was a big deal, but really he loved it. If anyone else had played with him like that, he might have killed them. But with me he was able to accept it as a standing joke, because he knew I cared about him.

Joe and I both got a lot out of our interactions, and I saw very clearly what Steiner meant about the contentment that comes from loving relationships. The unique thing about Steiner's approach is that he applies a mathematical economic model to relationships: You can actually measure, in mathematical units, levels, degrees, and frequency of social intimacy. The more social intimacy in a person's life, the "richer" they are. It's the only economic model where the more you give, the more you have. Seeing this helped me break through my old conditioning and my belief that giving means losing something.

Transactional Analysis and "giving in order to receive" were not popular concepts in the neighborhood where I grew up. Queens was a tough place, and if you went around talking about your need to love and be loved, you could expect someone to come up to you with a bat and show you how much they loved hitting you! In my family, the way you showed love was through humor and making others laugh. Learning to directly express my feelings about others took a lot of practice.

I worked for Brother Tom for 14 years and progressed from supervising a group of 10 boys to running the home with him, which consisted of group homes plus a main campus with up to a couple hundred teenagers. My contact with these boys taught me a lot more than I learned in college. They put me under a microscope and delighted in dissecting me mercilessly. If I was inconsistent, they'd immediately point it out. For example, though I didn't allow them to curse, I sometimes let out a curse myself. When I did, they were all over me about it. They forced me to be honest about myself and my motivations, which in turn helped me become more perceptive about other people's motivations. I consider them my professors of Transactional Analysis.

During my last 10 years with Brother Tom, I ran a flower business on the side because work in a nonprofit didn't pay a lot. It began when I bumped into a guy who was selling a flower shop in Manhattan. He agreed to let me work in the shop for a couple of weekends, to see if I liked it. I did, and so I scraped up the $10,000 purchase price and bought the store. Every year after that, I opened up a few more flower shops until the business was so big I had to devote myself to it full time.

I discovered that my former work running a nonprofit home for at-risk youth had been good training for my new career in the retail industry. Today, my job as CEO of 1-800-FLOWERS.COM is to find the right employees and then—as it was with the troubled teenagers—to get them to work in a group environment and to achieve more than they think is possible. I help them focus on their real goals and objectives, and encourage them all along the way.

Our customers need care and encouragement, too. As florists, we're in the business of helping them express themselves and connect to the people in their lives whom they care about. Again, it's that most fundamental of motivations—to love and be loved, to connect. So I see my work, whether I'm managing people or selling flowers, as helping people build positive relationships.

I owe a lot of my success, both in business and in life, to the main principle I learned from Claude Steiner's book: We humans are different from any other species in that in almost everything we do, we seek out social intimacy. The jobs we choose, the hobbies we pursue, the taverns we frequent, and the sports we follow—are all attempts to acquire and develop social relationships. I teach people in my organization to recognize their own need to love and be loved, and to accept, applaud, and encourage this instinct in themselves and in others.

Focusing on the positive has become second nature to me now, but at first I had to unlearn the lessons my dad had taught me. My brother Chris is president of 1-800-FLOWERS.COM, and he and I have worked on this together. Dad was a good man, but he grew up in a time when the prevailing attitude was that it's a tough world and you need to be tough on people. You should never smile at employees or give them a pat on the back because, as he put it, "You're paying them, damn it; they should do their jobs anyway." As a result, my dad was always complaining that he couldn't find good employees. What he never realized was that people will give their best if they have good relationships with the people around them.

For years now Chris and I have gone out of our way to find things that people are doing well so we can brag about them and applaud them. It's a simple formula, but it works: Everyone blooms with encouragement—including the one giving it.

Larry Jones

Larry Jones is president and founder of the international charity Feed The Children, a Christian, nonprofit organization providing aid and assistance to children and families in need in the United States and around the world. Founded in 1979, Feed The Children is the third largest charity in the country based on private nongovernment support, according to the *Chronicle of Philanthropy*. Over the years, Larry has received national and international recognition for his service to others, including the Humanitarian Award from the National Conference of Christians and Jews, the National Caring Award, and humanitarian commendations from Armenia, El Salvador, Guatemala, Iran, and Lebanon. Additionally, Larry is the author of numerous books, including *How to Bend Without Breaking*; *The Fifteen-Second Secret*; *Life's Interruptions, God's Opportunities*; and the novel *Black Box*. ▣

It all started with a simple question: "Can you spare a nickel?"

I was speaking at a church in Port-au-Prince, Haiti—which in my experience has to be the poorest place in the Western hemisphere—when I met a small, thin boy on the street. He told me his name was Jerry and then asked me for the nickel. When I asked him what the money was for, he answered, "So I can go to that store over there and buy me a roll. I haven't eaten all day."

As I reached into my pocket for some change, he said, "Do you also have three pennies? For three pennies they'll cut the roll in half and put butter on both sides."

I handed him the eight cents, saying, "You'll need something to wash it down with. How much is a Coke?"

"Twelve cents," he told me.

As I gave him the additional coins, I shook my head in wonder. Twenty cents to feed a hungry child—not a nutritious meal, but a meal nonetheless.

When I returned to my home in Oklahoma, I couldn't get Jerry out of my mind. I knew there were countless hungry children all over the world, but Jerry had put a face on the problem and made it real for me. I began to wonder what I could do about it. I knew that here in America we had too much food—the grain elevators were overflowing and I'd just read that we were storing millions of tons of wheat. Wasn't there a way to get some of our extra wheat to Jerry and the other hungry kids living in a country just 200 miles away?

I was a minister at the time, and I began to go on television and talk about this idea, asking, "Why should children be starving to death while we have surplus wheat in America?"

What happened next was a miracle and a test of faith all in one.

Though I wasn't making an appeal for action, the farming community heard me and suddenly the wheat came pouring in—two million pounds in less than two months. The next thing we knew, my wife Frances and I had founded Feed The Children. We had no clue about running a nonprofit, but we didn't have a choice. When you've got two million pounds of wheat waiting for distribution, you have to just dive in.

It wasn't the first time we'd felt overwhelmed at what was being asked of us. In the early years of our marriage, my wife and I left a church in Oklahoma City and went into a ministry with no visible means of support. Any money we received had to go directly into the ministry, so it wasn't long before we were destitute. We literally had 90 cents between us. At that point, we felt that God had forgotten us. We had one child and another one on the way; we had house payments to make and a car to run. Things were really rough.

We did what we always did. We prayed and read the Bible, but we drew strength from another book as well, *Hudson Taylor's Spiritual Secret*, a book I'd first read as a young man in 1960 and shared with my wife soon after. Written by Hudson Taylor's son and daughter-in-law, the book tells the inspiring story of a man whose faith was absolute.

In the 1800s, Hudson Taylor founded the China Inland Mission. His unwavering trust in God, in spite of the trials and tribulations he went through, is nothing short of miraculous. He was sent to China to open a mission, and if you can be dropped anywhere in the world in a worse situation, I can't think of where it would be. He could not speak the language, and the Chinese did not exactly welcome him with open arms. Then, several months after his arrival, he received devastating news from England: The funds that had been promised him were no longer available. He was on his own with no money and no ticket home.

But Hudson Taylor was undaunted. He had a phenomenal trust in God and knew that He was in charge, even in the hardest times. Taylor worked day after day in the most challenging conditions, and gradually his mission took shape. At the time of his death, more than a thousand missionaries were spreading the Gospel in China. They drew no salary and depended solely on Providence to supply their needs. Taylor's mission never made an appeal for financial help, yet was never once in debt.

Reading Hudson Taylor's story inspired courage in us once again, and the next day we received some unexpected funds, which gave us the faith to keep going until our finances eventually turned around. To this day, whenever I face adversity, his book always reminds me that we are the instruments of a higher purpose and that God will take care of us. And each time, I am amazed by the way things work out. Over the years, I've read the book many times and given hundreds of copies to friends.

Now, as we faced the monumental task of cleaning, bagging, and shipping the grain overseas, Frances and I read Taylor's book again. As always, it gave us the strength to trust that—somehow—things would fall into place. And sure enough, along with the wheat, there was an outpouring of help. For example, a guy from Florida called and said, "I've got a truck that goes from Miami to L.A., and it comes back empty. Where's the wheat?" Well, the wheat was only 17 miles off the highway in Texas, so the trucker dropped down, picked it up, took it over to Miami, and loaded it onto a boat. Then another man helped me ship a commercial wheat grinder to Haiti, and he traveled down to the island to set it up. Everything came together in this way.

I've seen it countless times in my life—when God asks you to do something, He also provides the means to achieve it. I used to try to figure out how He was going to make it all come about perfectly, but I quit doing that a long time ago. His ways are not our ways; they're totally beyond our comprehension. Frances and I have learned to simply trust that everything is exactly the way it should be. The result of this kind of faith is a deep experience of tranquility.

You've probably been with people who, whatever is happening around them, exude an overwhelming calmness. Several years ago, I had the privilege of spending two days with Mother Teresa. We stayed in the same monastery in Armenia after the earthquake. She was carrying the weight of literally thousands of projects and responsibilities, and yet she was utterly at peace. Though I'm not a Catholic, one morning I accompanied her to Mass. The priest overslept, and we stood outside in the snow. Mother Teresa was wearing socks and sandals, but she didn't complain or make any comment about the delay. She just waited out in the snow very calmly.

I picture Hudson Taylor this way. He was left out in the cold in China with only a telegram that read "We'll pray for you, but there won't be any money coming." And he accepted it and kept going. That was Hudson Taylor's spiritual secret: to solve a problem by immediately handing it over to God. Hudson said to God, "I'm here not because the missionary society sent me but because I have been appointed by You. Therefore, I am Your responsibility—please take care of everything."

Life is like that: Just when we think we've got the world by the tail, all of a sudden a storm—unemployment, death, divorce—hits us. We're left reeling, wondering how on Earth we're going to handle the situation. But if we have built our life on a strong spiritual foundation, we know that even in adverse times, God's master plan is unfolding and that, as the Bible puts it, "All things work together for good."

Once Feed The Children got off the ground, there was certainly never any shortage of work to do. I was once asked, "How do you determine where the need is?" to which I replied, "Take a map, turn out the lights, and throw a dart. Wherever it lands, that's where the need is." We've sent food to more than 100 countries, as well as to all 50 states. But our work is more than simply a campaign to end hunger. For example, by feeding 70,000 children in the slums of Nairobi, we have revolutionized education in the city. The kids are motivated to go to school—we've doubled enrollment in some neighborhoods—and now our next step is to get adequate school supplies into those kids' hands. Today, the international food delivery program started by two inexperienced people has become a thriving global literacy and education initiative.

I truly believe that whether you're a missionary, an insurance salesperson, a street sweeper, or the director of a hunger relief organization, if you are working to help others with faith and trust, you become unstoppable. As Hudson Taylor's life so beautifully demonstrated, when God calls us to do something, He opens a door that no one can shut.

Debbie Macomber

Debbie Macomber is the author of 124 books, including *Changing Habits*, *A Good Yarn*, and *Thursdays at Eight*. With more than 70 million books in print, Debbie has earned a worldwide, multigenerational following, first with her heartwarming, wholesome stories of love and commitment, and in more recent years, in the broader field of women's fiction. Debbie's books have appeared on every major best seller list, including those of the *New York Times*, *USA Today*, and *Publishers Weekly*. Her many honors include the recently presented "readers' choice" Quill Award. ■

For the last 16 years, I have been writing stories about love and life for a predominantly women's audience. Many of my readers write to me that they love to curl up with one of my books as a way to relax and leave the everyday world behind. I have my own favorite way to leave the world behind—and come back a better person. I discovered it 30 years ago when I took a chance and accepted an invitation.

I had never stepped inside a Protestant church in my life, so it was with some trepidation that I arrived at my first meeting of the Bible Study Fellowship. I had been raised Catholic, and although we read the Bible as part of the epistles and heard it as a part of the sermons at Mass, I had never sat down and just read a Bible. But I was in my early twenties and new to the area, and I wanted to be friends with the ladies in my neighborhood. So when a nice woman down the street invited me to join the group, I put my concerns aside. At the very least, I thought it would be something interesting and different to do.

At that first meeting, I found a chair in the meeting room in the basement of the church and introduced myself. As I had feared, I felt so uncomfortable just being in this church. Then the teacher stepped forward and introduced herself. To my surprise, her last name was Adler, my maiden name! It was as if God was saying to me, "You're home. This is family."

That day, the group was studying the book of Nehemiah in the Old Testament. I began reading it and found myself simply enjoying the richness and texture of God's words. But within a few meetings, I could tell that studying the Bible was having a deeper effect. Over time, it would have an overwhelming impact on my life, allowing me to feel a personal relationship with God.

Shortly after that first meeting, on the advice of one of my neighbors in the study group, my husband Wayne and I both attended a workshop at the church. The workshop focused on how the conflicts we have in our youth follow us into our adulthood. It was designed to help us integrate our Christianity with our everyday life. During the workshop, participants were asked if anyone would be willing to make a promise to read their Bible every day. I made that promise, and for the last 30 years I have kept it faithfully.

For many years, I read Bible verses—in no particular order—every day. Five years ago, I decided to start reading the Bible from cover to cover. I have read it through five times so far.

Right from the start, I noticed my feelings about God becoming stronger and stronger—it was like falling in love. And the more I learned about Him, the more grateful and cared-for I felt. Like most young people, I had a tendency to be self-centered, but over time, I gradually became more compassionate and more understanding of others.

I had a clear demonstration of this a few years later when my husband and I moved to a new area. We had a very difficult neighbor. I understand now that she had mental problems. At one point, we went through a terrible period when she felt I had done her some wrong. To this day, I can't imagine what it would have been. But whatever it was, she was determined to make our lives miserable. Every day for a week there was something. Our house was bombarded with raw eggs. Then our garbage was turned upside down in the street. I hung laundry out on the line and clothes turned up missing.

I called the police, but they couldn't do anything. We had no proof. I was so outraged. Our other neighbors had also had problems with her, so another woman on the block and I decided we would catch her in the act: We would dress up in camouflage and hide in the bushes, ready to leap out and confront her.

As I was getting ready to go, Wayne said to me, "You know how you always say that God is in control? Well, He's in control of this situation, too. Why don't you just let it rest with Him?"

He was right. What was I doing? I called my friend and said, "This is ridiculous. We can't do this." Then I sat down and started reading my Bible. But as we got ready for bed that night, I was still upset. I knew that there was probably going to be some incident, some new mess for me to clean up in the morning. I still felt so angry. I kept telling myself that I had to see this woman through God's eyes and love her through God's eyes. Finally I said, "Lord, I'm giving her to you. You take care of this situation."

At about 11 o'clock that night, after Wayne and I were both asleep, the phone rang. It was our difficult neighbor! She was calling to ask if my husband, who is an electrician, could help her. She said that their electricity had gone off, and they couldn't understand what was wrong. They had paid their bill and no one else was having a problem—they could see lights on in other houses in the neighborhood. My husband went over, and in a matter of about five minutes, he fixed it for her. We never had any problems with her again.

I have no doubt that if I hadn't been reading my Bible every day and doing my best to be the kind of person I felt God wanted me to be, I would have dealt with that situation entirely differently. Not only would I have tried to catch her red-handed, but I also would have retaliated—tried to hit back. Reading the Bible put my life in a much bigger context. I had an "alternative to self," and could look to someone else for better solutions to my problems.

To date, I have read five different versions of the Bible. Although I enjoy the different flavors of each, in essence they are all the same Bible—the same wonderful book that has given me a personal relationship with God, which I count as the most cherished and transformative thing in my life.

Last summer I was asked to speak at a conference that marked the twenty-fifth anniversary of the Romance Writers of America. I was very honored to be asked. When I sat down to write my speech, I knew that I wanted to convey, especially to young writers, the importance of the words we use. I wrote, "If we do our job correctly, the reader will feel what we feel. If we cry, they will cry. If we laugh, they will laugh. If we put our hearts out on the page, the reader's heart will link with ours."

The next morning when I opened my Bible, I realized this was just what God had done. He had put His words on the page so that we would know Him. He had laid His heart out there to connect with mine.

Arielle Ford

For more than 25 years, Arielle Ford has worked in nearly every aspect of public relations and marketing. Her clients have included nonprofit organizations, Fortune 500 companies, celebrities, world-class athletes, and even astronauts. For more than 15 years, Arielle has been the publicist for Deepak Chopra (whose career she is credited with launching) as well as for more than a dozen *New York Times* best-selling authors in the field of self-help, spirituality, and personal growth. She is the author of six books, including her most recent, *Everything You Should Know About Book Publishing, Publicity, Promotion & Building a Platform: A Step-by-Step Guide for Authors and Writers.* ■

In the autumn of 1984 I summoned my courage and did something I'd wanted to do for as long as I could remember: move to Los Angeles. It was a giant leap of faith, because I had visited Los Angeles only once before. Ever since that visit, though, I'd felt a strong magnetic pull to live there. So with very little money and no job prospects, I left South Florida, my home for all of my 31 years. I was exhilarated one moment, terrified the next, and I kept alternating rapidly back and forth between those two feelings throughout my first month on the West Coast.

I had only one friend in Los Angeles, Helen, but when I got there I found that she was busily packing to move to New York. That meant I had to find a place to live immediately. I found an apartment and got a job as a temp in a big public relations firm. The first three months went by in a blur. In between trying to keep up at work and trying not to get lost on my way home from work, my senses were on overload.

Unfortunately, the overload found its way onto my hips. I had been an avid jogger and fitness buff in Florida (as well as a former swimsuit model), but in L.A. the smog kept me from my usual workouts. Within a short time I gained 10 pounds. Soon the 10 became 20, and eventually my weight was up by 25 pounds. With the weight gain came the realization that I was depressed. And the more depressed I got, the more I comforted myself with chocolate.

I loved living in Los Angeles *and* I was constantly scared to death. Could I make it? Would I make it? What would happen to me if I lost my job? Would I end up pushing a grocery cart along the street, like so many of the homeless people I saw? Would I ever find a new group of friends? Would I get lost on the freeway and end up in a bad neighborhood? These thoughts ran through my head constantly. Only chocolate seemed to quiet the constant negative barrage of fear-filled thoughts.

One of my new friends, Stephen, suggested that I begin attending a weekly self-help group that he had found helpful. The groups were run by a psychologist named Esther, a sweet, grandmotherly type of woman whom I came to adore. I eventually began going to Esther for one-on-one counseling sessions. One day she gave me a gift. It was a book entitled *Key to Yourself*, by Dr. Venice Bloodworth. I opened the book and read a few lines. Instantly, I felt a shiver run up and down my spine and I got goose bumps. As I stood there, reading line after line of this magical book, the dark cloud of depression and fear I had been living under began to dissipate. I could feel layers of my old self—my anxiety about my future, my agitation and discomfort—peeling away until what was left was something I barely comprehended at first—the real me. This was my true self: optimistic, dynamic, and directed. As I continued to read, this experience intensified, and I had the overwhelming feeling that my life finally made sense and had purpose. It seemed to me that with this knowledge, I now had access to creating the life of my dreams.

Key to Yourself became my personal bible. I read parts of the book nearly every day. I highlighted passages, dog-eared many pages, and carried it with me everywhere. Every time I read that book, I felt the presence of more light around me. I began to put into action the things I learned. I began working out again and to my great amazement even cut down on my chocolate habit.

The concept in *Key to Yourself* that really changed my life was this: *thoughts are things*—the thoughts you think create the reality you live in. At that point in my life this insight was the most amazing thing I had ever learned. It turned everything in my world upside down . . . or maybe I should say it turned it right side up. I realized I had always focused on what I didn't want. Now, it became possible to change my thinking so I focused on what I *did* want.

My favorite line from the book became: "Decree a thing and it will be established unto you." The book also says not to tell the Universe how your desires should manifest, but to be open to be surprised by unusual delivery channels. I began to make decrees in every area of my life.

Over the course of the next year I lost the 25 pounds I had gained, I found a full-time job that really suited me, I made new friends, and best of all, began to trust in myself and the Universe. My fears of becoming a bag lady permanently disappeared. I bought dozens of copies of *Key to Yourself* for my friends and family. My sister, Debbie, who went on to become a highly successful workshop leader and best-selling author, found it to be as useful and important as I did. We both credit this book as the start of our search for spiritual and personal growth.

Expanding on the concept that thoughts are things, the book explains that thought is actually the only reality, and that the conditions of your life are the outward manifestations of thought. If you take this idea seriously and practice it sincerely, you become able to influence your health, your happiness, and your prosperity. If you are manifesting any undesirable condition, you simply change your ideas and a new set of conditions begin to appear. I applied this principle to everything in my life. It even worked on my chocolate issue! I changed my idea that chocolate makes me fat, and to this day I enjoy chocolate regularly without suffering "weighty" consequences.

The author of *Key to Yourself* also recommends that part of each day be spent in silence. I began to practice this, and the results were so amazing that I have continued to enjoy a period of silent meditation each day since then.

More than 20 years later, the lessons I learned from *Key to Yourself* are still with me. I begin each day with a meditation. I often decree what I want to have happen (though I still have trouble *not* telling the Universe how it *should* happen). I feel that my life's direction is my own hands, depending on the thoughts I choose to entertain.

Would I recommend this book to everyone? You bet. Because as the author says: "It does not matter what your present condition may be, it rests with you to change it and have your future be exactly what you would have it be. We are entirely responsible for our success or failure, happiness or misery."

If you're like me, you can benefit from hearing those wise words every day of your life.

Michael Toms

Michael Toms has been exploring personal, social, and spiritual transformation through his work as an electronic journalist, editor, and writer for more than 25 years. He is the founding president of New Dimensions Foundation, cofounder of New Dimensions Radio, and CEO of the New Dimensions World Broadcasting Network. He also serves as the executive producer and principal host of the award-winning *New Dimensions* internationally syndicated radio series. Michael was an editor of *The Inner Edge*, the newsletter for enlightened business practice, and is the best-selling author of *A Time for Choices: Deep Dialogues for Deep Democracy, At the Leading Edge*, and *An Open Life: Joseph Campbell in Conversation with Michael Toms* and coauthor of *True Work: Doing What You Love and Loving What You Do.* ▪

As a child, I was the bane of the nuns at my Catholic school. A rebel, I constantly posed thorny questions, such as "How could God, who is so loving, condemn anyone to eternal damnation?" Or "Why would babies who hadn't been baptized not go to heaven?" The nuns' answers never satisfied my voracious need to understand the basics of life. It seemed to me that like their clothing, the sisters' "mental habits" tended toward black and white as well! Still, I kept speaking up—wanting to know, wanting my questions to be heard.

I found powerful validation for my inquisitive nature when I was in sixth grade. Visiting the library near my home in Arlington, Virginia, one day, I was drawn to a leather-bound volume of Dante's *Inferno*. I pulled it from the shelf and sat at the wooden library table, engrossed in

Dante's words. Despite the sophistication of the language, I could tell that he was asking the same questions I was—even going as far as attacking the church! It struck a chord in me, strengthening my quest for the truth and real answers. It taught me that it was important to pay attention to my thoughts and feelings, especially the ones that gave rise to questions about reality.

I went on to attend a Jesuit prep school. Here was an intellectually lively environment where my questions were finally welcomed. At the beginning of my time there, when I was just 14, I happened on a book that took the message I had received from Dante's *Inferno* one step further. I was looking around in a drugstore one day when my eye was caught by a paperback titled *The Creative Process*, edited by Brewster Ghiselin. It was a collection of essays and articles by a variety of people, both current and historical: Yeats, Einstein, Housman, and Jung, among others. I opened it to a chapter and began reading Henry Miller's essay, "Reflections on Writing."

It was as if the hand of God came through the roof and hit me—I could not have been more struck by the words I was reading. Miller wrote about the importance of finding one's own authentic voice, using the styles and influences of others as guides, but searching for the expression that is original and wholly your own. My passion for making sense of the world around me had found a new dimension. Not only did I need to come to my own conclusions about life but I also needed to express them in my own unique way.

Dante had set the stage for this startling realization, and now Miller—whoever he was, for I had never heard of Henry Miller before that day—was pushing me to find my own destiny through the discovery of my authentic voice. I had no idea what that voice was, but I knew that I wanted to find it.

In 1954, when this event occurred, paperback books cost very little. I handed over a quarter and left the store with *The Creative Process* tucked safely into a brown paper bag. I was on my way . . . somewhere. Looking back, I see that this book set me on the journey that eventually evolved into my life's work.

As time passed, I remained an avid reader. I found inspiration in a variety of books, including Will Durant's *Pleasures of Philosophy* (originally titled *The Mansions of Philosophy*) and James Boswell's *Life of Johnson*. Each book added a piece to the puzzle I was working on—the puzzle of where I was going with my life, what was important to me, what I wanted to *do*.

When I was 19, my father died. The time for philosophy and purely intellectual pursuits was at an end. I stopped being a full-time college student, enrolled in night school, and by day, started training as a salesman. The job itself was interesting; I threw myself into it and began the climb up the corporate ladder. During this time of my life, I was not actively seeking to know my inner voice. Instead, engrossed in the information and systems I was learning, I enjoyed absorbing the technical expertise of the men around me. It was gratifying to accomplish so much and feel my competence grow. What was even better was the opportunity for travel that came with my work.

By the time I was 24, I was managing other salespeople and was based in the West, spending a lot of my time in San Francisco. In the sixties, San Francisco was a "yeasty" place, and I was exposed to a lot of culture and ideas that ran counter to the materialistic direction my life was heading. At one point a friend of mine asked me: "What are you doing in this job?" I thought about it long and hard but didn't have an answer at that point.

So while the question of my true direction in life simmered on the back burner, I continued working, traveling, and playing the role of the up-and-coming business executive. My sales territory expanded, and I began dividing my time between Las Vegas, San Francisco, Palm Springs, and San Bernardino. During that time, I met a young woman and we became engaged to be married. Surprisingly, it was this relationship that catapulted me back onto the path I had started to walk in that drugstore in Alexandria almost 14 years earlier.

Our wedding date was set, the arrangements had been made, the invitations had been sent. We were going to be married in a distinctly individual ceremony in Muir Woods in February of 1968. In December of 1967, back in San Bernardino after a visit to San Francisco to see my fiancée, I awoke one night with a start from one of those dreams that feel so real—in this one, my fiancée was telling me she didn't want to get married. Relieved that it was only a dream, I was still upset and couldn't go back to sleep. I began to clean the house as I listened to Beethoven's Ninth Symphony—anything to stop thinking about my nightmare. At 8:00 AM, just as the Chorale was reaching a crescendo, the phone rang. Instantly, I knew it was her—and I knew what she was going to say.

I was heartbroken. The weeks that followed were dark and deeply emotional. I wrote pages and pages of letters to my ex-fiancée, pouring out my heart to her. It was obviously cathartic, but it was more than that. I explored my feelings, thoughts, everything I had experienced up to that point. Despite the pain I was in, I began to feel the power of being connected to myself again. I was hearing my inner voice and pouring it out onto the page. I went as deep as I could, and then I remember one night simply surrendering, giving it all up and just sending out a plea: *Help me out here. . . .*

The next day I walked into a bookstore and found a book that seemed custom-made for me. Reading Albert Ellis's *A Guide to Rational Living*, I felt my despair begin to lift. Ellis pointed me toward a more useful, constructive way of being in touch with my innermost thoughts and feelings. It was the just the first in a long line of books that I read during that period—many of them about spirituality, Eastern philosophy, and religion—that brought me to a new understanding of my life, who I was, what I had to say, and what I wanted to do.

Within a few weeks, I was clear that I didn't want to work as a sales manager anymore. My rise to the heights of the corporate firmament was over. I resigned, much to the dismay of my colleagues and the executives at the company. They just couldn't understand me. No one believed that I was taking a personal sabbatical—time off to find myself. They were sure I had found a sweeter deal somewhere else and did their best to woo me back, offering me more money, more perks, better titles. I looked around and realized that every one of them was a company man—not one had ever done what I was about to do. And I saw where it had led them: no family life, no time for other interests. I wasn't interested.

I knew then that I was making progress. To stand up and say, "No more; this is not for me," even though I had no idea where I was going next, was a major milestone on the journey to find my own authentic voice.

Around that same time, I began to discover I had an inner knowing, a silent guidance that I could rely on when faced with decisions and choices. The more I trusted this guidance, the more automatic it became, and the next years of my life were marked by a continuous awareness of this inner knowing. I was led by my own promptings to relocate to San Francisco, find an apartment, find a job. All perfectly natural things to do, but it was the complete spontaneity and peace I felt while doing them that set them apart. During this period, I even returned to the world of marketing, starting the first Direct Response Marketing agency west of Chicago. I made a success of it, yet the whole time I knew that it wasn't my life's work. Even so, I trusted that I was moving in the right direction.

The weekend I met my future wife, I had turned down an invitation to go out of town with friends—I had *known* that something was going to happen.

Justine and I hit it off immediately, but it was months before we became a couple. Then, one evening, Justine came over to see me, to discuss questions she was having about her spiritual life. She was a Jehovah's Witness at the time and only wanted to talk about her version of the Bible. I reached behind me and pulled a copy of the Jehovah's Witness New World Translation of the Bible from my bookshelf, saying, "You mean this one?" We talked late into the night, comparing interpretations of Bible passages. I found myself beginning sentences over and over again with "Yes, but how about looking at it this way . . ."

That night was another turning point for me. Thus far in my life, I had made great strides in *listening* to my inner voice. Now, I felt that I was finally *expressing* that uniquely personal voice. My talent for looking at an idea from all sides and articulating all the possibilities found fulfillment in our shared exploration of our fundamental beliefs.

Nine months after that conversation, Justine and I began New Dimensions Foundation and created the radio program *New Dimensions*, which soon began broadcasting nationally on the National Public Radio flagship station KQED-FM in San Francisco. Today, more than 30 years later, we describe New Dimensions World Broadcasting Network on our Web site as "uncommon wisdom for unconventional times" and "a voice for positive change in the culture." Every week I get to interview one of the greatest thinkers of our time and explore the deepest questions, issues, and mysteries facing humankind.

Since that long-ago day when I first read Miller's essay, I have read every one of his books, as well as hundreds of other books by a wide variety of authors about consciousness, spirituality, and philosophy. My long and often roundabout quest for the complete expression of my own voice—inspired by the chance reading of a single work—has led me to initiate dialogues that, according to our listeners, have awakened, inspired, and transformed many lives.

Not a bad value for a quarter.

Bob Young

Bob Young is one of the most influential figures in the success of Linux and open-source software—computer software whose source code is made available to the public so all users can participate in its development. He cofounded Red Hat Inc. with Mark Ewing in 1993, helping to turn Linux into a household name. After being involved with Red Hat for more than 12 years, first as CEO and then as a member of the board of directors, Bob left Red Hat to found Lulu.com, a site that allows content creators and owners to bring work directly to market without surrendering control of their intellectual property. ▪

I was never much of a student—a C was a good grade for me—but reading was always fun. In fact, the only honor ever given to me in high school was being chosen as a student librarian. Usually the position of student librarian had to be applied for, but apparently I had checked out more books from the school library than any other kid in the entire school. The teacher who ran the library said, "The least you can do, if you're going to be constantly pulling books off the shelves, is to put them back on the shelves."

Because I was a shy, unathletic kid, my life was pretty quiet. But being bored wasn't fun, and to avoid it, I'd daydream. Books are really useful for getting some color into daydreams. If you don't read, you have the same daydream over and over again, but the more you read, the more channels you have on your internal "daydream TiVo." Reading and daydreaming were my ways of escaping the dull, regimented life of school.

I remember checking out *Don Quixote*, by Cervantes, even though it wasn't required reading, simply because I was curious about the guy who "tilted at windmills," which I knew meant to fight for causes that others think are imaginary or not worth fighting for. How could a book written hundreds of years ago in Spain have produced one of the English language's more interesting expressions?

I don't read quickly and tend to read a number of books at once—the boredom factor again—so it took me a while to finish its thousand pages. Like many things in life, there was no way of knowing at the time the significant effect *Don Quixote* would have on me. Cervantes wrote the book in 1605 as a satire on contemporary books about romantic chivalry. Apparently, that was a big theme in Spanish literature at the time and he was poking fun at it, yet he wrote about Don Quixote with a great deal of affectionate sympathy. One gets the sense that the author identified with the comical hero he'd created. Don Quixote was grossly incompetent, often doing more harm than good in spite of his noble intentions, and was clearly a daydreamer. (He seemed to have a large number of channels on his daydream TiVo, too.) What jumped out almost immediately was that Cervantes's crazy knight, who never stopped trying even though he always failed, came across as a very likable, even admirable, buffoon.

I reflected on how this applied to my own experience at school. Only a limited number of people can be really good students and be at the top of the class. That's just the nature of competition. For every person who's at the top in the class, there has to be someone who's at the bottom. In theory, you'd worry about the people in the bottom half of the class, because they're constantly being told for 16 years (assuming they go to university) that they're not very talented. How could they ever have the confidence in themselves to be successful? And in fact, I had sometimes worried about my future prospects in light of my mediocre academic performance. Yet after reading *Don Quixote*, it was clear that continuing to go for it—*especially* if you weren't an A student—was the only way to even stay in the running. In short, one has to play to win.

Over the years, I've seen the truth of this. More often than not, the people who have actually made huge successes of their lives are the ones who definitely weren't at the top of their class. Yet, they're the people buying the $5 million condos on the beach in Florida.

The reality, one could argue, is that academic ability is just one factor in success. So much else comes into play, such as persistence and hard work—the early bird really does get the worm and the turtle frequently does win the race. The Don Quixote world view is that huge benefits come from just showing up and being there to learn new things and benefit from the fortunate things that may happen. To succeed, you have to be ready and willing to seize the opportunities that come along.

After graduating from university, I decided to start my own typewriter rental business, mainly so my business card would read "Bob Young, President." My mother, who had been worried about her ne'er-do-well son who couldn't get a good grade to save his life, was very impressed with my title, even though I was the executive of a business without any customers or revenue. But with my résumé, no one else was going to give me an interesting job, so it was up to me to think big and create my own high-risk enterprise.

What I found was that although you might not be a genius, if—like Don Quixote—you put yourself out there, tilt at windmills, take on adventures, and are risk tolerant, good things will happen to you. Or at the very least, interesting things will happen to you.

Experience has shown me that taking risks has specific advantages. One, you learn things faster than the people who don't take risks. Two, you have a broader range of experiences. Three, you bump into more obstacles sooner than the people who play it safe, and, four, you learn to get around those obstacles. So it's not that you're smarter than the other guys; you just get a better education—quicker.

To be successful in business—especially in the computer industry, where there are so many brilliant people—I had to take *more* risks than the other guys took, because if we both played it safe, they were going to win. I might not win doing wild and crazy things, but at least I'd give myself a chance.

This kind of risk-taking has worked out well for me. There's an example of this that they still talk about at Red Hat. When we were first starting the company, I remember sitting at a table with my partner Mark, considering our options. We had taken free products, including the Linux open-source code, which anyone could download, and made them into the Red Hat operating system, basically the same way General Motors assembles cars out of parts.

The question was: How do you make money selling, in effect, a free commodity? In our case, we knew that if we could make our operating system popular, we could be very successful providing support, upgrades, and other services for it. But we needed money now to pay the rent; could we wait that long for income? Mark felt we had no choice but to charge people up front for it, even though the parts were free.

But I felt we had to give it away—and completely, with no requirement that they buy anything from us. It was a gamble, but it seemed to me the more broadly we could get people to use Red Hat, the more popular it would become and the more enthusiastically everyone would come back to us to buy products and services—especially the big Fortune 500 companies. It wasn't easy convincing him, but my partner eventually agreed to give our software away and trust that the big companies would very quickly require a reliable, trusted partner to provide a support system with an 800 number and techs—and would hire us to do that.

And that's exactly how the thing has played out. Today Red Hat sells multimillion-dollar contracts to major global financial corporations, despite the fact that these global corporations can download the current version of our software at no cost. These corporations understand full well that an operating system is an evolving piece of technology that every year will need to do new and better things than it did the year before. The real challenge for them isn't making the operating system work today; it's knowing that it will work for the new projects they'll have coming out 12 months from now.

Nowadays, this seems obvious, but it took quite a leap of faith at the time. In the early years, a lot of people took me aside and put a figurative arm around my shoulder, saying, "What you're doing is really fascinating, Bob, but I hate to break it to you—you can't make any money in the software business if you give away your software."

This was a case where doing things differently looked crazy, like tilting at windmills. But it was only by doing things differently that we figured out what did and didn't work.

My quixotic notion at that table over 10 years ago was inspired by insights taken from Cervantes. Don Quixote might have been deluded and even dead wrong as he mistook country girls for princesses and windmills for threatening giants, but he threw himself into every endeavor with all the passion and conviction he had. He'd take any risk to do what he felt was right, and that gave me the confidence to do the same. Over time, as a member of a small team going up against giant corporations, I've come to look at risk as an asset. If, as an entrepreneur, you aren't taking a chance on a different way of doing things, you're almost certain to fail. The big, established competitors are always going to be able to do things the conventional way better than you can. And besides, doing business this way is a lot more interesting.

The success of Red Hat fulfilled most of the goals I'd set out to achieve upon leaving university in 1976. Knowing that, my wife Nancy was recently kidding me, questioning why I was working so hard at Lulu. I gave it some thought and had to laugh at the answer: Cervantes's script still applies. Lulu is trying to do for the publishing industry what Red Hat did for the software industry—give users more control of the technology available. To me, the current multibillion-dollar publishing industry sure looks like a great windmill, or giant, to tilt at.

Craig Newmark

Craig Newmark is the founder of www.craigslist.org, a phenomenally successful Web site offering local community classifieds and forums to 190 cities in all 50 U.S. states and 35 countries—all for free, and in a relatively noncommercial environment. Every month, more than 10 million people use the site, and more than 6 million classified ads are placed. Founded in 1995, craigslist calls itself "a place to find jobs, housing, goods & services, social activities, a girlfriend or boyfriend, advice, community information, and just about anything else." ▪

I never wanted to call it craigslist. What started as a little list of places to go and things to do in San Francisco has grown into an effective international Internet "bulletin board." It's somewhat embarrassing, but I'm getting over it. I wanted to call it s-f happenings, but my friends all told me calling it craigslist would help to make the Internet seem more person-to-person and less intimidating, which was one of the purposes of my sending out the list in the first place.

In 1995, most people were still unfamiliar and uncomfortable with personal computers. The whole online phenomenon was just beginning, and the Internet was primarily used by computer types like me (who had grown up wearing a plastic pocket protector and thick black glasses taped together—the full nerd cliché).

At that time, I worked for the Charles Schwab investment firm, and my major contribution was to evangelize the Internet as a way for brokerages to do business. I quickly saw that the Internet could be used for so much more. I observed a lot of people helping each other out, and I figured I should do a little of that.

And so I started my list and sent it around. At first I just listed cool events, usually involving arts and technology. Then people asked for more stuff, such as job or housing postings, though at that time we weren't posting—it was just e-mails. Craigslist actually started as a little bitty e-mail list. People wanted more, so I did it. People wanted a little bit more and I did that. Soon I had too many people to send e-mails to, and I had to create a Web site: www.craiglist.org was born.

People often ask me about my decision to make the list free. At craigslist there is no charge to post anything (except employers' and apartment brokers' listings), and it is noncommercial—there is no advertising, especially banner ads. Doing this meant that I personally walked away from millions of dollars. That sounds like a hard choice to make, but people forget that I didn't start craigslist to make money; I was working at another job that paid me enough money to live comfortably and buy all the gadgets I wanted. Since craigslist started out free, the big decision was whether to charge anyone at all. We mean it at the site when we say we "give people a break." Some things, I decided, shouldn't be about money, and craigslist was one of them.

Craigslist had been up and running for about five years when I started hearing about a book called *The Cluetrain Manifesto*. It was written by four guys who each had written things on their own that I considered very intelligent. *The Cluetrain Manifesto* took my own deeply felt sense of what was true about the Internet and put it into words—concise and powerful words. In the first chapter, one of the authors, Christopher Locke, says that he believes the Internet has the power to finally make businesses "human" again. Just like ancient marketplaces, he says, the Internet is full of the sound of everyday life: voices in conversation. He, along with the other authors of the book, describes the Internet as "the great conversation"—a gargantuan international party line that belongs to the people who use it.

Reading the book made me consciously realize what craigslist was about. These ideas perfectly mirrored my own intentions for the site, reaffirming and strengthening them. The book validated what we had done so far and cemented my decisions for the future. I wanted to keep craigslist human: a big network of people helping each other out. From the beginning, craigslist has always been about the people who use the site—not about the people who run it.

The authors of *The Cluetrain Manifesto* have a lot to say about businesses that are not responding to the changes taking place all around them. If businesses aren't in touch with the people they are serving, they won't survive. In fact, the title comes from a quote about a firm in free fall from its position in the Fortune 500: "The clue train stopped there four times a day for ten years and they never took delivery." I decided I wouldn't let craigslist miss the clue train. So after reading the book, I made a commitment to stay directly connected to the people who use the site and became a full-time customer service rep at my company.

Over the years, craigslist has remained true to my original vision. It's really fairly simple. Basically, our customers run our site, and they do so by posting, by flagging, and by telling us what should be on the site. We get a lot of suggestions; we figure out which ones make sense and then we do them. Sometimes we're not perfect. There are flaws, but things work out.

I think the basic rule at craigslist is the Golden Rule. The one most people learn as kids—in my case I learned it simply by growing up in the family I did. Practicing the Golden Rule is not a big deal: It's just the right thing to do. Yet, reading *Cluetrain*, which emphasized the human dimension of all Internet applications, made me see how genuinely important this view was. I wanted to practice it in my business, as well as in the rest of my life.

There is a Jewish concept called *tikkun olom*, which is Hebrew for "fixing the world." It's a form of charity, of helping those in need. Craigslist was a vehicle to do that, and over the years, as the community spirit grew, we saw expressions of kindness and caring happening in small ways every day.

Then, after Hurricane Katrina in 2005, we witnessed it on a large scale. Within hours of the hurricane hitting land, we noticed that there was a surge of traffic on our New Orleans site. We saw that people were making use of craigslist to help find relatives, to offer people housing and, later on, to offer people jobs. Initially, we decided that we should stay out of people's way, let them use the site as they needed and simply try to accommodate them. We added resources that made sense, such as links for Katrina relief and support, and we also created a Baton Rouge site.

Many moving stories were posted after each of the big hurricanes of 2005, but I remember one particular posting after Katrina that was a good example of the way craigslist was of service to people in need. It was dated September 6, 2005; the subject was "Success Story":

> *Out of desperation, I posted with the utmost doubt that this list would help. Within 72 hours I received notice from a reader who knew the exact location of my parents. To make the success even more incredible, my parents are deaf and don't really use the internet. Posting this request for info seemed futile. Thanks to CraigsList, one more family has been reunited. Many tears of joy are being shed tonight. It has been a rough time for us. Thank you soooooooooooooo much CraigsList. THANK YOU THANK YOU THANK YOU!!!!!!!!!!!!!!!!!!!!!!!!!!!!!!!*

When I read things like this, it's clear that craigslist has become a community service site in the most simple, human way possible—through people talking to people and helping each other directly. The great conversation of the Internet described in *Cluetrain* as "unpredictable, messy and uncontrollable" is now allowing an unimaginably large number of people to interact every day. Like the authors, I believe this is a good thing and people will usually end up serving each other well, for my 10 years at craigslist have confirmed my belief that the overwhelming majority of people are trustworthy and good.

Kate Ludeman

In 1988, Kate Ludeman, Ph.D., founded Worth Ethic Corporation, which provides coaching and team building to senior executives in major corporations, such as Adecco, Amgen, the Gap, Dell, eBay, FDIC, KLA-Tencor, Microsoft, and the Red Sox. Kate has written five books, including *Alpha Male Syndrome*, a book about alpha males in the workplace. ■

Over the course of my career, I've learned that when the going gets tough, this tough woman . . . takes a bubble bath. It was during an unusually long, hot bath in 1984 that I read a book that transformed my life.

It was a cold, gray Sunday afternoon in February and I was still recovering from a terrible work meeting I'd led the previous Thursday. Just a month earlier, I had taken a position as Vice President of Human Resources at a Silicon Valley high-tech firm. The corporate culture at my new firm was competitive, analytical and, frankly, intimidating. One member of the executive team was a retired military officer, and every one of them was a dominant alpha-male type. The company had never had a woman in middle management, let alone an executive. Remember, this was over 20 years ago, and the world was different. To intensify the challenges, I was also the first professional human resources (HR) leader they had ever hired—up until this point in their growth, the CEO's former executive assistant had performed all HR functions.

Going into the position, I had inherited a significant compensation problem and had called a meeting with the management team to discuss the salary demands the engineers had presented to me in no uncertain terms. I told our top managers that we had to come up with a pool of several million dollars to stay competitive salary-wise. If we didn't, I was convinced many of our most valuable engineers would walk across the street to a competitor and immediately get a 50% salary increase. To ensure that the engineers felt the new funds would be distributed fairly, I recommended that everyone agree to follow a loosely structured compensation system.

The ensuing uproar wasn't pleasant. Each man tried to out-shout the others to recount his own nightmare story about a rotten HR manager rigidly following compensation guidelines, to his detriment. The general consensus, based on their own past experiences, was that like most HR leaders, I didn't know anything. First, I was too eager to give away their hard-earned dollars; I wasn't being firm enough with the employees and looking out for the company's bottom line. Second, I was attempting to turn this open corporate culture into a bureaucracy on par with the government. Angered by their aggressive, attacking tone, I matched their intensity, and at my worst moment, loudly told them all to shut up. The disastrous meeting finally ended with an agreement to meet in a week to resolve the issue.

I was shaken by the intensity of the meeting, which felt like a clear low point in my career. At the previous two companies where I'd worked, I had been *adored*! No one had ever yelled at me, and certainly no one had ever questioned my competence. I was convinced I had made a huge mistake in joining this company; I felt sure that they would have never treated a male executive in that way. I knew I had to get my act together and turn this thing around.

That Sunday afternoon, as I ran a bath, I looked glumly through the bookcases in the furnished house I was renting during my relocation, for a book to read in the tub. I found a small volume by Gay Hendricks titled *Learning to Love Yourself*. Although I had never heard of Gay Hendricks, I thought to myself, *I can certainly use that!*

I climbed into the tub, slipped into the blessedly hot water thick with bubbles, and opened the book. Within five minutes, I knew I had stumbled on something important. And as it turned out, the key to creating a happy life as well as satisfying work and career success resided in those pages.

I stayed in the bathtub for well over three hours and read the entire book. I had to refill the tub with hot water several times and even got out at one point to get a notebook and pen, so I could complete the numerous exercises in the book, which helped me uncover many self-limiting beliefs that operated beyond my awareness.

As I did the exercises, I realized that I'd wasted a lot of energy focusing on what I couldn't control. I couldn't control my gender, and I couldn't control whether people treated me differently as a woman. So long as I put my attention on those issues, I was focusing on the changes I wished *other people* would make. This heightened my stress, because inside I had little confidence that these changes would occur.

Another exercise asked me to think about an issue I was facing, and then to ask the question "How does this feel familiar?" Naturally I chose the compensation dilemma. Recalling the horrible meeting, I immediately was transported to my summers as a child, where I struggled to fit into the large pack of neighborhood boys. I tried to push my way in, but none of the boys wanted the girl to go with them. I desperately wanted to prove I was just as good as they were at collecting arrowheads, climbing trees, and riding horseback, and I was frustrated and hurt that they wouldn't include me. Looking back, I realized that I had been very one-dimensional in my approach. I had attempted to become a part of their group by being nice and by becoming as skillful as they were. When that didn't work, I withdrew into my own world and read a book. I realized that up until that moment, I had been following exactly the same pattern, including reading the book!

I saw that I needed to create a new type of acceptance and a new method for pursuing it. I combined what I'd learned from the two exercises: I put my attention on what I could control, how I communicated, and what actions I took, and I began to wonder how some of those powerful men got what they wanted. Instead of seeing my challenge as a gender issue that left me feeling resentful and somewhat victimized, I redefined the problem as something I could solve. I realized I needed more sophisticated people-influencing skills.

I read on, stopping often to reflect and complete the exercises. I was surprised at the power of this little book. I wasn't a stranger to the self-help world. I had a Ph.D. in psychology and had done a lot of reading and inner work. And yet I still had a lot of learning ahead of me.

The hardest exercise in the book turned out to be the most constructive in planning my approach to the upcoming meeting. I was instructed to "take something I don't like and love it just the way it is." I thought of the meeting that had gone haywire, and mentally surrounded it with the same quality of love I felt for my daughter. While I was doing this, I began to smile and feel happy. As my anxiety dropped, my creativity surged. Ideas began to bubble up, and I saw that what each of the senior executives really wanted was to be fully listened to, so his own money issues could be healed.

When I got out of the tub, I was as wrinkled as a prune but thoroughly exhilarated. I had a plan that I knew would create a breakthrough. The very next morning, I called on each of the executives separately. I listened to their concerns, heard their "HR horror story," and forged individual connections. It turned out that the disastrous meeting was really a blessing in disguise, as my recovery strategy gave me an opportunity to lay the foundation for a solid relationship with each of them.

Our second meeting was a high point in my career. Mrs. Fields Cookies was just taking off at that time, so before the meeting, I placed a platter of three dozen of her best chocolate-chip cookies in the center of the conference room table. I opened the meeting by making light of the debacle of a week ago, saying that at the last meeting they had thrown "rotten tomatoes" at me and at each other. I had gotten hit by some of them, and so if they were going to throw anything today, it was going to be cookies. "But," I continued, "I hope that you will eat some first and sweeten your dispositions a little bit."

The men had come in "loaded for bear," but my lighthearted, humorous approach disarmed them completely—as did the knowledge that I knew their concerns and history from our personal interviews together. I felt so much more confident . . . and they also felt more confident in me.

The tool from *Learning to Love Yourself* that helped me the most—and has continued to help me throughout my life since then—is a technique called deep belly breathing. Just before the meeting started, I took a breathing break for two or three minutes that left me feeling centered, calm, and confident. I didn't have a lot of anxiety about how my plan was going to be received. I just knew that it was going to work.

And it did work. They actually created a bigger pool of money for leveling salaries than I had asked for because *they* felt confident that the money needed to be spent. I had figured out how to give them the information they needed, and it gave me credibility with them. That meeting launched me to a whole new level at work; it integrated me into the company. Before, I had been the person everyone was testing; now I was someone they respected.

I had thought that I was strong—like steel—but in reading *Learning to Love Yourself*, I learned that I was more like a colander: I might have looked steely, but I was full of holes that were allowing my power and forcefulness to escape.

The book also gave me a mantra that I used at work for many years: *I want to be respected, not liked.* I focused on developing the tough-minded, pragmatic, and analytical side of myself rather than the charming, understanding and compassionate side I had already mastered. I saw that my usual MO was not going to cut it and could actually be a drawback; what I needed to do was to project a much more competent business persona that also reflected my style as a woman. As time went on, I found that I enjoyed being assertive and powerful. Using what I learned from this book I've worked with more than a thousand executives, including a hundred senior-level women, to discover new ways to leverage their strengths.

Over the last 20 years, I have bought hundreds of copies of *Learning to Love Yourself* to give to friends and business colleagues, because of the almost miraculous effects I experienced after reading it. Even if you aren't "in hot water," this little book truly has the power to change the way you look at yourself and others.

Amilya Antonetti

Amilya Antonetti left a flourishing corporate career to take on the multibillion-dollar corporate giants in the cleaning industry. Today, Amilya's Soapworks, a line of hypoallergenic, nontoxic cleaning products, are distributed in both America and Canada. Amilya is the author of *Why David Hated Tuesdays: One Courageous Mother's Guide to Keeping Your Family Toxin and Allergy Free* and *The Broken Cookie Syndrome: Your Life Can Be More Than Crumbs*. Her story has been featured on *Oprah*, *Extra*, and *The Early Show* as well as in *Time*, *People*, and *Entrepreneur* magazines. ■

My childhood was a struggle, marked by constant challenge. My father, fresh off the boat from Italy, and my mother, only one generation removed, worked hard, chasing the American Dream. I had my own dreams of leaving my mark on the world, but my parents considered me a foolish child with unrealistic notions. Growing up, I was told repeatedly that people who do important things in life go to Harvard, to MIT. The message was " 'Those people' will change the world, but not you." I was just a young girl of immigrant parents, with lofty ideas. They hoped I would snap out of it and marry well. But I kept saying, "Well, I want to be one of 'those people.' " And inside—somehow—I knew I could be.

In spite of the discouragement I received growing up, I always had an inner guide, a sense that I knew where I was going, even though I usually couldn't articulate it to others. People would say to me, "How do you know?" and I'd say, "I just do. I know this is the right way to go." Unfortunately, I haven't always been brave enough to follow this inner guide.

Life with my family was difficult. I didn't think it could get any worse, but when I was 17, my mother, always troubled by depression, committed suicide. I left home, determined to leave the negativity behind and test my own instincts. I still felt I could find the path to greatness, even though the big fancy college I'd always dreamed of was not in my deck of cards. I had no road map but charged full steam ahead anyway, working hard and learning from my mistakes and successes.

At first, I dabbled in entrepreneurial projects, but after a while, I felt I needed to understand the inner workings of corporate giants. I wanted to find out how they were achieving success and what their shortcomings were. In this way I hoped to learn what I believed others had already learned from attending universities. Taking jobs at the biggest companies that would hire me, including Siemens, MCI, and AT&T, I did well. I broke records in sales, received awards, and was promoted to positions usually filled by people who were much older than I—and who wore pants, not skirts.

Although I am grateful for all the experience I gained in corporate America, it was not an easy time. It felt all too familiar: I wasn't taken seriously because of my age, gender, and lack of education. In addition, my high energy, coupled with my constant questioning of procedures, was a challenge to the people in management above me. I was told repeatedly that "this is the way it's always been done," and I found the constraints on my creativity frustrating. I was puzzled by how these corporate giants stayed on top and continued to succeed. Despite my achievements, I felt empty and unheard. I didn't feel that I was making a difference.

Once again, I saw that I had to follow my own guidance in order to succeed. I couldn't let the voices around me drown out the voice inside. It was right around this time that I found a book that illuminated this truth and strengthened my conviction about it.

In 1993, *The Alchemist*, by Paulo Coelho, appeared in my life and became a touchstone for me, a reminder that my journey was my own to travel. I was sitting in someone's office at AT&T when I saw it lying on the desk. The title intrigued me. I had never heard the word *alchemist* before and had no idea what it meant. (I later learned that alchemists were the precursors to modern scientists and tried to find a way to turn metal into gold.) I asked, "Can I have this?" and my colleague said, "Sure.

Somebody left it here. Take it." I didn't know why I wanted it, but I followed my inner prompting and took it home and read it.

The book tells the story of a young man, a lowly shepherd, who dreams of living a life of great purpose. People keep telling him, "Your purpose is to tend sheep." Some even become angry, asking him what's wrong with being a "just a shepherd." But he sees himself as more. When he shares his dream of crossing the desert to find the Egyptian pyramids, people think he is crazy. Feeling lonely and alienated from the others in his village, he decides to set out on his journey despite what others think. He doesn't know how he's going to get through the desert, but he knows how to take the first step, so he starts. Along the way, the shepherd meets many people, including an alchemist who becomes his greatest teacher.

The author presents many lessons in this seemingly simple fable, but the one that stood out for me is that every person is on a journey, and the omens, as the author calls them, or signposts, for the journey can be seen only by that person. Other people can't see them because it's not their path. The journey and the choices made by the traveler may not make sense to anyone else, but that doesn't mean they aren't valid.

The first time I read the book, I hung onto every word, highlighting sentences and writing in the margins. It validated everything I believed in about the need to be directed from within. For the same reason, it was a challenging book for me to read. Could it really be true that I should listen to myself? Trust myself? Even if my hunches went against prevailing wisdom and accepted authorities?

Not long after I read *The Alchemist*, I put aside all thoughts of business success and making my mark on the world. Now married and awaiting the birth of my son, David, I was excited about this new chapter in my life. But when David was born, my excitement quickly turned to anxiety. Something was seriously wrong with my baby. He constantly cried, sometimes screaming in pain. For months we were in and out of hospitals, but the doctors could not discover what was causing the skin rashes and breathing problems that tormented him. Finally, as David continued to fail, they told me, "We think you should let him go." I had never been so scared, lost, and confused in my life.

David's early months had knocked me so far off my feet that I'd found myself listening to the nurses, doctors, specialists—everyone but myself—and doing everything everybody was asking me to do. I believed that the professionals must know more than I, a first-time mom, even though I could see David was not getting any better and the answers they were giving me just didn't feel right in my core. My instincts were telling me that I had to find the underlying cause of David's myriad problems.

Now at rock bottom, I felt that the doctors had given up and wanted me to do the same. I thought, *Okay, that's enough! I am going to do what I feel in my heart*. I sat by David's bed and I said, "God, if you let me keep him, I swear, I'll make a difference. I don't know what I'm going to do, but I will do something. Let me keep him." That night in the hospital, I decided to follow my inner voice. I knew I would rather fight and lose than wonder "What if?" for the rest of my life. I was not going to give my power away any longer. No one could make my journey for me; only I could see the omens and hear the guidance that I needed.

I took my baby home and began studying our daily life, looking for the cause of David's suffering. I kept records of everything. Eventually I saw that he suffered most on Tuesdays, the day I cleaned the house. I started investigating the products I was using, and bingo—things began to become clear. The chlorine, ammonia, and other synthetic ingredients in these products were triggering something or were somehow causing David's shortness of breath and skin problems. When I threw them all away, David's crying finally stopped and his health began to steadily improve.

I went nuts trying to find cleaning products that would work like the name brands I had been using but that would not make David feel so sick. I couldn't find anything. One night, in absolute frustration, I called my grandmother. She shared with me how women in her day made soap. Astonished, I asked her to come over and show me what she was talking about. It felt like I had gone back in time, as I stood in my kitchen making soap with my grandmother.

This led to hours and hours of research, gathering information and asking millions of questions, but finally I began to see my purpose. I felt strongly that I had a responsibility to other moms. I knew there were others out there like David—children and adults—who suffered from chemical-exposure diseases, skin irritations, and respiratory challenges, who needed solutions. With the help of a group of remarkable people, I began the long process of creating cleaning products that were hypoallergenic, nontoxic, and safe.

Today Amilya's Soapworks is competing successfully in the multibillion-dollar cleaning industry. My faith in myself and my desire to create something with a greater purpose—a company with products that are human- and Earth-friendly—are what have kept me going against frequently unthinkable odds.

Since 1993, I've read *The Alchemist* from start to finish two more times. The book seems to magically reappear at difficult times in my life—once when I knew a divorce was in my future and again when the company required that I push myself further than I thought I could. Reading *The Alchemist* reminded me that I had to take another deep breath, listen to my inner voice, and do what I believed to be right. I didn't know if things would turn out all right, but I had a strong feeling that if I jumped, a net would appear. And it did. Today my life is richer than I could have ever dreamed. Amilya's Soapworks continues to grow— especially after my appearance on Oprah Winfrey's show—the books I've written are selling and making a difference in people's lives, and David and I are thriving.

I still pull *The Alchemist* off the shelf whenever I need quick validation of my own wisdom or when I want to reconnect with its message: It isn't always easy to live the life you were meant to, but the lessons learned and the rewards are immeasurable.

This wonderful little book has also helped me to perform a kind of real-life alchemy: making something good out of the tough times I've faced. I see that everything in my life has had some value. In fact, I consider all my "challenge cards" the most powerful cards I hold. I call them my aces. Nobody bet on me. I was like a big Clydesdale horse, trying to run in the Belmont. All I heard was, "Look, girlfriend, it ain't going to happen for you." That just made me work harder to prove them wrong.

If I hadn't read Coelho's book, I might still be looking for validation from outside myself. I'd be going after the credential or the degree that said "You're okay." I've learned that the only place validation ultimately can come from is within—and that's the irony. The shepherd in *The Alchemist* went across the world and back again, only to discover that the treasure he sought was in his own village. It had been right there, where he started, all along. In the same way, I have learned that one of my greatest treasures—that small voice inside—is always right here when I need it, if only I choose to listen.

Jim Guy

Jim Guy is the chief marketing officer of Cambridge Investment Research, Inc., a national broker and dealer serving the needs of independent financial planners, headquartered in Fairfield, Iowa. ■

Fifteen years ago, I attended a business conference in Hawaii. It had been a busy day—I had gone to meeting after meeting, and now we were going out for the evening. I sat on the bed of our hotel room while my future wife Helen was in the bathroom, getting ready to go. While I waited, I looked around for a newspaper or magazine to read but found nothing. I opened up the drawer of the nightstand. There was a Bible—no surprise there—along with another book. The cover of the second book displayed a sunrise, the orange-and-yellow photo a backdrop to the words *The Teachings of the Buddha.*

Intrigued, I picked the orange book up, opened the cover, and read that the Japanese Buddhist Society had placed it there. (I later learned that all hotel rooms in Hawaii are stocked with these books.)

At that time, I knew nothing about Buddhism—except that I was drawn to statues of the Buddha. I had a few such statues, but aside from the pleasure I took in the tranquility that seemed to emanate from their various faces, I had only the vaguest sense of what the religion was about.

Not that I was interested in religion. I was an agnostic—with an attitude. I had been raised Methodist but had let it go as a teenager, rejecting what I considered a shallow understanding of reality. I didn't buy it—the set-up George Carlin describes as "the invisible old guy in the sky" who rewards or punishes humankind for good or bad behavior.

My father was an atheist, though my mother had made him promise to never let us kids know. Only after I became an adult, after he knew that it wouldn't influence or upset me, did my father tell me about the moment in his life when he rejected the idea of God entirely.

He had been 11 years old. His father, my grandfather, the only person in his life he felt really cared for him, was ill with pneumonia. For days his condition had worsened, and now it seemed that he wouldn't live from one hour to the next. All through that night, my father prayed. He remembers not sleeping, only praying, praying, praying that his father would recover.

His father died.

And my father came to a firm and bitter conclusion: There was no such thing as God. For the rest of his life, he had no use for religion—preferring to face the stark reality that this world was spinning on its own without the benefit of a kind and loving guardian to keep things on an even keel.

My own life had been easier than my father's. Growing up, I had both parents, siblings, a stable home, material comfort, and an adequate education. As an adult, I had a good job and enough money, but I can't say it made me happy. I was often tense and anxious and had struggled with depression from the time I was a young man.

Once when I was about 19 or 20, I was moaning about something or other to my dad. He looked straight at me and he said, "Jim, life isn't fair or easy or even very good. But you need to do the best you can with what you got." His words haunted me for a long time, especially as my own experience of unhappiness increased. Dad died suddenly one month before my twenty-first birthday. Why was life so hard?

Sitting on the edge of the bed in the hotel room, I began to read *The Teachings of the Buddha*. I was introduced to the Four Noble Truths and the Noble Eightfold Path. The First Noble Truth, "There is suffering in the world," resonated inside me as if I had been struck like a bell. The deep simplicity of this statement felt like a solid place to rest, to begin. I had experienced all too well the truth of it. There was nothing here that smacked of rewards or punishments, sin or saintliness; only a calm acceptance of present reality. I read the next three: There is a cause to suffering. There is an end to suffering. There is a path out of suffering.

Each Noble Truth seemed to propel me into a deeper place inside. Like a massive staircase leading down to a still pool, the steps were wide and required a pause before going to the next one.

I heard Helen come into the bedroom. With a feeling that felt suspiciously like serenity, I closed the book, looked up with a smile, and said, "Ready to go?"

Over the next few days, I read as much of *The Teachings of the Buddha* as I could. I filled out the order card I found in the book and sent it in with a check for six dollars. The Japanese Buddhist Society sent me my own copy, which I still have today.

Becoming a Buddhist was surprisingly easy for me. It didn't require belief in a deity or regular attendance at a place of worship. I studied *The Teachings of the Buddha* as well as many other books about Buddhism, and spent a lot of time contemplating the meaning of the ancient texts and trying to follow the Noble Eightfold Path, which led one out of suffering. I continued acquiring statues of the Buddha. I felt a more powerful connection to them as my spiritual life became stronger and stronger.

I remember the day I realized that this contemplation of the Buddhist teachings, which had become a meditative practice for me, was actually a form of prayer. As an agnostic, prayer had been something that I felt was never going to be part of my life. Pray . . . to whom? And for what? The whole asking-God-to-do-something-for-me thing felt ridiculous. But that day, as I pounded along the endless path of the treadmill, sweaty and panting in a T-shirt and pair of shorts, suddenly I saw prayer as just an expression of my own spiritual nature, an emanation of the Buddha within. I almost laughed out loud with the lightness and joy this realization brought to me.

There are other, more practical, benefits that I feel as a practicing Buddhist. Helen, now my wife, tells me I am nicer. Feeling more able to cope with the depression that still comes up sometimes, I've stopped taking antidepressants. Working as an investment advisor and then as an executive of a large corporation, I often feel the pressure that comes with massive amounts of responsibility, but now I have a way to help "unstress" myself. There is another dimension to my life—beyond the ups and downs of home and business—that simply makes my life richer.

I often wish that I could have shared *The Teachings of the Buddha* with my father. I think he would have understood and embraced this path. I think this because the hardest Noble Truth is the first one. My father *knew* the truth of suffering—had lived with the misery expressed in the first Truth all his life—but never lost sight of the value and goodness in life, and hadn't been a miserable man or even an unhappy one. Considering life worth the struggle, he had come to accept the suffering in the world, though it never ceased causing him pain.

I dream that for him, the other three Truths would have brought him the comfort of knowing that life can be a spiritual fight, which if well fought, perhaps along the Eightfold Path, can lead to the end of suffering.

As for me, it seems a minor miracle that I was thrown a life preserver—in the form of a book about religion, of all things—as I floundered in the same rough sea that had knocked my father around. But that book led me to discover the art of happiness and brought me peace.

Gary Heavin

Gary Heavin is the founder and CEO of Curves. With almost 10,000 locations in 40 countries, Curves is the world's largest fitness franchise and the tenth largest of all franchise companies in the world. Gary is considered the innovator of the express fitness phenomenon that has made exercise available to over 4 million women, many of whom are in the gym for the first time. He is the author of numerous books including the *New York Times* best seller *Curves*, which is revolutionizing America's approach to dieting. ■

With all the failures and corporate ethical lapses in the news today, many people are wondering how to build strong companies while maintaining their integrity. Ten years ago, I was wondering the same thing.

I found success at an early age. I owned my first health club at age 20 and grew it into a six-club chain. By age 26, I had a million-dollar financial statement. However, my youthful enthusiasm was no match for my lack of experience and wisdom. I had over-expanded and was underfinanced, in addition to making a few dozen other mistakes, and by age 30, I'd lost it all.

During my thirties, I became serious about my faith and the values derived from that faith. I became a committed Christian; I intended to learn from my mistakes and apply biblical principles to my life and my business. There's nothing like failure and humiliation to make you teachable.

One day, at a resale shop, I noticed an out-of-print book and purchased it for five dollars. It was *The Secret Kingdom* by Pat Robertson. The controversial founder of "The 700 Club," Pat has a great personal story of overcoming obstacles to achieve success. His book illustrates ten principles or values that the Bible teaches about life. Over the past ten years, I have applied those principles to my business with great success. Pat lists the principles in a different order and calls one or two by a different name, but the following descriptions relate my adaptations of them and how they have worked for me in my life.

The first principle combines honesty and integrity. Honesty simply means to tell the truth. Not half-truths, subtle deception, the end justifying the means, and so forth. Tell people the truth as best you can. Integrity is doing what you say. Many of the current corporate ethical debacles would not occur if just these values were made part of business conduct and personal character.

As I began to franchise my fitness concept, I applied these values to my decisions and the corporate culture we were creating. I was honest with prospective franchisees. I told them that this was only an opportunity; they were going to have to work hard to succeed. I told them to expect us to do the right thing and to hold us to a level of correction, rather than perfection. As we worked together to build their local franchise and our international business, we were careful to always follow through on the agreements we made, so an atmosphere of trust was created. Our franchisees speak so highly of us that we have become the world's fastest-growing franchise—simply by word of mouth.

This trust allowed strong relationships to be built and opened the way for another principle, the law of unity, to come into play: When two or more people agree to work toward a common goal, they can go much farther together than they can separately. While I personally cannot coach and counsel millions of women, ten thousand franchisees and I—working together—can.

The next principle is that of greatness—which, surprisingly, is also called the principle of servanthood. The Bible says that he who would be the greatest among you would be the servant of all. Over the years, I have experienced the truth of this principle. As the CEO of my company, I see myself at the bottom of an inverted pyramid. On my shoulders rest hundreds of employees who rely on me for the resources to do their jobs. On their shoulders rest the thousands of franchisees who need training and support, and on their shoulders are the millions of members who are getting in shape. Our focus has always been on service rather than on profit or company growth. We have an expression: if you serve, they will come. We have literally served our way to becoming the tenth largest franchise company in the world.

The next principle, the law of use, states that if you don't use what you've been given, it will be taken away. This law is illustrated in the biblical story of the gold talents (quantities of precious metal). In this parable, a man about to embark on a trip gives each of his servants a different amount of talents. When the master returns, he holds his servants accountable for what they were given. The one who invested his talents the most wisely is praised and given more. The one who buried his talents has them taken away and is severely reprimanded. How many of us have talents and opportunities that we have been given and do not take advantage of?

This principle was pivotal in my career. Ten years ago, my wife Diane and I owned two Curves locations that were successfully serving hundreds of women and providing well for us financially. Yet, we knew that *millions* of women needed these services. We had to make a choice: Utilize the opportunity of franchising and risk everything we owned once again, or just enjoy where we were. We chose to use what we had been given—investing our talents to help a larger number of people.

The next principle is that of responsibility: To whom much has been given, much is expected. As Curves grew, we began to invest in research, education, and innovation. Our program and the competence of our individual franchisees continually improve so that millions of women can manage their weight and protect their health more effectively. We have underwritten college courses and associate degree programs and have created professional certifications in the areas of health and wellness. Two thousand franchisees earned college credit through our Curves University program during the past year. If people trust us with their decisions about health and weight management, we've got to live up to that responsibility by continually educating ourselves and improving our methods.

The principle of change advises us to expect change—and even embrace it. Although most people hate change, it is the nature of business.

Being "good enough" is never good enough for long. Over the past decade, we have watched dozens of competitors try to copy what we have done. Understanding the principle of change, we have never rested on our laurels. Instead, we moved from an exercise business model to one that also provides weight management. We improved our equipment and training methods. We went international. Innovation is our company's driving force as we welcome and work with change. I believe that Curves is the leader in the fitness industry today because we are willing to change.

Another key to success that I learned from *The Secret Kingdom* is the principle of reciprocity, or giving back: If resources can flow through you to meet the needs of others, you'll be given more resources. In other words, the more you give, the more you get. Diane and I decided long ago to give away more than we keep. As we saw how we were blessed, we encouraged our franchisees to give back to their communities.

Last March, we held our ninth annual food drive and our franchisees raised more than eleven million pounds of food for their local food banks. Jay Leno of *The Tonight Show* mentioned us in his monologue, reading one of our newspaper ads that read, "Weight loss center has food drive." Though it does sound funny, our March food drive is one of the most powerful examples of the principle of giving back I know: for nine consecutive years, the month of March has been our best membership enrollment month.

To further model corporate giving, Diane and I offer a $1000 annual matching grant for franchisees who raise money for their local charities. That's twenty percent of their annual royalty, offered in exchange for their helping people in need in their communities. Being able to let go of money keeps it from becoming overly important and helps keep our focus on service. As my friend Zig Ziglar says, "You can get anything in life you want—if you just help enough other people get what they want."

In case you think building this company has been easy, let me mention the next principle: perseverance. If you are going to become competent at anything, you have to stick with it. In spite of losing everything I owned in the fitness business, I had a passion to help women protect their health. I like to tell people, "I'm not all that smart. I just made mistakes until there weren't any left." The key is to learn from those mistakes and not repeat them. The race of life isn't really won by the fastest runner—it's won by those who get up the fastest after they fall down.

The final two principles are the spiritual laws of miracles and dominion. The law of miracles teaches us to expect extraordinary opportunity, help and joy, and the law of dominion teaches us that we are here to make the world a better place. I relied heavily on these two principles at a point in my life when other people might have given up. At age forty, after having lost everything, I dared to dream that I could build the largest fitness franchise in the world—starting with no money, no credit, and no investors. I believed that I had a better solution to the weight management crisis than the experts, and so, with all the faith I had, I threw myself into making my dream a reality. I trusted that if I was working to make life better for others, I would certainly succeed.

The Secret Kingdom helped me find the way to true success in business and in life. It reinforced my belief that I was, and still am, endowed with the seeds of greatness; we all are. If you really, really understand who God is and who you are to Him, and you understand His character reflected in these principles, imagine what kind of life you could live—and what kind of business you could build.

Stephen Covey

Dr. Stephen Covey has been recognized as one of *Time* magazine's 25 most influential Americans. He is the author of several acclaimed books, including the international best seller *The 7 Habits of Highly Effective People*,® which has sold more than 15 million copies in 38 languages throughout the world, and his most recent best seller, *The 8th Habit: From Effectiveness to Greatness*.® In 2003, he received the National Fatherhood Award, which, as the father of 9 and grandfather of 44, he says is the most meaningful award he has ever received. Stephen currently serves on the board of directors for the Points of Light Foundation, which, in partnership with the Volunteer Center National Network, engages and mobilizes millions of volunteers from all walks of life to help solve serious social problems in thousands of communities around the country. ■

From my earliest days, I swam in a calm sea of unconditional love and encouragement. My parents were devout Mormons and believed in continually affirming people's worth and potential. They did this for each other, their friends, colleagues, and of course their children. It was a part of living by our religion.

I remember, as a boy, waking up one night to find my mother standing by my bed.

"What are you doing?" I asked, still half asleep.

"Just affirming you, dear. Go back to sleep now," she replied.

And I drifted back to sleep to the sound of her words: "You're going to do great on the test tomorrow; you're the most marvelous son," and so on. I became accustomed to this kind of loving interaction and have done the same things with my own children. I saw very early in life how much we can affect each other, and ourselves, with our words and intentions.

It was understood that I would follow in my father's footsteps and join the family business after college, but that plan changed during my mission, a period of missionary work undertaken by every young Mormon. I was 20 years old and serving in Great Britain when my mission president asked me to lead a seminar to train the local leaders of the church. The leaders were 40, 50, and 60 years old. I said, "I can't do this. There's no way."

But my mission president told me that he had complete faith that I could do it and eventually persuaded me to take it on. He helped me prepare for the event, and it ended up going extremely well. I found I experienced a great deal of satisfaction from extending myself and really helping other people change their lives. That, to me, was so much bigger than going into business that I knew that I'd found my calling— I wanted to be a teacher, helping people to have happier, more successful lives.

During my training for this profession, I soon discovered that my loving upbringing had one surprising drawback. Because I had been surrounded by happiness for as long as I could remember, I never had to create it for myself. Unconditional love had been handed to me—a gift of my birth—and I had internalized it. The personal freedom this provided had become natural to me. So when I began teaching, I found it was sometimes difficult to explain the mechanics of things that were spontaneous for me.

Luckily, another benefit of the way I'd been raised is that I have always been open to new ideas. Because I feel inwardly secure, I can afford to risk being vulnerable intellectually. This has allowed me to be open to completely new ways of thinking. Not surprisingly, this has made me particularly fond of books. They've had a tremendous impact on me throughout my life.

Two books I read early in my career have had especially far-reaching effects: *Man's Search for Meaning*, by Viktor Frankl, and *A Guide for the Perplexed*, by E.F. Schumacher. These books introduced me to the concepts of personal responsibility and choice, providing a framework and giving me tools that have allowed me to help my students, and eventually millions of readers, to be more effective and fulfilled in their professional and personal lives—no matter where they are starting from.

I read *Man's Search for Meaning* first, around 1962. The biggest understanding that I gained from Frankl was that you have the power to choose your response to any given set of circumstances. Frankl did this in the death camps of Nazi Germany, where he was subjected to inhuman treatment on all levels: physical, mental, and emotional. At one point, the Nazis burned his manuscript—his life's work. Instead of becoming despondent, he changed his initial reaction from "Why me?" and "Why is this happening?" to "What is life asking of me?" The answer, in the case of his manuscript, was, "Rewrite it; make it better." With this shift in thinking he could always find meaning in life, regardless of what was happening on the outside.

Almost 10 years later, I read Schumacher's book, *A Guide for the Perplexed*, which took the concept of personal choice to a more applied level. In the book Schumacher describes four levels of being. The highest level is characterized by the ability to be self-aware—that is, to be aware of being aware. This quality is the unique endowment of a human being. We're not simply the sum of our experiences; we can reflect on those experiences and how they interact, and then make a choice based on that awareness.

This idea has had a tremendous impact on my teaching, my writing, and my personal life, including the raising of my children. Even when they were small, my children knew they couldn't get away with giving an excuse or blaming someone else. If they said, "Well, she did this and this," I'd ask, "Why did you choose this response to that?" In our house, everyone knew that we always have the power of choice and that no one is a victim—ever. Each of us is responsible for our part of the equation, so we don't blame anyone else for our situations.

Sometimes a child would ask, "Well, what should I do?" I would invariably reply, "Use your R and I: resourcefulness and initiative," and we'd figure it out together. It became a joke in our family: Dad thinks "R and I" is the answer for everything. I admit it, I do think using our inner resources and creativity is the only way to respond to the challenges we face in life. Our resourcefulness and initiative—a gift of our self-awareness—empower us to most effectively answer Frankl's question, "What is life asking of me?"

When I read *A Guide for the Perplexed*, I was teaching at Brigham Young University. I liked the book so much that I made it required reading for my classes in Organizational Behavior and Management. I taught personal responsibility by having students write their own contracts with me, outlining what they were going to accomplish in the class, and, more importantly, what contributions they would make. Then they decided what kind of accountability system they would set up, so that they were accountable not only to their own conscience but also to the people they lived and worked with.

Putting the responsibility for learning back on these students literally transformed their lives. They often gained a new level of mastery over themselves, not just academically but also in terms of getting exercise, eating right, and living by their consciences. Many of them were sloppy and undisciplined and knew they needed to do these things. And since they had to evaluate themselves and be accountable to the people around them, they knew they couldn't scrape by in the old way—by simply playing the game and doing the bare minimum to pass.

I once had a student who had gotten by for years on his popularity, his good looks, and his athletic prowess. One day he came in to ask me how he was doing in class. I said, "Don't ask me. What does your conscience say? What about the people you go around with? What do they say?"

"Oh, you know . . . ," and he gave me all these excuses for why he wasn't doing well. I said to him, "Look what you're doing. You're telling me you are a victim of your circumstances. You're doing the very opposite of what we committed to up front. I'd say that you deserve the D-minus you're getting." Later that student told me, "You can't imagine the impact that had on my life, that someone would hold me to the responsible course in life." And like so many others who discover the link between personal responsibility and effectiveness in life, he went on to get an education—rather than just good grades.

Another important concept I discovered in *A Guide for the Perplexed* was the difference between convergent and divergent problems, a distinction I use constantly in my consulting work with organizations and individuals. I've learned that it's vital to know which type of problem you have, as they require entirely different solutions.

With a convergent problem, you just need more information. Let's say you have a problem with your car. You gather more data about what's wrong, and eventually everything converges to the solution. As you gather information, you eliminate options—it's not the fuel line, it's not this, it's not this . . . oh, here's where it is. Eventually you come to the solution.

But with a divergent problem, you've got to go deeper and discover the underlying values that are causing the divergence. More information will not solve the problem. Everyone has been in the situation of arguing with a partner, a spouse, or a child, and the more you talk to each other, the worse it gets. Both of you are treating it like a convergent problem, thinking, "I'll just give you more information. If you just understand more, you'll see I'm right." But the real problem is that you've got values that are divergent. That's what is causing the clash. So the first step in solving a divergent problem is to recognize that it's a values—not an information—issue. Then, if you can find a bigger, higher value that both parties agree on, you can take a convergent approach.

In my book *The 8th Habit*,® I talk about the idea of a "third alternative." If you say to the person you're arguing with, "Would you be willing to search for a solution that is better than what either one of us has been proposing?" you change a divergent problem into a convergent one. It puts you both on the same side of the table—looking in the same direction—and then you can start sharing information in a creative way, rather than being defensive and protective.

And to help my clients reach this convergent mode of functioning more quickly, I tell them that no one can make their point until they re-state the other person's point to his or her satisfaction. Doing this, they listen to each other with more empathy and are better able to look for a third alternative.

A great number of things I teach today were inspired by *Man's Search for Meaning* and *A Guide for the Perplexed*. The seeds sown by these books so long ago were able to sprout and grow in the fertile ground of intellectual openness that my parents had created in me. I am deeply grateful to them—and to Frankl and Schumacher, and my other teachers—for the resulting "harvest" I've been able to share with so many people around the world.

Maynard Webb

Maynard Webb has been chief operating officer of eBay, Inc., and has a distinguished record of technology and business management achievements during his career of more than 20 years. Prior to joining eBay, Maynard was senior vice president and chief information officer at Gateway, Inc., a Fortune 250 leader in computing technology, where he contributed to Gateway's rapid expansion and Internet-enabled business operations. He has also worked at Bay Networks, Quantum, Thomas Conrad, Figgie International, and IBM. ■

It was 1993. I was trying to lead my first large organization—a team of a couple hundred people. Although I had been in middle management before, this was my first executive position and I was charting my way through fairly turbulent waters: The previous guy in my position had been fired, his team was upset and somewhat junior, and we had lots of things to accomplish. What was worse, I didn't think we had all the principles and guidelines we needed to have in place in the organization.

I knew how I wanted to lead, but I was still learning how to inspire others to take action. Sometimes I would dictate what had to be done, but this didn't seem to motivate anyone to do it on their own. I was showing them how I did it, but I wasn't teaching them how *they* could do it. At the time, I simply didn't know how to express my vision in a framework that others could easily internalize and use.

Plus, when I looked around, I often had the unsettling feeling that some of the other executives didn't share my vision or my values. This came to a head when an important decision had to be made that would affect a large number of employees. I was uncomfortable with the way the decision was being handled.

I stewed about the situation for weeks and finally, one Friday afternoon, I talked about the problems surrounding the decision with a colleague who was also a personal friend. I knew he was having a difficult time with the same issue. He told me he had just read a book that had deeply affected him, and he recommended I read it, too. This was in the days before the BlackBerry and the Palm Pilot, so I wrote down the title in my day planner: *The 7 Habits of Highly Effective People*, by Stephen Covey.

The very next morning, I went to the bookstore and bought Covey's book. It was a Saturday, so as usual, I was spending the day with my family. Between driving the kids to baseball games, going to fast-food places to grab a meal, and hanging out together at home, I grabbed moments here and there to read the book. I found Covey's material tremendously engaging and inspirational. Throughout the day, I felt moved to read things out loud to my wife and talk with her about them.

One of the first chapters in the book, "Beginning with the End in Mind," switched a light on in me. Covey asks, "When you leave this world, how do you want be remembered?" I immediately found a piece of paper and did one of the exercises: writing down what I wanted carved on my tombstone. It was exhilarating to think in such terms.

The next thing that really hit me was Covey's model that lays out the framework of urgent versus nonurgent and important versus nonimportant tasks. Action items can be classified into four different groups, or quadrants:

1. Urgent (time-sensitive) and important
2. Nonurgent and important
3. Urgent and nonimportant
4. Nonurgent and nonimportant

I saw that quadrant 2 activities, nonurgent but important, were often passed over as people scrambled to get the urgent activities—both important *and* nonimportant—accomplished.

The technology field is filled with people who confuse "action for traction." An "everything is urgent" energy propels most people through their days. You can be busy and exhausted, and feel good because you are getting so much done—yet totally lose sight of what's important. The average tenure for most chief information officers is between two to three years, so there is a tendency for those folks to try to do the things that are immediate and not take on the big things that are really needed. They make people happy in the short term but end up taking the company off the edge of a cliff. I saw that Covey's quadrants provided a way to keep the big picture alive in one's everyday activities—at whatever level the person was working at the company.

This idea wasn't totally new to me. Even before reading Covey, I knew how to shut out the noise and do the things that mattered most. I think it's in my core DNA; it's just how I've always operated. But as a young executive, I was frustrated because I thought everyone should understand this concept and do it naturally. I didn't value the process of building a context for people.

I finished the book that night. I immediately decided to commit to using the tools myself in whatever way I could. But what excited me most was Covey's framework of priorities. It was a clearly laid out formula I could use to inspire others to do these things for themselves.

The next day I reflected on the best way to bring this information to the rest of the company. I had once worked for a boss who made us read a book every week and then report on it. We had to implement the author's practices the next day. I didn't want to force-feed the material to my staff in that way, so I made a list of people to talk to about it casually.

On Monday morning, I "socialized it," meeting with people one-on-one to see if Covey's ideas resonated with them. I'd say, "Hey, I was struggling with this, and in this book I read, there was a principle that really seemed to help." I'd explain the principle and ask, "What do you think about that?" Most people responded positively as they saw how it pertained to their own situation. Over time, people began picking up *The 7 Habits* on their own. Instead of being required reading, it simply spread from person to person by word of mouth.

In fact, during my tenure at that company, a large number of the staff ended up implementing Covey's ideas. As a consequence, the spirit of the team was high and we pulled off some major miracles. Unfortunately, I was at an early stage in my management cycle and made the mistake of allowing that enthusiasm and loyalty to be tied to me personally, rather than to the company. So when I left, many of the employees left, too. I've made a point of never letting that happen again. I make sure that employees know that they don't need me to succeed; they can implement Covey's principles in any setting and get the results they want.

Reading *The 7 Habits of Highly Effective People* changed the way I operated, both personally and professionally. It cemented my trust in my own instincts and gave me an effective method of sharing this valuable information with others. Today, I still take time out, usually on Sundays, to set my quadrant 2 goals and commit to getting them met for the coming week. And "Beginning with the End in Mind" is the one principle that has guided my life more than any other.

In my "fireside chats" with the team here at eBay, I talk about sitting on a park bench 20 years from now—when none of us will have titles and it won't matter what positions we held. "When people see you," I ask, "do they come up and give you a hug? Or do they run the other way?" We discuss how that's all tied to beginning with the end in mind.

I still work at these things myself. I have to, because by nature I'm driven—a perfectionist who is never satisfied. Covey's principles have helped me learn how to enjoy my life more, as well as accomplish more.

My big picture—what I want written on my tombstone—hasn't changed much since that Saturday in 1993 when I first read Covey's book and was moved to write it down: Maynard Webb: *He made the world a better place . . . and had fun doing it!*

M arc Bekoff

Marc Bekoff is a professor of biology at the University of Colorado at Boulder, and is a Fellow of the Animal Behavior Society and a former Guggenheim Fellow. He is the author of 18 books, including *The Ten Trusts* (2002, coauthored with Jane Goodall), *Animal Passions and Beastly Virtues* (2006), and the editor of *Encyclopedia of Animal Behavior* (2004). Marc is a member of the Ethics Committee of the Jane Goodall Institute, and in 2000, he and Jane Goodall cofounded the organization Ethologists for the Ethical Treatment of Animals: Citizens for Responsible Animal Behavior Studies. ■

In 1966, Vietnam was heating up and I was a college senior, casting about for my next step. One day, while browsing in the university bookstore, I discovered Petr Kropotkin's book *Mutual Aid*. Published in 1902, *Mutual Aid* is about the evolutionary impact and importance of cooperation in both animal and human groups. This idea appealed to me greatly. It validated my own world view that compassion and cooperation are inborn and that these qualities form the natural basis for successful societies.

Growing up, I always had strong feelings of compassion for both animals and people. I liked it when people cooperated, and I shied away from aggression and dissension. I was a pacifist; the bully at my grammar school constantly—and unsuccessfully—tried to get a rise out of me. One day, he became so frustrated with me that he actually picked me up and dropped me in a garbage can. Still, I wouldn't fight back. Even then, I knew that violence would just make things worse. There had to be a better way. When I read Kropotkin's book, I became aware that there were others, including scientists, who supported my point of view.

Although I was inspired by *Mutual Aid*, it had no immediate effect on my life. I filed the information away in my head and resumed my somewhat bumbling search for clues to what my career might be after I graduated.

That same year, Konrad Lorenz's book *On Aggression* was published. When I read *On Aggression*, something deep in me snapped to attention. *This is wrong*, I thought. *Wrong and dangerous*. The book upset me because of Lorenz's strong emphasis on the innate basis of aggression. Lorenz, a very famous ethologist (animal behaviorist) who went on to win the Nobel Prize, argued that there are very strong biological determinants of aggression and that while it is modifiable, in many ways it is unavoidable. Animals, and by extension, humans, he wrote, are biologically programmed to fight over limited resources. *On Aggression* generated a lot of interest because so many people then used it as an excuse for aggressive behavior and ultimately for warfare: "See, it's natural for us to be warlike. Animals do it, and they're our ancestors."

Suddenly, all the diffuse ideas I'd had about what I might do—go to graduate school, get a job, go to Canada to avoid the draft—coalesced into a single intention: I will prove this guy wrong.

The idea that I might like to study animals had been brewing in my mind for a while, so I decided to get a master's degree in biology. Two years later, when I graduated and lost my student deferment, my draft notice came. I remember thinking: *No more BS. It's time to take a stand*. I didn't—and still don't—believe in war. My path was simple; I wasn't going to support the promulgation of more war. Rather than leave the country for Canada, I registered as a conscientious objector.

If I hadn't read Lorenz, I know I would have felt as strongly, but I don't know if I would have acted as I did. I might have wrongly assumed that I had more comrades than I did in the compassion and cooperation camp. Now I knew that a frightening number of people subscribed to his theory that competition and warfare could be explained as simply being innate in our genes: It's just going to happen, it's inevitable, and you just have to live with it. Seeing that, I took a firmer stand. I thought that maybe the people who didn't like war could really make a difference if we spoke out. Part of Lorenz's gift to me was the clarification of my own values and the firm decision to live my life by them.

With the question of the draft settled, my quest to find the scientific refutation of what I considered Lorenz's dangerously one-sided thesis began to take shape. Of course I knew that animals and people could be competitive and aggressive, but from my own observation and reading, I felt that somehow, in the course of evolution, this had to be balanced by compassion, cooperation, and fairness. Anyone who studies animal societies knows that you can't have a wolf pack, for example, composed solely of aggressive, dominant alpha animals. There is always a spectrum of personalities and temperaments; you have to have dominant animals and you have to have more subordinate animals. I believed that the cooperative behavior displayed by the subordinate animals was as innate as the aggression displayed by the others, and I felt sure that the evidence for this could be found in the study of animal interactions.

I enrolled at Cornell University Medical College in a Ph.D. program in neurobiology and behavior. By then, I had quite a few unambiguous resolves: I knew I didn't want to go to war—in fact, that I *wouldn't* go to war. I knew that I wanted to study animal behavior; I knew that I wanted to find the biological basis for the force of cooperation discussed in Kropotkin's book. I also knew that I wouldn't experiment on animals. This last one eventually caused me to leave Cornell, as it became clear that my goals were not compatible with the program there.

I left Cornell looking for a situation in which I could study positive social behaviors and investigate the roots of the many positive traits I'd observed so clearly in numerous animals. I found a Ph.D. program at Washington University in St. Louis that was more in line with my goals. There I met professors, colleagues, and a mentor who supported and encouraged the direction my studies were taking me.

In the course of graduate work, I spent time observing play behavior in wolves, dogs, and coyotes. At that time, studying play behavior was considered a waste of time. There seemed nothing significant to be learned from it, as it combined actions from mating, fighting, hunting, and so on. Yet my experience told me quite the opposite. It's true that when you look at this behavior superficially, it makes no sense, until you realize that the animals are, in fact, playing by the rules. They are doing things that can be explained only by the fact that they are behaving fairly and cooperatively, not competitively. People had overlooked what I found so obvious: Play behavior is really the place to look for the biological bases of cooperation, fairness, and trust—what I now call "wild justice."

After getting my Ph.D., I became a professor at the University of Colorado at Boulder, where I have been since 1974. For the last 30-plus years, I've conducted research focused on the cooperative nature of play—how animals play fairly; how they trust one another, forgive one another; apologize to one another; how they are nice to one another. My work, along with that of many others such as Jane Goodall and Michael W. Fox, has shown that it's not always "Nature red in tooth and claw." Animal behavior is a combination: Sometimes animals, including humans, are aggressive and assertive and warlike, and sometimes they are compassionate, empathic, and cooperative. Aggression is not inevitable or any more "natural" than cooperation. The research that I've done has a strong quantitative, empirical, statistical basis that supports that.

In my mind the most important aspect of my contribution—the piece that finally balances Lorenz's impact—is the major lesson that humans can learn from this work: We find the roots of cooperation, fairness, justice, empathy, and trust in the behavior of animals. These qualities are the gifts of our ancestors. In fact, today, research using functional magnetic resonance imaging technology is clearly showing very similar neurological mechanisms in humans and other animals in terms of the neurological basis of different behaviors—including fairness and cooperation.

For many years, I kept Lorenz's book on my shelf; just seeing it there gave me fresh resolve. Periodically, I even reviewed it just to make sure I hadn't misread him. But each time I did, it only reinforced my feeling that I was doing the right thing.

Sometimes a book can transform your life by filling you with revulsion and catalyzing you into action. Would I have found the same life's work without any help from Lorenz? I don't know. As a young man, I wasn't always clear about what was true for me, but I was abundantly clear about what *wasn't true* for me, the moment I read it.

M ax Edelman

Max Edelman is a Holocaust survivor who was blinded in a Nazi concentration
camp in 1944. An advocate for persons with visual impairments, he is also a
writer who has had several articles focusing on equality for people with disabili-
ties published in Ohio's largest newspaper, the *Plain Dealer*, as well as other
publications. Max belongs to the American Council of the Blind and the National
Federation of the Blind and was instrumental in encouraging the two organizations to work together on a Braille literacy program for children in his area. Since
retiring 15 years ago from his career as a physical therapist, Max has devoted his
time to writing and talking to groups about the Holocaust and blindness. ■

In retirement, willingly or not, I occasionally reflect upon my 83 years of
life. As a Holocaust survivor, there are many things that are painful to
recall—one of them being the book I read as a teenager that completely
changed my life. *Mein Kampf*, by Adolf Hitler, that irredeemably evil
book considered the bible of Nazism, rearranged not only *my* future but
the face of the world as well. I have felt its effects—both destructive and
constructive—for more than 65 years.

In the 1930s, *Mein Kampf* outsold all other books in Europe except
the Bible. It was even popular in the small towns in Poland like the one
where I grew up, especially in anti-Semitic circles. Knowing this, sheer
curiosity drove me to get a copy of the book. I must confess, reading
Mein Kampf at the age of 16, I understood very little of the geopolitics,
world economics, or international treaties Hitler referred to, but his
distorted characterizations of the Jewish people chilled me to the bone.

Hitler was shrewd enough to realize that to draw many people to his cause, he had to give them one issue to attract their attention—too many issues would only confuse them—so he chose his favorite: anti-Semitism. It wasn't hard to understand why my anti-Semitic neighbors were so eager to read Hitler's book. Although my family's history in Poland went back a number of generations, as Jews we were still considered aliens and subjected to frequent persecution.

With Hitler fanning the flames of religious hatred, physical attacks on Jews markedly increased, even in my hometown. Life became less and less tolerable as time went on. I am often asked why my family didn't leave. We tried but had few options: The democratic countries in the world refused to take Jews in. Our only remaining hope was to obtain a permit to go to Israel, the land of our ancestors. But that too turned out to be wishful dream, and like millions of other Jews, we were trapped when World War II started.

I spent the next five years—from age 17 to 22—in concentration camps. For most of those years, I was imprisoned in camp Butzyn, in Poland, a satellite of the death camp Maidanek, and toward the end I was transferred to Flossenburg, in Bavaria, about 70 miles southeast of Nuremberg.

I learned quickly that my survival hinged on staying relatively well and going to work every day, if possible. This, under the prevailing conditions, was a tall order—indeed, too tall for many. Unlike millions of others, I managed to survive, but there were many times I was in a bottomless pit of despair with nothing to hold onto but the tiniest shred of hope.

Then on April 8, 1944, I lost my sight as a result of a terrible beating by two Nazi guards. I didn't expect to survive in the camp after becoming blind, but I was lucky. My friend Eric, the barracks supervisor, who was not a Jew but a German national political prisoner, and Sigmund, my brother, who was imprisoned with me, protected me from the fate of most handicapped prisoners, which was instant execution. Their actions fulfilled the biblical injunction to "be your brother's keeper" to the highest level. Because Eric was a German, the camp officers and guards trusted him. He used that trust to my advantage. He lied to them, made up alibis for me when necessary, and kept me out of their sight. Eric was fully aware of the consequences of being caught protecting a blind inmate, and a Jew at that. His kindness and that of others in the camps, both Jew and non-Jew, are what kept me from giving up on the human race.

On the day of our liberation, April 23, 1945, I was one of a group of hundreds of Jews from Flossenberg walking five abreast through the German countryside on a death march to an unknown destination. There had been 2,500 of us in that group when we'd left Flossenberg days earlier, but about two thirds had died along the way. The remaining 800 of us were barely alive. When our Nazi captors fled at the sound of the approaching American troops, we realized that our long nightmare was over. Although I was grateful to be free, I soon became overwhelmed with feelings of self-pity. *I am liberated all right,* I told myself, *but I am blind.* Except for my brother, my whole family had perished; I was practically alone. I became very scared—I was more scared of life than I had been of death in the concentration camp! Even though I was one of the lucky few to survive, the horror that Hitler's book had unleashed continued to have a devastating effect on me in peacetime.

I began the long and difficult process of rebuilding my life. In December of 1945, Sigmund made an appointment for me to see Dr. Hans Vesseli, the head of the University of Munich Eye Clinic. After a thorough examination, he only confirmed what four other doctors had already told me: My blindness was permanent and nothing could be done to change it. Dr. Vesseli, who was a Freemason and had been no fan of the Nazis, sensed my mood. "Bitterness and disillusionment won't do you any good, my young friend," he said. "Instead, resolve to prove to the world that Jews are not the evil beings Hitler made them out to be. Carry the torch of advocacy for tolerance and respect for human rights. Make it your legacy: a memorial to your loving family destroyed by the Nazis."

That little speech had a profound and positive impression on me. Yes, I was beaten and I was blind—but I wasn't broken. I trusted that an unimpaired mind could overcome an impaired sense. I decided to dedicate my life to replacing Hitler's lies with the truth.

Acting on Dr. Vesseli's advice, I immediately enrolled in the college-level rehabilitation school for the blind in Bavaria. I was the only Jew; the rest of the students were all ex-SS officers and soldiers. One Sunday after lunch, we sat in the dining room socializing. Suddenly, a group started to sing Nazi songs. I immediately stood up and went to my dorm room. Two minutes later, one of the instructors came in to apologize for the incident. "It is all right," I answered calmly. "That bunch of Nazis have yet to learn that Hitler is mercifully dead, and that bigotry and prejudice no longer have a place in the post-war world. I and my fellow Jews do not remotely resemble the Jew Hitler depicted us to be in *Mein Kampf.* I have made it my mission to show the world this truth, and such incidents will not throw me off course."

It was this mission—inspired by Hitler and his hateful book—that gave me a strength and focus that helped me through the many challenges I faced in the following years. I graduated in 1948 with a degree in physical therapy. And again, it was Dr. Vesseli who helped me to find a job. Although there were Germans who murdered my family and destroyed my eyesight, I can never forget there were also Germans who helped me: one who stuck his neck out to save my life in the concentration camp and another who helped save me from the bitterness and hate that threatened to engulf me, and then guided me in building a new life.

A German Catholic young lady decided to take a chance with this blind Jewish physical therapist and married me, even though I was dedicated to exposing the evils of some of her own countrymen. We established ourselves in America and raised and educated our two sons in the Jewish faith, doing our part to secure the Jewish people's continuity.

Helen Keller once wrote, "The highest result of education is tolerance. No loss by flood and lightning, no destruction of cities . . . by hostile forces of nature, has deprived man of so many noble lives and impulses as those which his intolerance has destroyed." The Holocaust is a perfect example of this sad truth. It is why I continue to write and speak about human dignity and the evils that result from intolerance and disrespect of human rights.

Not too long ago, I was invited to give a presentation about my Holocaust experiences to a class at a local high school. After the presentation, a student came up to me and said, "Mr. Edelman, my grandfather was a Nazi," and started to cry. I reassured that young lady by saying she had absolutely no reason to feel responsible or to have any guilt feelings about who her grandfather was or for what he had done. I believe that each new generation can overcome the mistakes of the past by choosing to treat all people with tolerance and respect.

The negative effects of Hitler's book are obvious. I still become emotional when I think of the terrible things we had to endure as a result of his hate-filled words. But when I was finally free to create my own future, I had to choose how I would live with the scars of my ordeal. I could so easily have focused on the evil I had seen and become bitter and full of hate myself. Instead I chose to take my revenge on the author of *Mein Kampf* by showing the world how much this Jew could accomplish in life and contribute to society. My wounds that will never heal have created a fire in me that will never go out.

Diane Wilson

Diane Wilson, a fourth-generation shrimper, began fishing the bays off the Gulf Coast of Texas at the age of eight. By 24 she was a boat captain. In 1989, she read a newspaper article that listed her home of Calhoun County as the number one toxic polluter in the country and thus began her life as an environmental activist. Her work on behalf of the people and the aquatic life of Seadrift, Texas, has won her a number of awards, including: National Fisherman Magazine Award, Mother Jones's Hell Raiser of the Month, Louis Gibbs' Environmental Lifetime Award, Louisiana Environmental Action Network (LEAN) Environmental Award, Giraffe Project, Jenifer Altman Award, and the Bioneers Award. Diane's first book, *An Unreasonable Woman*, was published in 2005. ■

Fate sometimes presents itself if you're quiet and listen hard enough. I was a woman familiar with quietness. I was, after all, a fisherwoman, a loner. I had just spent fourteen of the quietest days of my life on a shrimp boat in Lavaca Bay on a hunger strike, protesting a polluting chemical plant that wanted to dump fifteen million gallons a day of toxic waste into our "struggling-to-survive" Texas bay.

My 14-day hunger strike had been yet another departure from my life as the original Texas gal whose first 40 years had been spent tending kids and tending gardens and patching shrimp nets when she wasn't captaining a 42-foot shrimp boat single-handed off the Gulf coast of Texas.

Lately I hadn't done any of that stuff, except of course being a mom. A few years back, the seemingly endless supply of shrimp and fish in our bay had slowed to a trickle and no one knew why. Shrimping had hit rock bottom, the fisheries were in a crisis, and the town was dying. To make ends meet, I had tied up my shrimp boat, the SeaBee, and taken a job at my brother's business, Froggie's Shrimp Company. At least I could get a paycheck, managing the few shrimpers still left on their shrimp boats. But life's never that simple, because, in addition to the fish and shrimp dying in droves, a series of mysterious calamities had struck our Gulf coast region: brown and green and red algae—thick as a shag carpet—had blanketed the bays, and dolphins, numbering in the hundreds, had beached and died in our inland waters. Plus, way too many people were getting cancer. What was going on? I connected the dots when a federal EPA report came out, ranking Calhoun County, the county of 15,000 souls where I'd been born and raised, as first *in the nation* for toxins to the land—accounting for 51 percent of Texas's total toxins. That sure was enough to catch my attention. Calhoun was also home to six large chemical companies. I knew there had to be a connection.

So my seafaring life vamoosed and I went landlocked for a while. I zeroed in on one of the chemical companies, demanding they stop discharging chemicals into our bay, and became a full-fledged activist. I called meetings—not well-attended ones—for the next several, divisive years. Petitions and lawsuits followed. Eventually, with the support of pretty-near nobody, I began launching solo hunger strikes.

There was plenty of backlash on a more personal side: corporations threatened countersuits, politicians declared me a maverick and a nut, the newspapers had a heyday with my solitary antics, and the local fishermen were flat-out embarrassed (and apathetic) and tried to avoid me at all costs. They didn't approve of a woman making all that fuss and trying to shut down the chemical plant—the only other source of livelihood they had if the shrimping got too bad. Plus, associating with me might hurt their ability to do business, as the banks and local government were all aligned with the corporations. Then my brother, who owned Froggie's, got alarmed that his fish house might lose business because of me, so he fired me. And another brother got hired on at the same chemical company I was fighting and stopped talking to me. My marriage was blinkity-blinking worse than a neon café sign on its last leg. It was hard going all around.

I understood everybody's anger. I hated that what I was trying to do could affect workers' lives; I'm a working-class woman myself and I felt for those workers. But I knew that if we thought only in terms of short-term economics, over time, we would *all* lose. I couldn't let things continue the way they were.

Home from my latest hunger strike, I went about my business as best I could, considering all the scorn I faced. I was encouraged by the success of my hunger strike, which had wrested an agreement from the chemical company to do an environmental impact study, but I felt overwhelmed by the enormous amount of effort still ahead of me. I was a woman "out front"—an unnatural and undesirable thing to be where I came from—with hardly a person on my side. How long could I keep this up?

Then a few days later, out of the blue, a word popped into my head and wouldn't leave. *Myth.* Now, why the heck was I thinking about that? The next day I took my mystery word and loaded my truck with my five kids and we all drove to a library 35 miles away. At the library, I loosed the kids like chickens from a coop and, with my baby in my arms, I strolled over to the library's card catalogue and looked up my new confounding word. There, along with the word "myth," was a name and a book title I'd never heard of: Joseph Campbell, author of *The Hero with a Thousand Faces.*

The Hero with a Thousand Faces had something to say about the current mess I found myself in, even though the book was a cross-cultural tracing of myths, humanity's most ancient stories. Didn't matter how old the stories were. Didn't matter how dead the heroes—like Hercules and Theseus and Diana and Arthur—were. Because the Hero's Journey—an archetype found in all the world's mythologies—survives into modern times. According to Joseph Campbell, the latest incarnation of the Hero could well be sitting on a shrimp boat in Lavaca Bay staging a hunger strike.

I liked that idea plenty. So I wasn't just a fisherwoman with no resources or allies. I could be the bones and blood of the Phoenix Bird, whose mythical role was to burn totally and completely, and then be reborn. It felt like my life was going up in flames—but if I were the Phoenix, what was there to get upset about? Everybody knows the Phoenix Bird's path. If you've ever heard that pithy saying, what doesn't kill you makes you stronger—well, then, you're tromping in its territory. Joseph Campbell laid out the steps fairly pat in his book. He says when our day comes (and it surely will) and death closes in, there is nothing we can do except die and be resurrected, dismembered totally and then reborn.

I liked what he said about being reborn, too. Once reborn, he says, "Where previously we found an abomination, we shall find a goddess." Wasn't I waking up to my own strength and goodness? "Where we had thoughts of slaying others, we shall slay ourselves; where we had thought to travel outward, we shall come to the center of our own existence." My battle to save our bay was also changing me. I was "slaying" the person I had always been, and finding a deeper, more powerful way to be. "Where we had thought to be alone, we shall find the world." My days of solitary sailing were over. I was no longer just my little bitty self; I felt connected to the world and the bigger picture.

Applying Campbell's words to my own situation changed my perspective radically. My mission to strike at the heart of the chemical company (a sort of mini-Death Star that dominated our small, rural, Texas county) contained many of the classic elements of myth. The shrimper who first gave me the news of our county's pollution was not *just* a cancer-ridden fisherman taking chemotherapy every weekend in Houston; he was my sacred ally delivering "The Call to Adventure." All the hurdles I had to clear—physical, emotional, and legal—were my version of "The Road of Trials." A hunger strike was no longer about not eating or about winning something; it was a walk through grinding pillars of stone where I could be obliterated if I lost my courage or my focus. It was a test of my commitment.

But the biggest shift was realizing that the battles I fought, which I'd always thought were *outside me,* were actually within me, and had been all along. Campbell says the Hero's Journey takes place on many levels, including the level of the spirit. I realized I was also battling my own demons of low self-worth, pettiness, and fear. Some of the worst monsters I faced were parts of my own psyche.

For a fisherwoman whose closest link to spirit was the freshly netted dead shrimp, called ghost shrimp, that lay heaped on the back deck of her boat, this was heady stuff. All that I was doing took on a new dimension— a mythic dimension. My personality took a 180-degree turn and I became fearless. Until that point, most of my activism had been solitary—filing lawsuits, sending petitions, and going on hunger strikes. I'd reluctantly called meetings, but only when it was absolutely necessary. All my life I'd hated to talk. I wouldn't even get on the phone. At school, I certainly hadn't raised my hand or spoken up about anything. But after discovering *The Hero with a Thousand Faces*, I began talking in front of increasingly larger groups on a regular basis. Since then, I've given speeches to groups of more than five thousand people. I've gone places and done things I never would have thought I was capable of.

The most extreme example of this was when I decided to take my shrimp boat out and sink it in order to draw attention to the chemical company's refusal to stop poisoning the bay. When I saw what I was doing as a Journey—a hero's quest to slay the dragon—my boat was not this big important thing anymore. The life of that bay was so much more valuable. I loved that boat, but I didn't have a moment's hesitation. People told me I'd go to prison over it, but all I said was, "Let 'em hop to it! Let 'em put me in jail."

I took my boat out in the bay and headed toward the shallower water near the chemical company's waste pipes. I wanted my mast to stick up out of the water there—to mark the spot where the damage was being done. When the chemical company saw what I was trying to do, they called the Coast Guard. Soon, I had three Coast Guard boats chasing after me, trying to confiscate my boat. Men in uniform were shouting through bullhorns at me, saying I was a terrorist on the high seas and threatening to put me away for 15 years and fine me $500,000. It didn't take long for them to board my boat and arrest me.

But then a miracle of truly mythic proportions occurred: the fishermen—the ones who had been against what I was doing all this time—saw what was happening, and a bunch of them—more than 30 people—got in their boats and came out into the bay. The long-standing racial tension between the Anglo, Vietnamese, and Hispanic fishermen was put aside as they all steered their boats back and forth across the bay in protest. The Coast Guard was flabbergasted.

When the chemical company saw this, they knew I had them beat. They said to me, "What's it going to take to shut you up?" And I said, "Zero discharge. You've got to recycle your waste stream." And they did it. That's how I got the first plant to do zero discharge. A month later, another plant followed. Eventually, the county government and the workers joined me in demanding zero discharge from all the corporations. It was a great victory, even though, on a larger scale, there is still such an enormous battle out there. Today, I'm trying to make zero discharge the national goal of the Clean Water Act, and I'm fighting for the environment on a more global level as well.

If I hadn't read *The Hero with a Thousand Faces*—if I hadn't put my own face atop the body of the Hero—I don't know if I would have been able to do all that I have done since then. Campbell's book helped me tap into a larger source of energy, to do what needed to be done and avoid the burnout that activists can feel over time. I once gave a speech and at the end of it, I paraphrased a quote by George Bernard Shaw, saying, "Reasonable women adapt to the world and an unreasonable woman makes the world adapt to her." Today I am proud to be the unreasonable woman I am—a Phoenix Bird burning and rising, over and over again—in service to the Earth.

Gary Erickson

Gary Erickson is the founder and co-owner with his wife, Kit, of Clif Bar & Co., a leading maker of all-natural energy and nutrition foods. He is also a competitive cyclist, jazz musician, mountain climber, wilderness guide, and the author of *Raising the Bar: Integrity and Passion in Life and Business: The Story of Clif Bar Inc.* ■

I was minutes away from selling my company. It was April 2000 and the negotiations to purchase Clif Bar—which I had started in my mother's kitchen 10 years earlier—were complete. The executives from "Company X," a huge multinational corporation, were waiting for us in San Francisco to meet with them to sign the contract.

All the experts had told my business partner and me that we weren't going to make it on our own and that we needed a large "money infusion" to take Clif Bar to the next level. Our top two competitors had already been bought by multinational giants. The experts warned us that unless we sold our company, we'd be buried and end up with nothing. So we had followed their advice. In less than an hour, Clif Bar would be able to remain competitive, and my business partner and I would be out on the street with $60 million each—"more money than Carter has pills," as my dad always said. I'd never have to work another day in my life.

As I stood in the office, waiting to go and sign the contract, I started shaking and couldn't breathe. I was having an anxiety attack, my first ever. I told my partner I needed to walk around the block. As I walked,

I wept, overwhelmed at what was taking place. Then halfway around the block I stopped dead in my tracks, hit by an overwhelming realization: "I don't have to do this!" I started laughing and I instantly felt free. I had the thought, *I'm not done yet.*

I sprinted back to the office. My partner was on the phone with our attorney. I said to her, "Send them home. I can't sell the company."

My partner wasn't happy about it, but she knew she couldn't sell the company without me. I spent the next seven months in negotiations with her, arranging to buy her out. Although what I was doing made no financial sense, I had no doubt it was the right thing for me to do.

There was a lot of turmoil in the company in the next few months because we had told everyone we were selling, and then we didn't do it. Everyone asked, "Now what? You've told us Clif Bar couldn't make it without the big money the big company would bring, and now you're telling us we can make it?" The management team had been living with a lot of fear for years, and now, instead of going away, that fear got worse.

Hardest for me personally were the stressful negotiations with my soon-to-be ex-partner. Although it was now clear to me that the right thing to do for Clif Bar was to remain private, she had been ready to take her half of the fortune and retire. I had derailed that outcome. I needed to buy her out but still have enough money to run—and grow—the company. It was tough going trying to hold everything together.

Around that time, a woman named Leslie, who had been an assistant to someone who had recently left Clif Bar, came to me and asked if she could be my assistant. I had always liked Leslie and agreed immediately. One day, seeing the stress I was under, Leslie walked up to me, handed me a book and said, "You need to read this."

It was *The Legacy of Luna*, by Julia Butterfly Hill, the autobiographical story of a young woman who graduates from college and goes to Northern California, trying to figure out what to do next in her life. She wants to find her purpose and to be of service to the world. Settling in Humboldt, she hears about the local ancient redwoods that are endangered—and the tree-sitters who are trying to save them. The redwoods in the area are massive trees, 200 or 300 feet high, that have been there for a thousand years. People who tree-sit climb the trees and don't come down, even eating and sleeping up in the trees. Although Julia wasn't a declared environmentalist, she felt that she wanted to join this nonviolent protest to keep the loggers from cutting down those trees. She decided to tree-sit for a couple of weeks, the typical length of time that tree-sitters spent in the trees before others came to replace them. People often think she was some wild outdoors person who had spent a lot of time roughing it, but she wasn't. To climb the tree, she first had to learn how to make the difficult ascent using ropes, safety lines, harnesses, and slipknots.

The tree-sitting was even harder. Besides the primitive arrangements for eating, drinking, sleeping, and sanitation, the people who owned the property were unhappy that the tree-sitters were there, stopping the logging operations. They often threatened to cut a tree down while a person was in it. They did everything they could to keep people from supplying food to the tree-sitters, and even tried to scare the sitters out of the trees by flying helicopters close to them.

For the next two years and eight days, from December 10, 1997, to December 18, 1999, Julia lived in the tree called Luna, without ever leaving it. She spent two severe winters up there—with winds blowing 50 to 60 miles an hour, being pelted by hail and rain day after day—in a makeshift bivouac at the top of the 200-foot tree. She didn't come down until she had secured a contract protecting Luna permanently.

I remember how excited I was reading this book. I don't read a lot— I prefer being outdoors, hiking, climbing, and cycling—but I couldn't put *The Legacy of Luna* down. It helped me to truly understand the momentous decision I'd made not to sell my company—and the opportunities that choice had given me.

Clif Bar was my tree. It was my chance to influence the world for good. I saw so many parallels between the events in my life and the book. Like Julia, I had taken the first step unaware of what I was really getting myself into. I had just wanted to create an energy bar that tasted good. I had no idea that Clif Bar was going to be the main focus of my life for the next 15 years—and probably much longer.

Once I was involved with Clif Bar, I wanted to see it through, despite all the warnings. Julia stayed up in Luna because no one would take her place. The experienced tree-sitters, the experts, were saying, "Look, Julia, this is too dangerous. Just get down. You're done; you did your thing."

But she didn't listen to the experts in her field. She said, "No, I'm not getting down. I don't care that it might cost my life. I'm not getting down," and she stayed. She used the tree as her office, calling people on her cell phone and working with lawyers to secure a contract protecting Luna. She did phone interviews with journalists all over the world. People came to see her, some of them, including Bonnie Raitt, Joan Baez, and Woody Harrelson, even climbing the tree to visit her.

If I had signed away the company, metaphorically I would have been getting out of the tree—and then what? Clif Bar's future wouldn't have been protected and I would've been walking away from something that wasn't finished. At that point, we were just getting to the "tipping point" of knowing what we were all about. Just like a kid growing up, a business needs time to figure out who it is.

I knew I would have been selling out, in the same way that Julia would have been selling out if, a year after climbing Luna, she had said, "You know what? I've had enough," and the tree had been chopped down. In the same way, if we had sold the company, Clif Bar would have been chopped down. We would have lost all the values that we were starting to build into the company. My partner and I had told ourselves those values would somehow be carried on by the new owner. But I had been fooling myself.

At the end of seven months of negotiating, my partner "left the tree" and received a deal that in five years would more than equal what she would have received from the near-acquisition. This was not my desired outcome, but she didn't believe we would survive and forced me to buy her out. And we're still paying off the settlement because we're doing it all on our own—with no investors—but we're getting much closer now. That huge debt has been like helicopters flying overhead, trying to knock us out of the tree. Every penny of profit has had to go to pay the debt off, so we've been strapped for the last five years. It hasn't always been comfortable, but neither was Julia's little platform as the months and years went by.

But in the end, it's been worth it. Today, we have become much more ourselves. Our values deepened tenfold after the company was taken off the market. At that point I made a decision. I told the Clif Bar team, "I'm not going to wait until the debt's paid off to start going organic or spending time doing community service, or donating 1% of all of our sales to charitable organizations or environmental groups. That's what we're committed to doing—and we're going to do it *now*."

Julia Butterfly Hill didn't stop when she had finally saved Luna. She started a nonprofit foundation, Circle of Life, to help educate people about the interdependence of all life. I was so inspired after reading Julia's book that I contacted her. Today, I am a member of her foundation's advisory board.

And like Julia, I didn't stop at simply staying at Clif Bar—that was just the first step. My partner had always resisted organics because they cost more. Today, we're more than 60% organic. We also buy wind energy to offset the energy we use in our bakeries and offices, and last year, we helped fund a Native American wind farm in South Dakota. We use only 100% post-consumer recycled material for our boxes and all the paper used in the office. Our food wrappers are still a problem because we just can't yet achieve the protection and the 11-month shelf life that we need with a material that's biodegradable or recyclable, but we've got a task force on it, and it's just a matter of time.

We're doing all those things, and somehow, we're able to keep growing. I call it "the grand experiment." Instead of measuring our performance by just one bottom line, we have five: Sustaining our Business, Sustaining our Brands, Sustaining our People, Sustaining our Community, and Sustaining our Environment. It's a business model that's about more than just creating shareholder value.

When I didn't get off my "tree," I didn't really understand why; I just did it and knew it was the right thing to do. I'm grateful to Julia for helping me understand why it was the right thing—and where to go from there.

M o Siegel

In 1970, Mo Siegel founded Celestial Seasonings Tea Company with only $500 of capital. Mo and his friends harvested the first two years of tea production by combing the mountains of Colorado in search of exotic herb teas growing wild. He led the company to a successful acquisition by Kraft, Inc., in 1984 and left the company in 1986. Two years later, he returned to the Celestial Seasonings board of directors when the company became independent by buying itself back from Kraft. In 1991, Mo once again became chairman and CEO and then took the company public. In 2000, he oversaw the merger of Celestial with the Hain Food Group to become the Hain Celestial Group. For two years Mo stayed to oversee the transition between the companies. Mo retired in September 2002 to begin a new era in his life. Today he serves on numerous corporate boards of directors, actively invests, travels, climbs the "fourteeners"—the 55 Colorado peaks that exceed 14,000 feet in height—and loves being a dad and grandpa. ■

I am a Colorado country boy, chiseled out of the snow and rock of these mountains. The year I was born, my father, who was raised in Chicago, moved our family to a dairy ranch on the side of a 9,000-foot-mountain pass in Colorado. The stormy weather at the ranch proved too harsh for the cattle, so that spring my father moved to us to Palmer Lake, a little mountain town at an elevation of just over 7,000 feet—still high by most standards—where I spent my childhood.

When I was two years old, my mother was killed by a drunk driver, leaving my traumatized father to raise three young children alone. Although my father, a self-styled Jewish John Wayne, was deeply religious, he had always led an unconventional spiritual life. He'd married my mother, although she was a Protestant, and felt closest to God while riding horses in the mountains; he prayed by the rivers and spent little time in formal religious environments. At home his religious word stood supreme, at least in his presence. But like my dad and his father before him, I grew up curious about religion, unconventional in my ideas, and in quest of deeper spiritual meaning. As a consequence—and to the terrible annoyance of my dad—I asked a lot of questions about God and religion. During my formative years I was especially troubled by the apparent conflict between science and religion over the subject of evolution.

I spent my last two years of high school living at a Catholic monastery and attending their college prep school. I entered the monastery school as a confused agnostic and graduated as a searching Christian. At the monastery, one of the priests introduced me to the teachings of the brilliant Catholic theologian Teilhard de Chardin. Teilhard's elegant writing on the relationship between religion and science propelled me to read a broad array of books on evolution. Before long, Charles Darwin became one of my life heroes, and his theories laid the foundation for my thinking on the subject. While searching bookstores for books on evolution, I also scoured the religion sections. I spent a number of years reading a wide range of religious books at an almost frenetic pace, ranging from Norman Vincent Peale to Taoism. The more I read on religion and science, the more I was convinced that science reflected the divine nature of God, rather than contradicting it. I wanted to understand how the world was the way it was. The idea that the universe was created in 6 days, or even 6,000 years, was something that wasn't working for me. I was rapidly moving toward centrist Christianity with a complete endorsement of scientific fact.

It was in 1969 at age 19 that I first encountered *The Urantia Book*. A number of friends had praised its teachings on evolution, and that Christmas a girlfriend gave it to me. I was surprised at its daunting size: 2,097 pages long. What confounded me the most was that the book contained 875 pages on the life and teachings of Jesus, including the missing years of his life—from age 1 to 12 and then from age 13 to approximately 30—not chronicled in the Bible. *How strange and intriguing*, I thought. *Dinosaurs and Jesus all in one text.* I didn't read it right away;

instead, I lent it to a friend. But over the course of the next few months, people kept telling me about *The Urantia Book*. So late one night, after hearing, "You really have to read this book," for what seemed like the hundredth time, I knocked on my friend's door and told him, "I need my book back." For the next year, I was absorbed in reading it—and I've been reading it ever since. Even today, I still host a weekly *Urantia Book* study group at my home.

Initially, I found the foreword to *The Urantia Book* utterly confusing, but I kept reading anyway. What followed was a fascinating intellectual and spiritual adventure that shook up everything I thought I knew. The first two parts of the book describe God, the Trinity, the organization and structure of the universe, life on other worlds, life after death, angels, and other personalities, and heaven. When I read Part Three, I felt as though I'd won the lottery. That section deals with the origin and history of our world, starting from the origin of our sun more six billion years ago— when it spun out of the disintegrating Andronover Nebula—and ending with the birth of Jesus. From ice ages to saber-toothed tigers, from the first human family to the evolution of modern government; from the story of Adam and Eve to the birth of prayer—*The Urantia Book* presented a logical story of physical and social evolution. It was the bridge between science and religion that I had been searching for, and I was finally at peace with the subject that had consumed me for years.

The fourth section of the book recounts the magnificent life and teachings of Jesus. Before I read *The Urantia Book*, I loved the story of Jesus in the New Testament, but I had always felt disappointed that it covered only a few years of his life. I wanted to know his entire life story and have it fit into a bigger context. Being born to a Christian mother, raised by a nonconformist Jewish father, and having spent two years in a Catholic monastery, my smorgasbord of religious education had taught me to question everything. How did the idea that Jesus was the only son of God relate to Moses, Buddha, and other prophets? And if you were born in India and had never heard of Jesus, would you really go to "hell"? When I read the section in *The Urantia Book* about Jesus, I was profoundly moved: Jesus—both the human being and the Son of God— came alive in the most superbly written biographical literature that I have ever come across. In addition to reframing Jesus for me, it made me far more respectful and appreciative of my childhood training in both Judaism and Christianity. Simply put, Part Four transformed my life from one of doubt to one of faith, from one of insecurity to one of trust in God—with Jesus as the lens through which God becomes visible. As a spiritual adventurer, I was thrilled that the Jesus of *The Urantia Book* built on the Bible, and then took me a hundred miles farther.

The Urantia Book changed three major things inside me. First, it made me examine my values and commit myself to doing something worthwhile with my life. After college, studying and peace marches were replaced by the ordinary tasks of living: making money and raising a family. After studying the teachings in *The Urantia Book*, I knew that it would feel selfish and wasteful to simply focus on material success. So, as a young man, when I began thinking of what I could do to make a living, I immediately turned to the health food industry. I was adamant that whatever product or service I sold should be healthy and make a positive difference in people's quality of life.

Growing up in Colorado, I had developed a love for hiking and spending time in the mountains. Not long after I read *The Urantia Book*, I decided to start collecting the herbs that grew wild in the canyons and valleys of the mountains around Boulder. With the help of friends, I collected and dried 500 pounds of my first blend, called Mo's 36 Herb Tea.® It was packaged in hand-sewn muslin bags and sold to a local health food store. This was the start of Celestial Seasonings Teas, which today is the largest manufacturer and marketer of specialty teas in North America.

Like all businesspeople, I have had to make choices every step of the way. My materialistic side could easily have hardened me, forming me into one tough businessman. But the ideals I internalized from *The Urantia Book* kept pushing me to choose good over greed and to care about the people I worked with as well as the people who bought our products. In fact, those ideas were the inspiration for the uplifting quotes we print on the side of our tea boxes and on our tea bag tags!

The second thing the book did for me was instill the importance of family. One line in the book reads: "The family is man's greatest purely human achievement." Everything I have done since reading *The Urantia Book*—from my career to my mountain-climbing—has been influenced by my decision to put my family first. I vividly remember the moment when I first understood the choices this commitment required. It was December 24. I was 26 years old and was sitting in the beautifully appointed office of the first billionaire I'd ever met. It was an important meeting: The billionaire and another executive in the company—also extremely wealthy—were talking to me about investing in Celestial Seasonings. Although the offices were emptying as employees departed to celebrate Christmas Eve, these two men just wanted to talk to me. It was snowing like crazy and I realized I might get stranded at the airport if I stayed much longer. I thought, *I'm going to miss Christmas with my wife and three young children . . . chasing after money!*

After a while, when the building was empty except for us, I asked one of the men where he was spending Christmas and what he was doing that night. He broke down and told me of his many divorces and how his children hated him. It turned out that he had nowhere to go. The billionaire also had been through multiple divorces and had no one waiting for him at home. They were hanging around their luxurious offices, entertaining a 26-year-old kid—because they didn't have anywhere better to go. The combination of the snowstorm, the two lonely men in that super-rich office, and the quote in *The Urantia Book* about human achievement and family hit me hard. I asked myself, *What's important in life?*

The answer was obvious. I stood up and said, "Excuse me. I've got to catch a plane." I left them, those two sad older men, and went home to spend the holiday with my wife and kids.

The third and most valuable thing that *The Urantia Book* did for me was to make God real. I once saw a sign on the inside of a friend's front door that said "God is knocking on the door; let's see whose face he's wearing this time." I loved that idea, but it wasn't yet my experience. Finding God on an everyday basis—and in everyone I met—seemed an almost impossible task for me. After reading and absorbing *The Urantia Book*'s specific and detailed teachings about the real fragment of God that dwells within all of us, I slowly grew to trust that a very real part of God has been implanted in our minds to guide our decisions toward God. This part of God—the still, small voice of Christianity and Judaism, the Atman of Hinduism, and the Tao of Taoism—lives with us in our joys and our sufferings. Experiencing God as something real and tangible inside of me and inside of you, and not just some kind of wispy spirit, was pivotal for me. This reality has shaped every single day of my life since that time.

When I first heard people discussing *The Urantia Book*, they said it was a revelation, written not by human beings but by angels, which I thought was just the goofiest thing I'd ever heard. I ended up reading it in spite of all that. After I read it, I was not concerned about who had written it or how it had been written, because it was so powerful. I'd wanted bold; I found bold. I'd wanted spiritual adventure, and I was on the ride of my life. I'd wanted truth, and the book was loaded with it. Since that time, I have looked into it deeply and I cannot find any author associated with the book. But that is not the point, because I love what it says and I'm a much better person because of its teachings. I've learned not to pick fights with the books I read—I'm appreciative and I grow from them.

Doris Haddock (Granny D)

Doris "Granny D" Haddock is a political activist, speaker, and author. Granny D first gained national attention when at the age of 89, she began a 3,200-mile walk across the country to demonstrate her concern for campaign-finance reform. She walked through over 1,000 miles of deserts, climbed the Appalachian Range in blizzard conditions, and skied the last 100 miles into Washington, D.C., when a historic snowfall made roadside walking impossible. In 2004, Granny D ran for the United States Senate at the age of 94. Her book, *Granny D: You're Never Too Old to Raise a Little Hell*, was published in 2001. Granny D still walks two miles a day before breakfast. ∎

Born and brought up in the great state of New Hampshire, I am what you call a real Yankee. For most of my life, I was a working woman—I had jobs in various offices, and for the last 20 years before I retired, I worked for the Bee Bee Shoe Company, managing their costing department. Before 1998, I wasn't a political person, and I certainly never considered myself an activist—someone who instigated protests or started movements. What happened through the years was that if anything fell into my lap that I could do something about, I did.

But in 1998, at the age of 88, I actually did become an activist, initiating an ambitious grassroots plan to promote something I believed in. It was the writings of another "older activist" named Peace Pilgrim that gave me the courage I needed to make my own plan a reality.

The seeds for my activism had been sown many years earlier. In 1960, my husband Jim and I were involved in an effort to stop a nuclear bomb being exploded in Alaska because it was going to ruin an Eskimo village. We were very interested in this because we had been to that village. We had a lawyer friend who said, "If you want to put together a national petition, contact your friends in the various states and ask them to help."

So we found relatives or friends in every single state of the Union, called them, and asked them if they would do the same thing, try to find people or friends of theirs. It spread like that, and we were successful in stopping the planned explosion.

My husband died of Alzheimer's disease in 1993, and for the next few years I didn't do much of anything. I had been his caretaker for the last 10 years of his life, and I was very tired. One day in 1998, I was reading the *Boston Globe* and saw an op-ed article written by Common Cause, which is a watchdog organization that keeps an eye on what is going on politically in the United States. The article said that *in the middle of the night,* two members of the House of Representatives had added an appendix to a bill that was going to President Clinton the next day to be signed. The appendix was for $50 billion to go to a particular tobacco company.

I was deeply troubled by this and decided to call Common Cause. I asked if the facts in the article were true. "And," I wanted to know, "did you stop that money from going to the tobacco company?"

They told me that the facts were true and that this time the appendix had been caught and made public, and it had been addressed. But they told me that they didn't know how many of these things went through that they didn't catch.

I was horrified. "But this is corruption," I said.

I think they were surprised by my naïveté, "Well, what do you think is going on there? Of course it's corruption."

I wanted to know what I could do about it. They said, "Well, if you can get people interested in passing the McCain-Feingold bill, it would stop the flow of that kind of money." The McCain-Feingold bill, named for the two senators who sponsored it, was campaign-finance reform legislation aimed at reducing the amount of money that could be given to candidates during elections. It was hoped that this would eliminate the influence of money on our lawmakers once they were in office. Common Cause, along with many other groups and individuals, felt the bill was necessary because the concerns of voters were being increasingly overridden by the money and clout of powerful industries and interest groups.

I thought, *Well, I can do that.* I found a few friends to help me start a national petition, just the way my husband and I had for the Eskimo village. We circulated our petition all over the country begging the Senate to pass the McCain-Feingold bill as soon as possible. After collecting thousands of signatures, we sent the signed petitions to all 100 senators.

The senators began writing back cookie-cutter letters basically saying, "Don't worry about this. We're taking care of it. We're going to pass the McCain-Feingold bill next time it comes up." But the next time it came up, it was filibustered. That's what had been happening to every campaign-finance reform bill since the days of Watergate. They were just impossible to get passed. Representatives would pass the bills in the House, knowing full well they would never make it past the Senate.

When McCain-Feingold didn't pass after all of our hard work, I got quite depressed. My son who lived next door to me was concerned. He was driving to Florida for a fishing trip and thought I should come with him. I had a sister living in Florida at the time, so I decided to go.

On the way down, in the middle of nowhere, we saw this old man walking along carrying a little pack with a cane. I said, "What in the world is that old man doing way out here?"

My son said, "I guess he's on the road again." And he sang the first line of the Willie Nelson song.

I knew my son was joking, but it got me thinking. "You know," I told him, "here I am, eighty-nine years old, and I haven't got anything left to do. I think I'm going to walk across the United States and wake this country up."

My son just said, "Well, people do that all the time, Mother. There's no sense in doing it if you don't have a cause."

"Oh, but I do have a cause: campaign finance reform!"

He was alarmed, "You're almost ninety!" But he could tell I was serious, and finally he said, "You can only go if you train for it."

Once I decided to do the walk, I got a little scared. How was I going to train? Could I really walk that far? I spent the whole of my vacation in Florida trying to work out exactly how I would do this mind-boggling thing I had committed myself to doing.

When I returned to New Hampshire, I told a friend of mine, a woman I'd been playing Scrabble with for many years and who went to my church, about my idea to walk across the country. She told me I should read *Peace Pilgrim*.

Before I read her book, I had never heard of Peace Pilgrim. Although she was not a young woman, she walked continuously for 28 years, logging more than 25,000 miles. I was immediately intrigued by her story, and over the course of a few days, I read the book twice. I needed to know her strategy for walking across the country, whether she had problems, how she had trained.

Peace Pilgrim started walking in 1953, at the same time that Joe McCarthy was conducting his witch hunts. She called herself simply Peace Pilgrim—she never gave her name or her age—and she walked for peace. She carried nothing with her, "walking until given shelter, fasting until given food," but eventually had been supported by many different churches. What inspired me most was her simple philosophy: overcome evil with good, falsehood with truth, and hatred with love. She never wrote any books, just a few little booklets. After she died in 1981, a few people compiled all of her ideas and experiences in a book, *Peace Pilgrim: Her Life and Work in Her Own Words*—the book my friend told me to read.

I remember one particular passage that gave me special comfort. The book describes one cold night when Peace Pilgrim found herself in an unexpected snowstorm, walking in snow up to her knees with no traffic on the road. She came to a bridge, climbed down under it, found a big carton with newspaper in it. She wrapped herself up in the newspapers and was able to survive the night. It convinced me that someone not of this world was protecting Peace Pilgrim—and would watch over me as well.

Reading about Peace Pilgrim was just the thing I needed to help me go forward with my idea. If she could do it, so could I! I was only going 3,000 miles—she had gone more than 25,000! Since I didn't believe that I would be supported by churches or anyone else, I began training by carrying a 29-pound pack on my back with a sleeping bag, a bottle of water, and 5 pounds of trail mix (in case I ever found myself without food). I started slowly and walked a little farther each day, until I could walk 10 miles at a time.

I knew what I wanted to accomplish: I thought I could get attention, because no one had ever walked across the country by themselves at the age of 90. Once I had everyone's attention, I could tell them how important the passage of the McCain-Feingold bill was. I wanted to stop this futile charade of introduction-then-defeat-by-filibuster, and I felt it would take a grassroots effort to somehow push the bill through.

The day finally came to begin my long trip; I walked behind the Rose Bowl parade—and just kept walking. I left Pasadena, California, on January 1, 1999. For the next 14 months, I walked 10 miles a day, traveling as a pilgrim, without money, without bringing support of any kind. Common Cause sent a letter to all of their members on my walking route, telling them that I was determined and meant what I said. They asked their members to show their support. I was delighted when people turned up to help. Many carried water, others offered me food as well as places to stay at night, and some just walked with me.

About a week after I left Pasadena, when I reached the desert, I realized I was in trouble. I couldn't carry enough water to get me through—it was too heavy. Dennis Burke, who was director of Common Cause in Arizona and later became the coauthor of my book, arrived at Twenty-nine Palms, California, with a little camper. He had gotten word that this crazy old lady was going to walk across the desert and she would not survive. Everyone told him he had better get over there and do something about it because "she's going to keel over on your watch."

When he arrived, he said to me, "I will follow you and bring you water. And at night, you can sleep in the camper and not have to sleep on the ground with the snakes. You either can do this or you had better go home, because you'll not survive the desert."

I had absolutely no intention of having a support car with me and wouldn't have if he hadn't insisted. But I knew he was right.

So I made my way across 12 states, camping or staying in private homes, supported by people who believed in what I was doing. I talked to everyone I met about how we needed to take our country back. Many who saw me said that I reminded them of Peace Pilgrim. I felt as though she were with me on my walk, and even today I feel her influence in my life. I truly believe that we are "sisters in spirit."

I arrived in Washington, D.C., on February 29, 2000. More than 2,000 people, including some members of Congress, met and escorted me down the city streets toward the Capitol building.

The publicity generated by my walk increased the number of calls coming in to Washington about the bill, putting more pressure on the House and Senate to pass it. Still, my work was far from over. For the next two years, I continued my lobbying. Then, in 2002, an unusual thing occurred: They voted on the bill in the Senate—*first*. It passed, which put the House in the position of really having to make it happen. On the day before the House started the debate on the bill, I took another— shorter—walk: Both Senator John McCain and Senator Russ Feingold walked with me to visit the leader of the Democrats and the leader of the Republicans—Feingold is a Democrat and McCain a Republican. It was a friendly gesture, meant to emphasize the bipartisan nature of the bill.

During the weeklong debate, I walked around the Capitol building every day. On the last four days and nights, I walked all night long as well, stopping every two hours for a 10-minute rest. There was no one there but me and the chickens, but I did it, and the members of Congress knew that I was doing it—so this put pressure on them. Unfortunately, in the end, the bill that was passed was a terrible compromise. It really didn't do what I had worked so hard for it to do, which is why I am still on my mission.

I have 16 great-grandchildren—and it's for them that I keep work- ing. I want them to live in a country where our elected representatives can govern in the right way, independent of money from corporations and other special-interest groups. For the last few years, I have been speaking all over the country about the importance of public funding in our elections.

You're Never Too Old to Raise a Little Hell, my book about my walk and my fight to establish true political democracy in this country, is used today in college classes as an example of the Power of One. When I am invited to speak anywhere, I always mention Peace Pilgrim in my talks. I think she is one of the greatest examples we have of the Power of One. I am grateful to her for her inspiration and for the courage she gave me to do something that I believe will make a difference in this world.

Lois Capps

Congresswoman Lois Capps took office in March 1998, succeeding her late husband, Congressman Walter Capps. Before joining Congress, Lois was a nurse and health advocate for the Santa Barbara School Districts and director of Santa Barbara County's Teenage Pregnancy and Parenting Project and the Parent and Child Enrichment Center. She now draws on this extensive health care background as founder and cochair of the House Nursing Caucus and serves on numerous health-related caucuses, as well as the Subcommittee on Health. Lois earned master of arts degrees in religion from Yale University and in education from the University of California, Santa Barbara, and received honorary doctorates from Pacific Lutheran University and Pacific Lutheran Theological Seminary. ■

My story begins with a journey back to the Sunday mornings of my childhood: my father, the pastor up in the pulpit, and I, sitting on the hard wooden pew in the front row under his gaze, listening as he preached. The texts he used were sometimes searing, like this one from St. Matthew's Gospel (New English Translation):

"... For I was hungry and you gave me food, I was thirsty and you gave me something to drink, I was a stranger and you invited me in, I was naked and you gave me clothing, I was sick and you took care of me, I was in prison and you visited me."

When the righteous question the Lord, asking Him when they did those things for Him, He answers, "I tell you the truth, just as you did it for one of the least of these brothers or sisters of mine, you did it for me."

And, He says to the others, the reverse is true: ". . . just as you did not do for one of the least of these, you did not do for me."

My response to this and the many other spiritual injunctions of my youth was to make public service the focus of my life. Although I never dreamed I would have a career in politics, today I am a U.S. congresswoman representing California's 23rd District, which includes Santa Barbara, my home. On my way to this surprising destination, I was a public health nurse and the wife of a professor and scholar who became a congressman.

And while there is no single book that got me to where I am today, except perhaps the "Good Book," as my father called it, I recently read a book that I feel could transform my future—and, I hope, the futures of over one billion people living in extreme poverty in the world today. *The End of Poverty: Economic Possibilities for Our Time*, written by Jeffrey Sachs, provides an exciting and effective way to fulfill my humanitarian aspirations—political, medical, and spiritual.

Those aspirations, as I've said, were formed by my upbringing. I come from Midwestern Scandinavian stock: My great-grandparents homesteaded in Iowa, and I was raised in Wisconsin. We were people of faith—clergy for two generations. I can recall hearing many reinforcements of biblical texts that fell into the pattern of "to whom much is given, much will be required." There was an unspoken expectation that we would serve others—through church work, teaching, and things like that. As a child, I took all this to heart, but I didn't feel called to those professions. I was fascinated by the field of health care. Since no one had ever pursued a career in medicine in my immediate family, it was a way for me to strike out on my own yet still live a life of service.

So I went to college and became a nurse. Not long after that, I met my husband, Walter Capps. Like me, Walter came from a traditional, Republican, "God-fearing" household, and we shared many of the same goals and values. We ended up at Yale Divinity School—Walter to earn his Ph.D., and I to get a master's degree. While we were in school, I worked part time as a visiting public health nurse in the communities around New Haven, Connecticut, where Yale is located.

This was during the early 1960s, the civil rights era. Walter and I heard Martin Luther King Jr. preach at Battel Chapel on the Yale campus. We were caught up in the spirit that motivated the Freedom Riders, both black and white, to ride buses through the South to protest segregation. When President Kennedy was shot, we immediately got into our car and drove to Washington, D.C., to join the throng of mourners making their way through the Capitol Rotunda. Along with many of our fellow Americans, Walter and I found the values and creeds of our upbringing stretched and challenged to include contemporary social justice issues. This led to political involvement.

Despite my family's emphasis on "helping those less fortunate," it wasn't until I was an adult that I was really exposed to poverty. I saw poor people in the emergency room where I worked in New Haven and, as a public heath nurse, was often in people's homes and observed how they lived. Now as a member of Congress, I've traveled to India, South Africa, and the West Bank and seen people in "extreme poverty," which Sachs defines as living on less than $1 a day.

Today I understand that the intertwined challenges of hunger and poverty call for more complex responses than simply reaching in my pocket as the offering plate is passed. When my children were teenagers, we joined the pilgrimage to assist families living in the Tijuana dumps. Each day in my work as a school nurse, I saw children who came to school hungry and whose families lived in garages or doubled up in small apartments. Now as an elected representative, the faces of the homeless vets who gather around Santa Barbara's Moreton Bay fig tree and the families seeking refuge in our local shelters strongly inform my life.

I'm not alone in my concern. Americans are a generous people. Natural disasters, both at home and abroad always draw an overwhelming outpouring of support. Yet it's astounding how few people know the tiny fraction of our national budget that goes to foreign aid. Most assume it is much larger than the .015% it is. As singer Bono made clear to the G8 countries (Canada, France, Germany, Italy, Japan, the United Kingdom, the United States, and Russia) in September 2005, if we all lived up to our pledge of .07%, we could greatly improve the quality of life on this planet for all of us, the rich as well as the poor. The world is so small today; we're all in this together. As a global economy, we simply can't afford extreme poverty in such a large percentage of the population. Plus, extreme poverty is the prime breeding ground for disease—it's in the poorer countries that avian flu is most likely to spread and intensify. And it's clear that poverty contributes to terrorism. This is a point of view focused on self-interest, but I know from my experience in government that until we look at it like that, it's not going to be addressed effectively. Now, thanks to the work that Jeffrey Sachs and others have done, we finally have a chance to do just that.

In *The End of Poverty*, Sachs—a world-famous economist, the director of Columbia University's Earth Institute, and an economic advisor to the United Nations—presents a plan to end extreme poverty by 2025. Over the past 20 years, Sachs has demonstrated a new way to create economic development in a variety of crisis situations around the world—in Bolivia, Poland, Russia, and India. Most recently he's been working in Africa. His formula has proved effective again and again: Don't wait for governments to change but get permission to work on the level of the village; take intensive steps, carefully attuned to the community's specific needs and run by the villagers, with strong support from outside donors and experts. The results are life-changing. If you're willing to provide intensive support for five years, you get a generation of girls going to school, so they stop having babies so young. You get roads being built so vehicles can deliver goods and services. You get potable water available to eliminate common diseases. It's a comprehensive formula: These are just a few of the results you get from going into the village with a checklist of specific things to do that empower the people living there.

Sachs's book is not light reading; it's dense with statistics, charts, and graphs. But his conclusions are compelling, inspiring—and profoundly exciting. It has finally given me a way to come to terms with the scripture passages of my childhood—like the one from Matthew—and say, "We can do this." Yet even more than that, it eliminates an aspect of helping others that I've always found troubling. Before, helping the poor was always in the context of "benevolence" and "charity." There's a dark side to both of those words, in my opinion—a feeling that "we who have so much can afford a few crumbs." Now, with Sachs's methodology, we can treat poor people with respect. We can look the person right in the eye and treat their poverty matter-of-factly. There is no blame or shame;

poverty is just a condition, like a boil, that can be treated and healed. And then the person is whole. It's not the fault of those who are born into these terrible situations, and it's not something that we do out of largesse; we do it because we're human beings and it's what we have to do. And now that Sachs has shown it's doable, there is no excuse for not doing it.

I know from my years of working in public policy that poverty is the linchpin. If we can eradicate poverty, so many other fundamental and chronic problems can be addressed. I have searched all my life for a methodology that can rise above partisan politics in the arena of international policy. Jeffrey Sachs provides it. Knowing poverty can be treated in a scientific way—the way you would dress a wound or put on an antibiotic—we have a platform to work from. Knowing Sachs's detailed research shows that economic growth spreads automatically from village to village, we have ammunition. It takes time and commitment, but it's doable; it's no longer pie in the sky.

My story comes full circle with a personal dream. At the University of California, Santa Barbara, where my husband taught for 30 years, the Walter H. Capps Center for the Study of Ethics, Religion, and Public Life has been established. There, Sachs's methodology could be taught, creating a generation of people skilled at eliminating poverty. And we could start by addressing the needs right in our own congressional district. I hope to see the day when extreme poverty will be considered a thing of the past.

Recently, Nobel Peace Prize winner Archbishop Desmond Tutu visited Santa Barbara, where people filled a large hall to hear him speak about his Truth and Reconciliation Commission, which dealt with the aftermath of apartheid in South Africa. The event ended with a question-and-answer period. One person asked, "What do you think is the one thing we can do to bring peace to the world?"

"End poverty," Tutu said. And then he turned and walked off the stage.

The End of Poverty has given us the tools to make this a reality.

List of Contributors
and Their Books

Guide to the Art of Long-Term World Travel, by Rolf Potts

ARIELLE FORD   *Key to Yourself*, by Dr. Venice Bloodworth

ELLYNANNE GEISEL   *Gone with the Wind*, by Margaret Mitchell

MICHAEL E. GERBER   *100 Selected Poems*, by E.E. Cummings

PHILIP GOLDBERG   *Franny and Zooey*, by J.D. Salinger

FARRAH GRAY   *The Seven Spiritual Laws of Success*, by Deepak Chopra

JOHN GRAY   *The Science of Being and Art of Living*, by Maharishi Mahesh Yogi

JIM GUY   *The Teachings of the Buddha*

DORIS HADDOCK   *Peace Pilgrim*
(GRANNY D)

EARL HAMNER   *The Time of Man*, by Elizabeth Madox Roberts

MARK VICTOR HANSEN   *Resurrection*, by Neville Goddard

LOUISE HAY   *The Game of Life and How to Play It*, by Florence Scovel Shinn

GARY HEAVIN   *The Secret Kingdom*, by Pat Robertson

GAY HENDRICKS   *The Enchiridion*, by Epictetus

LOU HOLTZ   *The Magic of Thinking Big*, by David Schwartz

LARRY JONES   *Hudson Taylor's Spiritual Secret*, by Dr. and Mrs. Howard Taylor

SHERYL LEACH   *The Power of Now*, by Eckhart Tolle

KENNY LOGGINS   *Siddhartha*, by Hermann Hesse

KATE LUDEMAN   *Learning to Love Yourself*, by Gay Hendricks

JIM MACLAREN   *The Passion of the Western Mind: Understanding the Ideas That Have Shaped Our World View*, by Richard Tarnas

DEBBIE MACOMBER   The Bible

JIM MCCANN   *Scripts People Live*, by Claude Steiner

MALACHY MCCOURT	A biography of Mahatma Gandhi
JACQUELYN MITCHARD	*A Tree Grows in Brooklyn*, by Betty Smith
CRAIG NEWMARK	*The Cluetrain Manifesto*, by Rick Levine, Christopher Locke, Doc Searls, and David Weinberger
LISA NICHOLS	*The 7 Habits of Highly Effective People*, by Stephen Covey
CHRISTIANE NORTHRUP, M.D.	*Natives of Eternity*, by Flower Newhouse
PIERCE O'DONNELL	*Profiles in Courage*, by John F. Kennedy
CATHERINE OXENBERG	*The Power of One*, by Bryce Courtenay
NANCY PEARL	*Space Cadet*, by Robert Heinlein
RUDY RUETTIGER	*Psycho-Cybernetics*, by Maxwell Maltz
MO SIEGEL	*The Urantia Book*
BERNIE SIEGEL, M.D.	*The Human Comedy*, by William Saroyan
JOHN ST. AUGUSTINE	*Instant Replay: The Green Bay Diary of Jerry Kramer*, by Jerry Kramer
MICHAEL TOMS	*The Creative Process*, edited by Brewster Ghiselin
DOREEN VIRTUE	*Man's Search for Meaning*, by Viktor Frankl
MAYNARD WEBB	*The 7 Habits of Highly Effective People*, by Stephen Covey
PAT WILLIAMS	*Veeck—As In Wreck: The Chaotic Career of Baseball's Incorrigible Maverick*, by Bill Veeck
DIANE WILSON	*The Hero with a Thousand Faces*, by Joseph Campbell
WYLAND	*The Silent World*, by Jacques Cousteau
BOB YOUNG	*Don Quixote*, by Cervantes

The Transformational Book Circle

Now, you can read the books that changed the lives of Louise Hay, Deepak Chopra, Neale Donald Walsch, and today's most respected transformational leaders. The Transformational Book Circle is a new concept in book clubs, a worldwide community that can change your life in profound and positive ways.

We asked the luminaries listed above and others, including Barbara DeAngelis and Kenny Loggins: What book changed your life? On the basis of their answers, we arranged for a beautiful special edition of each book to be printed, along with a CD of experiential activities that bring the book to life. Subscribers get one book (and the accompanying CD) each month for a year. In addition to the book and CD, you also get to participate in Web seminars and teleconferences with these luminaries.

For those who purchase this book, a special discount has been arranged. For more information and to get your special discount, please visit www.transformationalbookcircle.com.

Who Is Jack Canfield?

Jack Canfield is the cocreator and editor of the *Chicken Soup for the Soul*® series, which *Time* magazine has called "the publishing phenomenon of the decade." The series now has 105 titles with more than 100 million copies in print in 41 languages. Jack is also the coauthor of seven other bestselling books, including *The Success Principles™: How to Get from Where You Are to Where You Want to Be, Dare to Win, The Aladdin Factor,* and *The Power of Focus: How to Hit Your Business, Personal and Financial Targets with Absolute Certainty.*

Jack has recently developed a telephone coaching program and an online coaching program based on his most recent book, *The Success Principles.* He also offers a seven-day Breakthrough to Success seminar once every summer, which attracts 400 people from 15 countries around the world.

Jack is the CEO of Chicken Soup for the Soul Enterprises and the Canfield Training Group in Santa Barbara, California, and founder of the Foundation for Self-Esteem in Culver City, California. He has conducted intensive personal and professional development seminars on the principles of success for over 900,000 people in 21 countries around the world. He has spoken to hundreds of thousands of others at numerous conferences and conventions and has been seen by millions of viewers on national television shows such as the *Today Show, Fox and Friends, Inside Edition, Hard Copy,* CNN's *Talk Back Live, 20/20, Eye to Eye,* and *NBC Nightly News,* and *CBS Nightly News.*

Jack is the recipient of many awards and honors, including three honorary doctorates and a Guinness Book of World Records certificate for having seven books appearing on the *New York Times* best seller list on May 24, 1998.

To write to Jack or for inquiries about Jack as a speaker, his coaching programs, or his seminars, use the following contact information:

Jack Canfield
The Canfield Companies
P.O. Box 30880
Santa Barbara, CA 93130
Phone: 805-563-2935; fax: 805-563-2945
E-mail: info@jackcanfield.com
Web site: www.jackcanfield.com

Who Is Gay Hendricks?

For the past 30 years, Gay Hendricks has been one of the major contributors to the fields of relationship transformation and body–mind healing. He received his Ph.D. in counseling psychology from Stanford in 1974. After a twenty-year academic career as a professor at University of Colorado, he and his wife, Dr. Kathlyn Hendricks, founded the Hendricks Institute, which offers seminars in relationship enhancement and somatic wellness annually throughout North America, Asia, and Europe.

Gay has published more than 25 books, including such best sellers as *Conscious Loving*, *The Corporate Mystic*, *Conscious Living*, and *Spirit-Centered Relationships*. He has appeared on more than 500 radio and television shows on various networks, including *Oprah*, *CNN*, *CNBC*, *48 Hours*, and others. He and Kathlyn have their own weekly relationship program on Sirius Satellite and the Lime Radio Network. Along with business partner Stephen Simon, Gay founded the Spiritual Cinema Circle, www.spiritualcinemacircle.com, which distributes inspiring movies to subscribers in more than 70 countries.

The Hendricks make their home in Ojai, California, and may be contacted through their website, www.hendricks.com. For information on their relationship seminars, please e-mail them at enroll@hendricks.com.

Who Is Carol Kline?

Carol Kline is the coauthor of five books—with more than five million sold—in the best-selling *Chicken Soup for the Soul*® series, including the number-one *New York Times* bestselling *Chicken Soup for the Mother's Soul 2* and the recently released *Chicken Soup for the Dog Lover's Soul* and *Chicken Soup for the Cat Lover's Soul*.

A freelance writer and editor for more than 20 years, Carol, who has a B.A. in literature, specializes in narrative nonfiction. She has written for newspapers, newsletters, and magazines, and in addition to her own *Chicken Soup* books, has also contributed stories and her editing talents to many other books in the *Chicken Soup for the Soul* series.

Carol is also a speaker, self-esteem facilitator, and animal rescue volunteer. Since 1975, Carol has taught stress-management systems to the general public. At present, she is at work on several writing projects on a variety of topics.

To write to Carol or to inquire about her writing or speaking services, please use the following contact information:

Carol Kline
Carol Kline, Inc.
P.O. Box 521
Ojai, CA 93024
E-mail: ckline@lisco.com

Permissions

pg. 76 Rudy Ruettiger's story printed by permission of Rudy Ruettiger.

pg. 81 Danny Edward Scott Casalenuovo's story is reprinted by permission of Danny Edward Scott Casalenuovo. Copyright (c) 2003 Danny Edward Scott Casalenuovo. This story appeared, in a different form, in *Serving Time, Serving Others: Acts of Kindness by Inmates, Prison Staff, Victims, and Volunteers* by Tom Lagana and Laura Lagana, published by Fruitbearer Publishing, 2003.

pg. 87 Farrah Gray's story printed by permission of Farrah Gray.

pg. 92 Louise Hay's story printed by permission of Louise Hay.

pg. 95 Rhonda Byrne's story printed by permission of Rhonda Byrne, creator of "The Secret."

pg. 100 Mark Victor Hansen's story printed by permission of M. V. Hansen and Associates, Inc., copyright (c) 2005 by Mark Victor Hansen.

pg. 105 Michael E. Gerber's story printed by permission of Michael E. Gerber.

pg. 111 Tim Ferriss's story printed by permission of Tim Ferriss.

pg. 118 Christiane Northrup's story printed by permission of Christiane Northrup, M.D.

pg. 123 Doreen Virtue's story printed by permission of Doreen Virtue.

pg. 128 John Gray's story printed by permission of John Gray.

pg. 132 Philip Goldberg's story printed by permission of Philip Goldberg.

pg. 137 Bernie Siegel's story printed by permission of Bernie Siegel, M.D.

pg. 142 Dave Barry's story printed by permission of Dave Barry.

pg. 145 Sue Ellen Cooper's story printed by permission of Sue Ellen Cooper.

pg. 150 EllynAnne Geisel's story printed by permission of EllynAnne Geisel.

pg. 157 Earl Hamner's story printed by permission of Earl Hamner. In Earl Hamner's story, the authors are indebted to *Goodnight, John Boy: A Celebration of an American Family and the Values That Have Sustained Us Through Good Times and Bad* by Earl Hamner and Ralph E. Giffin, copyright (c) 2002 by Earl Hamner and Ralph Giffen, published by Cumberland House Publishing, for source material.

pg. 161 Nancy Pearl's story printed by permission of Nancy Pearl, author of *Book Lust* and *More Book Lust*, and in 2004, the 50th winner of the Women's National Book Association Award.

pg. 165 Wally Amos's story printed by permission of Wally Amos.

pg. 174 Jim McCann's story printed by permission of Jim McCann.

pg. 179 Larry Jones's story printed by permission of Larry Jones.

pg. 184 Debbie Macomber's story printed by permission of Debbie Macomber.

pg. 188 Arielle Ford's story printed by permission of Arielle Ford, author of *Hot Chocolate for the Mystical Soul*.

pg. 192 Michael Toms's story printed by permission of Michael Toms.

pg. 198 Bob Young's story printed by permission of Bob Young.

pg. 203 Craig Newmark's story printed by permission of Craig Newmark.

pg. 207 Kate Ludeman's story printed by permission of Kate Ludeman.

pg. 212 Amilya Antonetti's story printed by permission of Amilya Antonetti.

pg. 218 Jim Guy's story printed by permission of Jim Guy.

pg. 222 Gary Heavin's story printed by permission of Gary Heavin.

pg. 227 Stephen Covey's story printed by permission of Stephen Covey, copyright (c) 2006 by Stephen R. Covey.

pg. 232 Maynard Webb's story printed by permission of Maynard Webb.

pg. 236 Marc Bekoff's story printed by permission of Marc Bekoff.

pg. 240 Max Edelman's story printed by permission of Max Edelman.

pg. 245 Diane Wilson's story printed by permission of Diane Wilson.

pg. 251 Gary Erickson's story printed by permission of Gary Erickson. In Gary Erickson's story, the authors are indebted to *Raising the Bar: Integrity and Passion in Life and Business: The Story of Clif Bar Inc.* by Gary Erickson, copyright (c) 2004 by Gary Erickson, published by Jossey-Bass, for source material.

pg. 256 Mo Siegel's story printed by permission of Mo Siegel.

pg. 262 Doris Haddock's story printed by permission of Doris Haddock (Granny D).

pg. 268 Lois Capps's story printed by permission of Lois Capps. In Lois Capps's story, the authors are indebted to LeGrace Benson and the *Santa Barbara Independent* for source material.